English

Sustained Innovation Management

Sustained Innovation Management

Assimilating Radical and Incremental Innovation Management

Gaston Trauffler

and

Hugo P. Tschirky

in association with the European
Institute for Technology and
Innovation Management

First published 2007 by
PALGRAVE MACMILLAN
Houndmills, Basingstoke, Hampshire RG21 6XS and
175 Fifth Avenue, New York, N.Y. 10010
Companies and representatives throughout the world.

PALGRAVE MACMILLAN is the global academic imprint of the Palgrave Macmillan division of St. Martin's Press, LLC and of Palgrave Macmillan Ltd. Macmillan® is a registered trademark in the United States, United Kingdom and other countries. Palgrave is a registered trademark in the European Union and other countries.

ISBN-13: 978–0–230–00197–8
ISBN-10: 0–230–00197–1

This book is printed on paper suitable for recycling and made from fully managed and sustained forest sources.

A catalogue record for this book is available from the British Library.

Library of Congress Cataloging-in-Publication Data
Trauffler, Gaston, 1975– and Hugo P. Tschirky
    Sustained innovation management: assimilating radical and incremental innovation management / Gaston Trauffler and Hugo P. Tschirky.
        p. cm.
    Includes bibliographical references and index.
    ISBN 0–230–00197–1 (cloth)
        1. Technological innovations – Management. 2. Diffusion of innovations – Management. I. Title.
HD45.T67 2006
658.4—dc22   2006045775

10 9 8 7 6 5 4 3 2 1
16 15 14 13 12 11 10 09 08 07

Printed and bound in Great Britain by
Antony Rowe Ltd, Chippenham and Eastbourne

Contents

List of Figures

List of Tables

List of Abbreviations

ABB	Asea Brown Boveri
AG	Aktiengesellschaft
AT&T	American Telephone and Telegraph
BA	Business area
BASF	Badische Anilin- und Soda Fabrik AG
BA-U	Business Area-unit
BD&L	Business development and licensing
BG	Business group
BU	Business unit
CCD	Charge-coupled device
CD	Compact disc
CEO	Chief executive officer
CHF	Swiss francs
CIBA	Chemische Industrie Basel
CIO	Chief Information Officer
CMOS	Complementary metal oxide semiconductor
CoP	Community of Practice
CT	Corporate technology
CTI	Commission for Technology and Innovation
CTO	Chief technology officer
CVD	Chemical vapor deposition
Din	Deutsche Industrie Norm
Dpi	Dots per inch
Dr	Doctor
DSM	Dutch State Mine
EBIT	Earnings before interest and taxes
EBO	Emerging Business Opportunity
ETH	Eidgenössische Technische Hochschule (Swiss Federal Institute of Technology)
EU	European Union
EUR	Euro
FCF	Free Cash Flow
FISH	Fluoresence in situ hybridization
FLOPS	Floating point operations per second
GPRS	General Packet Radio Service
GSM	Global system for mobile communication
H	Hours
IA	Innovation architecture

IBM	International Business Machines
IP	Intellectual property
kb/s	Kilobyts per second
Km	Kilometre
KTI	Kommission für Technologie und Innovation
LCD	Liquid crystal display
MC	Market commercialization
MoB/KoS	Make or Buy / Keep or Sell
MOT	Management of Technology
NIBR	Novartis Institutes for Biomedical Research
NIC	National Intelligence Council
NIH	Not invented here
NPD	New Product Development
OECD	Organisation for Economic Cooperation and Development
OEM	Original equipment manufacturer
OL	Opportunity landscape
PoF	Pictures of the Future
PVD	Physical vapor deposition
R&D	Research and development
RFID	Radio frequency identification
R&T	Research and technology
ROI	Return on Investment
RTG	Research and Technology Group
SA	Société Anonyme
S&P	Standard and Poor's
SBA	Strategic Business Area
SBU	Strategic business unit
STF	Strategic Technology Field
SWOT	Strengths, weakness, opportunity, threats
SWX	Swiss Stock Exchange
TIO	Technology innovation officer
TTM	Time to Market
UMTS	Universal mobile telecommunications system
USD	US dollar
V&BD	Venture and business development
VC	Venture capital
VW	Volkswagen

List of Company Cases
and Examples

Preface

This book is the result of my research activities at the Swiss Federal Institute of Technology (ETH Zurich) Technology and Innovation Management Group chaired by Professor Hugo Tschirky. The research contribution to the state of the art in theory and practice would certainly not have been possible without the great support from people in academia and practice, professional and private life.

I am greatly indebted to Hugo Tschirky from ETH Zurich. First, for his professional input, his dedicated time and his general support for my research project, which greatly influenced the quality of this publication in a very positive way. He encouraged my projects in industry and fostered my academic exchange at international conferences and in joint research undertakings all over the world. The distance covered during my three years as a research assistant with Professor Tschirky took me about three times around the globe: 148,990 km. Second, he provided me with freedom and support for innovative ideas and created the excellent atmosphere in our team, which made my research activities a great pleasure. Third, he challenged and fostered my personal development in the course of the research projects, without which the finalization of this publication would not have been possible.

Many thanks go to Professor Urs Meyer from ETH Zurich for co-advising my research. Collaboration was a great pleasure and his challenging remarks, questions and support for my research and industry projects influenced this book very positively.

Also, I would like to thank my friends and research colleagues at the ETH Technology and Innovation Management Group: Dr Tim Sauber, Dr Valerie Bannert-Thurner and Dr Philip Bucher, Andreas Biedermann, Dr Jean-Philippe Escher, Dr Stefan Koruna, Karin Löffler, Dr Martin Luggen and Shoko Okutsu. This team – my dear friends – was the reason that at no time of my research did I not enjoy working on my PhD. Many thanks go also to numerous students in our department and junior assistants in our team. Special thanks to Martin Reisel and Thomas Jäger for their outstanding diploma thesis on 'Best Practices in Managing Radical Innovation and Disruptive Technologies', and to Mischa Csendes, Corinne Igel and Valerie Keller.

The laboratory of this research was industry. Thus, I would like to express my gratitude to my many research and interview partners. Without their openness to addressing highly sensitive topics and their contribution and remarks on my concepts, this publication could not make any contributions.

Last but certainly not least I would like to express my gratitude to my beloved ones – my family and to Karin Schultze. Your understanding, support and particularly your encouragement helped me very much in finalizing this publication.

Zurich   GASTON TRAUFFLER

Foreword

No crystal ball is required to predict safely that innovation competency will continue to be a critical factor distinguishing successful companies from failures. 'Innovate or stagnate' is an often used saying. Although this vision might be widely accepted, the number of companies with sustained innovative growth – including incremental *and* radical innovations – is still quite limited.

Companies coping with technology change often focus primarily on incremental product and service innovations. Only seldom is appropriate attention paid to other equally essential innovation domains such as process innovation, organizational innovation, marketing innovation and above all entire business innovation. And very rarely are radical innovations included in ordinary innovation planning, although such successfully implemented innovations are of high strategic value (often critical to survival).

A main reason may be the fact that radical innovations, as opposed to incremental innovations, explore new technologies, provide substantial improvements of known product features, and enable entirely new sets of performance features, and they therefore require taking considerably higher entrepreneurial risks than incremental innovations. As a result radical innovations obviously do not fit the pattern of attributes that characterize projects of ordinary innovation processes.

On this account the question intuitively arises as to whether radical innovations can result from any type of managerial process or whether they come about in a non-predictable manner like the 'post-it' product in the often referenced 3M story. If indeed such a process were conceivable, the next question would refer to its design and management.

Answers to these questions constitute the basis of this book. Its content is the result of a doctoral dissertation research project carried out at the Swiss Federal Institute of Technology. Its origins, on the one hand, lie in case studies of radical innovations that were generated in companies belonging to different industries. On the other hand, global cases of 'best practice' in dealing with incremental and radical innovations were investigated. The findings were then interpreted on the basis of an integrated approach to technology and innovation management. This concept differs from ordinary management of technology approaches insofar as the holistic perspective of managing innovation-driven enterprises is dominant.

The ambitious size and scope of this project required extensive networks of academic and industrial collaboration. Two of them to be mentioned explicitly are the European Institute of Technology and Innovation Management (EITIM) and the Global Advanced Technologies Innovation Consortium (GATIC). EITIM consists of a collaboration eight European institutes of Technology and Innovation Management with the shared motivation to make a substantial contribution of improving Europe's still trailing innovativeness. The latest book carries the title *Bringing Technology and Innovation into the Boardroom*, reflecting the above mentioned holistic management perspective. GATIC, on the other hand, consists of a joint collaboration of technology-oriented universities and innovation-driven companies from the US, Japan and Europe.

As a result, a remarkably well-elaborated compendium is presented. On the one hand, it provides a valuable insight into state-of-the-art current sustained innovation management in theory and practice. On the other, it contains numerous suggestions on how to cope with the *challenge of sustained innovation* consisting of different but closely related processes for incremental and radical innovations. Relating to the questions raised above, it is thus demonstrated that meaningful processes focused on radical innovations can be established. These suggestions are underlined with a large number of 'best practice' cases. The cases are well depicted thus allowing a relatively easy learning transfer into comparable business situations.

This book is addressed to management practitioners in technology-based companies to help them cope effectively with the challenges of technological change. Moreover it provides a most useful piece of reference for scholars *and* students searching for field-tested solutions of integral technology and innovation management issues.

Zurich   HUGO P. TSCHIRKY

1
Introduction

The rapid rate of technological change (Gertsen, 2003: 801; Petrick and Echols, 2004: 82) over the past few decades has begun to show an alteration of its very nature. Until only a few decades ago the nature of technological change and, thus, the trajectory along which changes happened used to increase, for the most part relatively steadily. Companies operating in such a technological environment competed by innovating continuously along predictable technological trajectories.

Technology change continuously evolved; it was mainly driven by innovation focused on improving existing technologies. Foster (Foster and Kaplan, 2002: 32) called this period the a time of continuity, where companies were concerned with maintaining stability by innovating embattled products and services (Scigliano, 2003: 10f.). This type of innovation is incremental: it takes place within existing infrastructures of companies, building on existing knowledge in existing markets without challenging underlying strategies or assumptions (Miller and Langdon, 1999: 4).

However, the stability that organizations are naturally striving for (Scigliano, 2003: 9) has clearly disintegrated over the last few decades (D'Aveni, 1994: 227; Nault and Vandenbosch, 1998: 171). While in the past, acquired competitive advantage used to insure stability for many years, even decades, today such stable competitive advantage turns out to have become more and more transient (D'Aveni, 1995: 255). Evidence of this pattern can be found in the average lifetime of companies listed in the S&P 500.[1] At the beginning of the twentieth century the expected average lifetime of a company in the S&P 500 was 65 years, in 1988 this had diminished to an average of only 10 years (Foster and Kaplan, 2002: 33f.). Extrapolating this pattern means that companies founded today will be challenged by an ever increasing struggle to survive in the S&P 500.

The aspiration of companies to sustain continuity can be explained historically as firms were focused on the production of products and services and not on their own further development (Foster and Kaplan, 2002: 45). However, the last decade of the millennium with its technology hype

(Cooper *et al.*, 2001: 3) can be regarded as the end of this continuity and clearly heralded what Peter Drucker had already described in 1969 as the age of discontinuity.[2] Considering when Drucker's theory was published this is not an entirely new phenomenon. The work of Schumpeter (1934), Mensch (1979), Marchetti (1980) and Perez (1983) on technological innovation, as well as that by Kondratiev[3] on economic prosperity-recession-depression-recovery cycles, suggests a long wave[4] pattern of continuously evolving technology change interrupted by discontinuities. From a technology change point of view, Tushman and Anderson (1986: 726) described these waves as incremental change that are punctuated by revolutionary breakthrough changes. What is new is that in recent times the frequency with which the technological waves are punctuated by this revolutionary change increased considerably (Foster, 1986: 48). This new nature of technology change is hence increasingly discontinuous (Sohn and Moon, 2004: 72).

Discontinuous technology change is characterized by the fact that it breaks with the existing technological experience. It destroys acknowledged paradigms (Dosi, 1982: 152) disrupting the status quo or interrupting expected evolutions in an industry (Tushman and Nadler, 1986: 76; Kunz, 2002: 14).[5] In order to adapt to such changes in an industry, companies generally need to master creative destruction (Schumpeter, 1934), which is the ability to destroy or break up traditional competitive structures and to change its rules by creating innovations (Scigliano, 2003: 1). Innovations with this power are usually not of an incremental character. There is more needed than mere improvements of existing approaches. The kinds of innovation with the power to change given rules in an industry are known as radical innovation (Damanpour, 1988: 546; Strebel, 1995: 12f.; Leifer, 2000: 4; Scigliano, 2003: 1) also called breakthrough (Nayak and Ketteringham, 1986: 181; Noori *et al.*, 1999: 545; Mascitelli, 2000), revolutionary (Abernathy and Clark, 1985: 12) or discontinuous innovation (Tushman and Nadler, 1986: 76; Reid and Brentani, 2004: 170).[6]

An innovation is said to be radical if it involves the application of significant new technologies or significant new combinations of technologies leading to new market opportunities (Tushman and Nadler, 1986: 74f.). Radical innovation 'departs dramatically from the norm' (Anderson and Tushman, 1990: 604) and 'transforms the relationship between customers and suppliers, restructures marketplace economics, displaces current products, and often creates entirely new product categories' (Leifer *et al.*, 2000: 2).

Despite the present need to master radical innovation in order to adapt to an increasing discontinuous technology change, the strategic management of it is poorly understood (Miller and Langdon, 1999: xii). When speaking of strategic management we refer to strategic planning. Strategic planning can be defined as 'a self-discovery process that recognizes and responds to environmental pressures and opportunities within the limits of resources' (Nahm, 1986: 45). Its objective is 'to identify the key problems that may develop in the future before they become critical and to examine what strategies can be adopted to prevent the coming about of undesirable consequences' (Chambers and Taylor, 1999: 27). The management of discontinuous technology change increasingly can be considered a standard problem of strategic technology planning (Harmann, 2003: 1f.) and needs to be integrated in the planning process (Lehmann, 1994: 1).

There are many examples of companies, especially established ones, that have failed to adapt to discontinuous technological change (Hamel and Prahalad, 1994: 79; Stoelhorst, 2002: 262). Many of them were destroyed or at best lost a significant part of their market share (Martino, 1993: 278) due to strategic planning mistakes. Such mistakes will be shown in the coming section. It describes examples of companies that failed to overcome a discontinuous technology change in their industry due to weak strategic management. This is the evidence that proves the urgency for improvement in the strategic management of discontinuous technologies and radical innovation. This is the call from practice.

1 Evidence and the call from practice

Technological discontinuities happen in every industry (Floyd, 1996: 5; Kunz, 2002: 1). Computer optical storage systems, watches, medical diagnostics, digital mobile telephones, high-performance polymers, digital photography, biotechnology, nanotechnology and genetic engineering are all examples of the technologies that are changing the world we live in, creating opportunities for some companies and putting others out of business (Lynn *et al.*, 1996: 34f.). From all of these examples, three cases of discontinuous technology changes have been selected. The first two are well-known examples of discontinuous changes observed over the last few decades in the semiconductor and in the hard disc industry. The third case more extensively describes a discontinuous change that can be observed right at the moment: it is the unstoppable shift from analog to digital photography.

A study in the semiconductors industry conducted by Tushman and O'Reilly (1996) analyzed how discontinuous technological change affected companies in this industry. Driven by the miniaturization in the computer industry in the period between 1955 and 1995, vacuum tubes were substituted with transistors, which were then replaced by integrated circuits. In this period, market leadership in the semiconductor industry completely changed several times. Most of the companies in this industry had stayed too long with their existing products even with the appearance of the first signs of the technological shifts. Focused on improvements of the old technology, most of the established market-leading companies were not thinking about planning radical innovations; they lost their leading position.

In another study describing the progress of the hard disc industry in the same period, Christensen (1997) shows that the strategic management of established, market-leading companies in the computer industry repeatedly failed to recognize the need for a radical technological innovation as a technology shift was emerging. Thus, with every technological leap during the analyzed 30 years, the leading companies were displaced from their market position. These were the same companies that, only a few years before, had invaded the industry with a radical innovation. They had succeeded in acquiring the leadership with the previous technology shift. However, once they had reached a leading position in the industry, their motivation for radical innovation had shifted to incremental innovation. It was this shift in motivation that finally caused them to fall as a further radical innovation, coming from industry outsider companies, invaded their business.

A current example of a discontinuous technological change is the one happening in the photography industry. The fusion of electronic and optical technologies that started in the 1960s has disrupted the photography industry over the past few years, increasingly displacing the conventional silver ionic film technology. The shift has been triggered by the radical innovation of a light-sensitive chip technology.[7] It is a semiconductor accumulating energy depending on the amount of light to which it is exposed. Since this digital technology demonstrated its benefit over the analog technology in the early 1990s with the first consumer cameras, its popularity has risen steeply. For example, in Germany the total revenue of digital cameras sold from 2000–2 has doubled to a total of 600 million euros, while sales of conventional cameras are steadily declining (*Der Spiegel*, 3/2003). The boom seems far from slowing. In France the market volume increase in the period from 2002–4 has been estimated at 72 per cent (Meslem, 2003: 159).

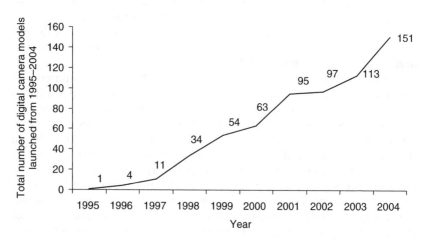

Figure 1.1   Number of digital cameras launched from 1995 to 2004
Source: Digital Photography Review, 2005.

Figure 1.1 illustrates the increasing number of digital technology camera models launched in the world market in the last few years.

The shift induced by digital technology is truly discontinuous for the photography industry. It completely changes the rules of the industry. Hence the traditional camera constructors have to deal not only with their known competitors but also with a great number of companies new to the camera industry such as Sony, Sanyo, Toshiba, Casio, HP or Panasonic. At the same time, these companies from the electronics industry have tremendously increased the research and development pace in this traditionally slow industry that they have penetrated. This has had a considerable effect on the product lifecycle of cameras: while in the past new cameras were launched annually, now new digital camera models are delivered to the market as often as every three months.

Not all companies are taking advantage of this new reality and its accompanying boom. Besides the successes of Canon, Olympus, Sony and Fuji some formerly trend-setting and industry-leading companies, such as Minolta, Konika and Leica, are struggling to catch up (*Der Spiegel*, 3/2003). Figure 1.2 illustrates the number of products launched between 1995 and 2004 in the industry. The diagram reflects which companies are most engaged in the development of digital cameras.

These three examples show that the management of discontinuous technology changes and radical innovation has been an important topic for many years. They show that for some reason established companies still

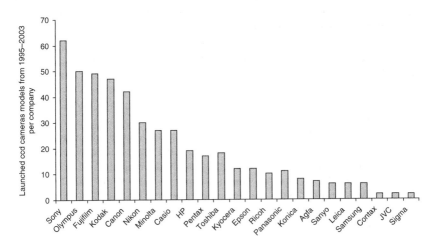

Figure 1.2 Number of digital cameras launched per company, from January 1995 to 2004

Source: *Digital Photography Review*, 2005.

have problems adapting to discontinuous technology change and that they have difficulties generating radical innovation.

The next section elaborates on the question of why established companies have such difficulty overcoming discontinuous technology change and why they apparently hesitate to engage in radical innovation. Knowing what is at the origin of the problems allows the focus of this book to be narrowed.

2 The origin of the management problems

Looking for the origin of the problems in handling discontinuous technology change and radical innovation in the above examples and in many others analyzed by scholars, one common point becomes clear: for far too long, established companies have continued updating their existing technology instead of acknowledging and reacting to the emergence of new technology. They have put most of their effort into improving the existing technological approach in order to defend it against the emerging discontinuous one. Although these efforts are not to be underestimated, as in some cases the existing technology did experience a considerable performance boost when attacked by an emerging one, it is true to say that usually its limits are quickly reached compared to the emerging technology. Tushman and O'Reilly (1996: 727) put it this way: 'Managers that try to adapt to discontinuities through incremental adjustment are unlikely to succeed.' Foster (1986: 52ff.) calls such incremental adjustments trying to challenge emerging discontinuities the 'sailing ship effect'.[8]

The case of the photo industry well illustrates the pattern of the 'sailing ship effect'. The Advanced Photo Systems, known as APS, can be interpreted as an effort to boost analog film technology when the first consumer digital cameras were emerging in the early 1990s. It was an initiative by the world's biggest established camera companies such as Canon, Fuji, Kodak, Minolta and Nikon. The APS technology was basically a new film format of the existing silver ionic film technology. Its extra-thin film layer was entirely enclosed in a special compact cartridge allowing smaller camera dimensions. Besides its advantage in size, the film also included optical and magnetic data trails enabling the exchange of information between the camera, the film and the picture-developing laboratory. With these and some other new features that were meant to facilitate handling, developing and ordering of picture copies, APS technology was first commercialized in 1996. However, its success was limited. With the rising popularity of digital cameras at in the end of the millennium, APS cameras hardly sold. Their commercialization was discontinued only a few years after their launch.

Many companies prefer to concentrate on incremental improvements rather than engaging in radical innovation in order to prepare for or to shape the next generation of technologies. Once the technological transition is accomplished and products based on the existing technology lose market share, it is extremely difficult for companies to catch up with the new technological and market situation in their industry (Miller and Langdon, 1999: 5).

A study conducted 2003 in Germany analyzing 432 innovation projects in 39 industries shows clearly that managers most appreciate innovations that are of the type of an old product's care, maintenance and improvement (Berth, 2003: 18).[9] Innovative, radical, or even visionary types of innovations are rather unpopular. Most striking in this study is, however, the discrepancy between the estimated rates of return established by managers for the different types of innovation. Projects with a low degree of innovativeness, such as the case with mere improvements, were estimated far too highly whereas radical and visionary innovation projects turned out to be far more lucrative than managers expected.

Uncertainty as the root of the problem

One of the main reasons that companies hesitate to engage in radical technological innovation is that these innovations trigger major changes and inherent uncertainty[10] within the companies' organization. Individuals are uncomfortable with uncertainty and thus work to structure, organize and interpret the world they experience in order to create routines (Burkhardt and Brass, 1990: 106) and reduce any sort of uncertainty. However, these management routines are generally not designed to handle the characteristics of radical innovations, which are shaped by the high degree of newness of these innovations. Companies cannot fall back on experience (Macharzina, 1984: 6). The consequences of engaging in these radical innovations are thus hard to predict, which again increases the level of uncertainty. As a result radical technological innovations are often high risk for companies (Day *et al.*, 2001: 23): they need long-term commitment (Rice *et al.*, 1998: 58), they are founded on numerous and poorly developed technological solutions (Abernathy and Utterback, 1978: 45) and they open new uncertain markets that need to be created (O'Connor, 1998: 151; Herstatt and Lettl, 2004: 163). Thus, radical innovations are basically difficult to plan strategically. All these characteristics do not fit well with most company's management approaches in today's competitive environment.

Today companies are looking for quickly visible short-term growth in order to satisfy shareholders' expectations (Clarke and Varma, 1999: 414). Customer orientation in well-defined, existing markets with a limited number of proven and well-developed technological solutions are essential (Tushman and O'Reilly, 1996: 730). These latter characteristics are typically those of incremental innovations with moderate degree of uncertainty (see Figure 1.3).

A company that exclusively plans for incremental innovation with mere market orientation might be successful in the short term; however, it might be surprised by a technological discontinuity that does not support the course of its incremental innovation (Ansoff, 1981: 234; Zehnder, 1997: 98).

Characteristics	Incremental innovation	Radical innovation
Technology change	Continuous	Discontinuous
Time horizon	Short term	Long term
Technological solutions	Limited, well developed	Numerous, poorly developed
Risk	Moderate	High
Market	Existing	New, to be created
Planning possibilities	Good	Difficult
	Moderate uncertainty	**High uncertainty**

Figure 1.3 Characteristics of incremental versus radical innovations

In such cases the time left for action tends to be zero if the company is not strategically prepared (Macharzina, 1984: 6).

Ideally, strategic management should be designed to handle both types of innovation challenges, radical and incremental. *It should be able to handle a medium degree of uncertain incremental innovations and to, at the same time, reduce the high level of uncertainty of radical innovation opportunities. However today, most organizations are designed to excel in only one type of innovation. Typically established*[11] *companies well master incremental innovation whereas small start-up companies excel in radical innovations* (Noori, 1990: 103).

Towards sustained innovation[12]

It can be summarized that companies tend to ignore the emergence of discontinuous technology change and prefer to stick with their existing technologies. Managers in such companies feel more comfortable maintaining and improving technologies that they already know rather than engaging with change through radical innovations. This attitude, as well as the incorrect estimation of managers regarding the rate of return of highly innovative projects, indicates that, on the one hand, the management of radical innovation and discontinuous technologies is very poorly understood in practice (Miller and Langdon, 1999: 5) and that, on the other hand, management literature does not sufficiently address this strategic planning issue of technology and innovation management to produce relief. As will be described in more detail in Chapter 3, most managers have difficulties planning for or reacting to discontinuous technology change or preparing their company for the strategic management of radical innovations as applicable strategic planning concepts are missing. This is the gap in practice.

Chapter 2 will show that managers find little support from strategic management theory when looking for practitioner-oriented planning concepts that treat this subject adequately (Stoelhorst, 2002: 262; Harmann, 2003: 40). Although there are authors that suggest planning concepts for the management of discontinuous technologies and radical innovation, *none was found that kept in mind that such a concept needs to be compatible with as well as integrated in the management of incremental innovations.* This integration of both approaches is needed in order to cover the two alternating sides of technology change (Wyk, 2002: 25): both the continuous evolution of technology change where the ability of incremental innovation is required and the discontinuous breaks in technology change where the ability to innovate radically is required. *It is only by simultaneously mastering both innovation approaches, radical and incremental, that the long-term competitive advantage of a company will be insured throughout the altering technology change* (Gertsen, 2003: 801): *radical innovation in order to explore*[13] *and build up distinctive and inimitable competences*[14] *followed by incremental innovation in order to exploit*[15] *and use these competencies to secure growth* (Hunger and Wheelen, 2002: 52f.).[16] *We call this twofold approach the **sustained innovation approach**.*[17,18] Today there is no systematic strategic planning concept that respects the approach of sustained innovation in an integrative way. This is the gap in theory (see Chapter 2, Section 3).

In a nutshell this book pursues two related goals: the first is to create an improved understanding of what is necessary for a successful strategic planning of discontinuous technologies and radical innovation in order to contribute in closing the gap in theory. The second goal is to propose a concept for systematically[19] managing discontinuous technologies and radical innovation with regards to integration with existing concepts of incremental innovation. The goal is to deliver an *uncertainty-reducing procedure that is, at the same time, of a systematic nature and practitioner-oriented.* The procedure should enable the manager *to constantly and anticipatively implement company internal changes in order to adapt to different kinds of external environmental changes*: continuous and discontinuous changes. The elaboration of such a strategic concept is the contribution of this work in closing the gap in practice.

The corresponding research question is: 'How should processes, structures and methodologies of strategic planning with discontinuous technologies and radical innovations be designed, directed and developed in order to achieve the implementation of sustained technological innovation?'

3 Research backing the insights of this book

This book is based on a scientific research conducted over 2002–5 at the Department of Management, Economics and Technology at the Swiss Federal Institute of Technology. This publication used a variety of research methodologies such as in-depth literature research, corporate case studies, interviews and action research to collect a large amount of scientific data. The aggregation and cross-analysis of this data enabled the insights published in this book.

4 Structure of this book

The structure of this book is derived from its initial scientific publication. It comprises the present first chapter, which basically describes the call from practice and the management encounters when challenged by the management of radical innovation and discontinuous technologies.

Chapter 2 reviews the existing literature on discontinuous technology and radical innovation. This provides a preliminary understanding of the aspects relevant to the management of discontinuous technology and radical innovation; furthermore, gaps in the existing research are identified.

In Chapter 3, 'Managing radical innovations – corporate case studies' state of the art management practice is analyzed. For this purpose three case studies conducted by a series of in-depth interviews were carried out in order to reconstruct the management approaches and their consequences in three companies aiming to transfer discontinuous technology into radical innovations. Analyzing and cross-comparing the cases leads to the identification of a number of issues related to management processes, methods and structures. These issues reflect the state of the art in the management of discontinuous technologies and radical innovations. They discuss the performance of this management and their implications. The issues are the basis for the formulation of nine propositions that reflect requirements for management processes, methods and structures. The propositions can be understood as the requirements for the design of a management approach for discontinuous technologies and radical innovation within the context of sustained innovation.

In Chapter 4 the propositions are used to develop a new management approach for strategically managing radical innovations. While doing so, a second phase of case studies is conducted in order to continuously improve the concept. The interviews conducted in this second phase are done to identify companies that already fulfill today one or more of the concept's propositions. Such cases were considered 'best practice cases'. They show companies where practical applications of management solutions developed in the concept of this research have already been designed and/or successfully implemented. Thus, their analysis shows how the concept's propositions can be effectively implemented in reality.

Beside those best practice cases, Chapter 4 also includes 'practice cases'. The practice cases have also been identified during the interviews mentioned above. They are used to illustrate statements and findings described in the text by referring to real practical cases.

This chapter presents one possible solution derived from the propositions. However, it does not claim exclusivity. Thus, a partial validation of the presented solution was done through action research.

Chapter 5 describes management principles that purely address management's concern in management summary style. Their objective is to support management in their decision-making process. Thus, this last part represents the final statement of this book.

Chapter 6 contains an outlook as well as the management summary.

2
State of the Art in Management Theory

This chapter first builds the theoretical basis of this publication, then gaps in state-of-the-art management theory will be elaborated in detail. In the first section some definitions and basic concepts are given. The second section reviews in detail the research done in the field of discontinuous technologies and radical innovation. The third section shows how this insight is used today for the purpose of strategic planning of discontinuous technologies and radical innovation. The chapter will close with a conclusion of this analysis formulating the gap in state of the art in theory.

1 Underlying definitions and basic concepts

This section gives a representative overview of the definitions and concepts of strategic management, technology management and innovation management that are relevant for this research. This overview provides the reader with state-of-the-art management knowledge of strategic planning with discontinuous technologies and radical innovation.

Strategic management

The strategic management issue is probably the most philosophical topic in management literature. As will be shown later, there are diverse schools and a series of approaches to dealing with the strategy question. From an initial point of view, strategic management is understood as planning to run and change the business in order to achieve the business's mission and goals (Wright, *et al* 1992: 3).[1] Terms such as 'thinking', 'acting' and 'decision-making' are tasks central to this purpose (Gälweiler, 1990: 65). Before going into these details, strategic management is first classified within an integrated context of management and its basic functions are explained.

Basic functions of management in an integrated company context
Strategic management is an essential element needed to constantly develop the company modeled as a complex system within a dynamically changing

environment (Malik, 2001b: 135ff.). In order to realize this development, strategic management cannot be considered as a stand-alone mindset. Rather it needs to be linked to a top-level character of management, the normative management, and to an executing character of management, the operative management (Ulrich, 1984: 329). *Normative, strategic and operational* management represent essential elements of an integrated management context (see Figure 2.1). Normative management provides the values and ethics; it forms the culture a company needs to sustain in a rapidly changing environment. It gives the company a distinct identity that justifies its activities. This identity is typically formulated in a vision that states the benefit of the company for its customers. Strategic management follows the guidance of normative management. It shapes the companies' activities, defining their objectives and their methods of implementation.

Together normative and strategic management have the function *to design* the development of a company. Design has the goal to create a working system. For this purpose the required resources and institutional domains will be defined and merged into a consistent organization: design as a management function means the draft of an institutional model, where the designation of the targeted properties of the institution is essential. Therefore such designs can be called 'design models', which have to be clearly differentiated from scientific explanation models, which try to explain an existing reality, and differentiated from decision models, which display a specific problem situation in an existing system. In contrast, design models are analogous to design drafts: they aim to create a not yet existing reality. The development of this design model is therefore an effective and constructive procedure (Ulrich and Probst, 1988: 260).

Execution of this design is the responsibility of operational management. It runs the measures that are needed in order to implement the designed model. Operational management has, thus, the function *to direct* the development of a company (Bleicher, 1992: 68). This means that the company objectives are aligned in real time to the created objectives of the design model. The created objectives can be new structures or new processes that help to execute company objectives. This requires a constant debate with the environment conditions in addition to the situation of the company itself. The outcome of this is a constant need to evaluate changes of planned projects, which demand a further decision and its implementation. To direct is therefore a function that is essential in a system so that this system can achieve its objectives under evolving conditions with concrete activities (Ulrich and Probst, 1988: 261).

After the system has been designed and directed, it needs to be continuously *developed* so that it can adapt to the constant social, technological and industrial changes that result in changed conditions and assumptions for designing and directing the company as a system. Thus, in the foreground there is the further development of the company in terms of constant

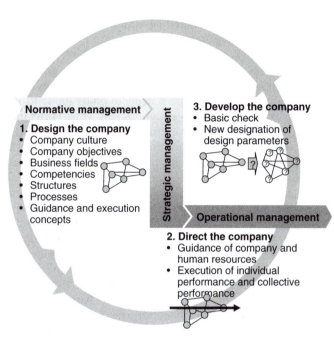

Figure 2.1   The basic management functions in an integrated management context
Source: Adapted from Tschirky and Bucher, 2003: 27.

improvement or qualitative learning. In the short term it is essential for the company to learn to function better with given objectives, to subsequently eliminate deficiencies and not to repeat mistakes. In the long term it is essential to encourage the innovativeness[2] of the company (Ulrich and Probst, 1988: 263).

In sum, strategic management can be understood as a mindset within an integrated context of the company (Hammer, 1998: 57). It is the mindset that takes care of planning, steering and coordinating the development of the company (Welge and Al-Laham, 1992: 2356). This development should not be understood as a passive reaction to an external changing environment but rather as an active design of internal configurations of the company. It designs the organizational structures and influences the company culture.

Based on this understanding of strategic management, the terms of strategy and strategic planning will be discussed in the next section.

Strategic management views in a competitive environmental context

In modern strategic management aligned with the management of enterprises in a competitive environment three basic views can be distinguished: the market based view, the resource-based view and the knowledge-based view (Müller-Stewens and Lechner, 2001: 11f.).

The market-based view was motivated by Porter (1980). It is founded on his work on Industrial Economics and the concepts on corporate policy developed at the Harvard Business School. This view promotes the idea that the competitive advantage of a company depends on its ability to analyze, in the first place, its external competitive environment. Thus, Porter proposes to analyze the structure and competitive situation in the industry and the market. These two elements are the key for the company's strategy development.

The resource-based view emerged in the beginning of the 1990s based on the thoughts of Chamberlin (1933), Robinson (1933) and Penrose (1959). These economists emphasized the uniqueness of firms' assets and capabilities rather than market and industry structures. The idea is promoted that management's most important task is the development and deployment of internal resources in order to gain competitive advantage over other companies.[3]

The knowledge based-view proposes that a firm's source of unique advantage resides in its ability to integrate knowledge of different individuals in the production of goods and services (Ghoshal and Moran, 1996; Grant, 1996). Thus, strategy development from the knowledge-based view consists of building up unique competencies that allow the company to gain competitive advantage. Prahalad and Hamel (1990) call these competencies core competencies. Competencies are those core attributes of an enterprise that enable it to come up with unanticipated products and services, to invent and shape consumer demand, and to enter new markets rapidly and successfully – in other words 'competencies are considered core if they differentiate a company strategically' (Leonard-Barton, 1992: 111).

Strategy

There is no common definition of the term strategy. Although strategy has become a key word in management practice and literature, definitions vary from author to author. Strategy is still defined according to its use (Schendel and Cool, 1988: 23). However, what most of these definitions have in common is that they agree on two specific elements that a strategy needs to incorporate: first, the goals that the company should realize and, second, the ways or path by which these goals should be achieved. 'Strategy can be defined as the determination of the basic long-term goals and objectives of an enterprise and the adoption of courses of action and the allocation of resources necessary to carry out these goals' (Chandler, 1962: 13). In the same context Tschirky and Bucher (2003) refer to strategic path and strategic goals (see Figure 2.2). Some representative examples of this understanding of strategy are:

- 'Strategy is the determination of the basic long-term goals and the objectives of an enterprise, and the adoption of courses of action and the allocation of resources necessary for carrying out these goals' (Chandler, 1962: 13).

- 'A strategy is a plan or a pattern that integrates an organization's major goals, policies, and action sequences into a cohesive whole' (Quinn, 1980: 7).

- 'Corporate strategy is the pattern of decisions in a company that determines and reveals its objectives, purposes, produces the principal policies and plans for achieving those goals, and defines the range of business the company is to pursue, the kind of economic and human organization it is or intends to be, and the nature of the economic and non-economic contribution it intends to make to its shareholders, employees, customer, and communities' (Andrews, 1987: 13).

- 'A strategy makes statements about goals, measures and means in order to achieve sustainable competitive advantage' (translated from German) (Hammer, 1998: 57).

- 'A strategy of a corporation is a comprehensive plan stating how the corporation will achieve its mission and objectives. It maximizes competitive advantage and minimizes competitive disadvantage' (Hunger and Wheelen, 2002: 7).

Beside this differentiation in strategy according to goals and path, Abell (1999) suggests the consideration of strategies according to different time horizons. He describes the dual-strategy approach: 'today-for-today strategies' and 'today-for-tomorrow strategies'. Furthermore:

This distinction between a present and future orientation is not the usual short-term, long-term distinction – in which the short-term plan is simply a detailed operations and budgeting exercise made in the context of a hoped-for long-term market position. Present planning also requires strategy – a vision of how the firm has to operate (given its competencies and target markets) and what the role of each key function will be. The long-term plan, by contrast, is built on a vision of the future – even more importantly, on a strategy for getting there. (Abell, 1999: 74)

Figure 2.2   Strategic path and goals
Source: Adapted from Tschirky *et al.* (2003).

This strategic thinking according to different time horizons is in alignment with the differentiation made by Tschirky and Bucher (2003: 27f.). It distinguishes between strategic management for today, tomorrow and the day after tomorrow. Company development according to this strategic mindset is realized by the distinction of two different strategies that are run in parallel. On the one hand, the development from today to tomorrow is designed by a competitive strategy. This strategy defines short- to middle-term strategic objectives that secure and expand the company's actual competitive position. Thus this strategy should gradually transform the company. On the other hand, the development of the company from tomorrow to the day after tomorrow is realized by a development strategy. This strategy is meant to secure the changes that the company cannot realize through only gradual alterations. Its objectives are 'sustainable changes in the company's culture and values, substantial scientific and technological change as well as structural changes' (Tschirky and Bucher, 2003: 28–9). These are the kind of changes that are needed in order to react to or to initiate radical changes. The operational realization of these different strategies is done through fundamentally different project types. While gradual change is realized by competitive strategic projects, radical changes are realized by development strategic changes.

Furthermore, different levels and fields of strategies within an organization can be distinguished. Porter (1987) describes the difference between strategies on a corporate level from strategies on a business unit level. While 'corporate strategy describes a company's overall direction in terms of its general attitude toward growth and the management of its various businesses and product lines' business strategy 'emphasizes improvement of the competitive position of a corporation's products or services in the specific industry or market segment' (Hunger and Wheelen, 2002: 7). Fields of strategy can be clustered according to products, sales and marketing, financial, human resource, technology and innovation. These clusters of strategies are also called functional strategies, which are 'concerned with developing and nurturing a distinctive competence to provide a company or business unit with a competitive advantage' (Hunger and Wheelen, 2002: 8). All functional strategies should integrate to become the business strategy.

Based on the above understanding of strategy, a strategy is, according to Mintzberg and Waters (1985: 15), associated with setting directions, focusing efforts, defining the organization[4] and providing consistency.

Strategy formulation and strategy implementation

The previous sections outlined the understanding of strategy. This section will now go on to describe what it means to formulate and implement a strategy. The distinction made in this publication between strategy formulation and implementation has been promoted by Andrews (1987), arguing that thinking and acting should be separated. Following this course, first, different approaches of strategy formulation will be explained, followed by an explanation of strategy implementation.

Strategy formulation

Strategy formulation develops a plan in alignment to normative[5] and operational[6] aspects of the company: a plan that is consistent with its environment, resources, managerial values and organizations (Noori, 1990: 132). Various approaches exist for the formulation of a strategy; Mintzberg and Lampel (1999) analyze different strategy formulation concepts clustering them into ten different basic approaches: the ten schools of strategy formulation. The differences between the schools depend from the level of systematization (versus intuition), in the choice for a basic procedure – bottom up versus top down – in the use of analytical practice or in the choice of supportive methods and tools.

The author of this book tends towards a well-structured, transparent and understandable strategy formulation. These characteristics are best depicted by the planning school, the design school and the configuration school. These schools promote a systematized step-by-step procedure led by senior management and aided by analytical management tools. Thus, in the following chapters the strategic management concept that should allow managers to handle sustained innovation will be developed within the boundaries set by these two schools of strategy formulation. Hence the concept that will be presented is no longer to be understood as a strategic management concept but more accurately as (1) *a strategic* **planning process** *that will concentrate on the systematic elaboration of a strategic plan* (according to the design and planning school). This process has to be understood as part of strategic management respecting the basic strategic functions design, direct and develop. Thus, it mainly (2) *focuses on* **strategic perspectives** and to a much lesser extent on normative and operational aspects. Nevertheless, the strategic planning process should not be an isolated process; the interfaces with normative and operational aspects as such should still be respected. Furthermore, the developed strategic plan should represent one functional strategy that fits with all other functional strategies within the company. Additionally, the strategic *planning process should be* (3) **supported by checklists, tools and techniques** (according to planning school) *or more generally speaking supported by management methods*. Finally, the (4) **organizational structures and configurations** *that are necessary to enable* the process and to realize the internal transformation of the company will be described (according to configuration school). In this book organizational configurations will be more generally called structures. Table 2.1 summarizes the main boundaries set by the chosen strategy schools.

Strategy implementation

Strategy implementation is the operational realization of the strategy (Kantrow, 1980: 28). It can be understood as all of the activities and choices required for the execution of the strategic plan. 'It is the process by which strategies and policies are put into action through the development of

Table 2.1   Boundaries set for the development of a concept for sustained management

Boundaries set by the three schools of strategy formulation for the development of a concept for sustainable management	
1. Planning process	The concept should be designed as a process
2. Strategic perspective	The concept should address the strategic management perspective
3. Supportive tools and techniques	The concept should be supported by management tools and techniques
4. Enabling organizational structure	The concept should be enabled by distinct organizational structures

programs, budgets, and procedures' (Hunger and Wheelen, 2002: 9). Strategy implementation is for the most part a structural matter that has to consider the three following questions (Black, 2002: 121):

• Who are the people who will carry out the strategic plan?
• What must be done?
• How are they going to do what is needed?

The process of strategy implementation might involve changes that affect the entire company culture, structure, or management system; thus, strategy formulation should not be done without bearing the consequences for the organization in mind (Hunger and Wheelen, 2002: 9).

These considerations about strategy implementation emphasize the need for all strategic planning processes to be supported by organizational structures that take care of its implementation. It thus confirms the choice of the configuration school made above.

Technologies and technology management

Technologies

Technologies are the basic unit of technology management. There are controversial discussions about the term technology. This publication closely follows Tschirky's (Tschirky and Koruna, 1998: 226) definition: 'Technologies enclose specific individual and collective knowledge in explicit and implicit forms for product and process-oriented usage based on natural, social and engineering-scientific knowledge.' In this definition of technology the application of scientific knowledge and theories[7] is strongly emphasized. One might say that science 'turns' into technology after a step of application-oriented research or development.

Within the scope of technology management, the term technology has two fundamentally different forms: while a product technology insures that a specific technological impact comes about, a process technology enables and/or optimizes the occurrence of the technological impact. In the pharmaceutical industry, process technologies would be high-throughput screening technology applied in research or novel separation technologies applied in production, while the product technology would be the active substance in the drug. Common to both cases is the fulfillment of a specific function: in the first case a product function, in the second a process function (Tschirky and Koruna, 1998: 228).

Integrated technology management

The purpose of technology management is the deliberate handling of technologies. For decades, several authors have developed various approaches to technology management.[8] This book is in alignment with Tschirky's (Tschirky and Koruna, 1998: 267) concept of the 'integrated technology management' that drives the idea behind enterprise science (Tschirky, 2000).

Initial motivations for the concept of integrated technology management were to create technology awareness in general management. The aim was to resolve the *missing link* between engineering and science and general management by technology management. As a result, technology and its management consist in this concept as integrated parts of general management (see Figure 2.3).

For the realization of Tschirky's concept Bleicher's (1991: 56) notion of integrated management for the technology dimension of companies was found most suitable. The vision of the concept of integrated technology management is 'bringing technology into management'. 'Its basis is the postulate that "technology issues" will no longer be solely of concern in the context of direct technology-related managerial functions such as R&D and production management but will be of prime concern for general management at all levels' (Tschirky, 2000: 417). Tschirky (Tschirky and Koruna, 1998: 269) differentiates the following three levels of management:

- On the **normative level**, a clear commitment to the importance of technology as a vital concern for the technology-based company should be anchored in the company policy. At the same time, technology-awareness should permeate company culture, at every hierarchical level.

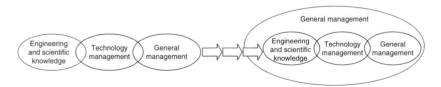

Figure 2.3 Technology and its management, integrated as parts of general management
Source: Tschirky, 2003b: 28.

- The **strategic level** is the transformation of company policy to comprehensive (technology) strategies. The principle of effectiveness is dominant. A primary concern is the trilogy of technology decisions (refer to Figure 2.8), which will be discussed in detail later in the section 'Technology strategic choice'.
- On the **operational level**, responsibility is taken for transforming strategies into practice in the context of short-term goals. Milestones in R&D projects, resource allocation and formal information flow are, for example, typical tasks at this level. The principle of efficiency is essential.

According to this view, technology management can be conceived of as an integrating function of general management, which is directed towards the normative, strategic and operational management of the technology and innovation potential[9] of an organization (Figure 2.4). The technology potential, as a socio-technical subsystem of an enterprise, comprises the available product and process technologies, their personal, informal and material carriers and the organizational structures and processes required for the technology application (Tschirky and Koruna, 1998: 246). The innovation potential comprises the available innovation competence of individuals and

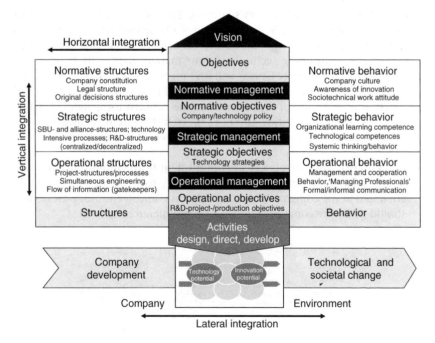

Figure 2.4   The concept of 'integrated technology management'
Source: Tschirky and Koruna, 1998: 270.

groups on all levels of the organization, which enable organizational inventions regarding the social and technical system, inventions related with the market impact of product and process technologies and business inventions (Tschirky and Koruna, 1998: 264).

After the conception of the integrated technology management, Tschirky extended the integrated view of technology management to 'enterprise science' (Tschirky, 2000: 418) in order to establish the correspondence between theory and reality in technology-based companies. Enterprise science is motivated by deficiencies found in current approaches of general management (see Figure 2.5):

> On the one side *describing* the reality of enterprise activities has to rely indispensably on the indicated main scientific knowledge. On the other though the analyzed [general management] concepts claim to be in the position of *explaining* the reality of enterprises and *even making recommendations* on their management, however they miss entire disciplines of reality relevant sciences. Therefore this claim appears to be inherently inconsistent and even contradictory. In this view it is postulated that the legitimacy of explaining the reality of enterprises and recommending principles of their management must arise imperatively from a concept which is based on all reality relevant sciences. *This is the core idea of the Concept Enterprise Science.* (Tschirky, 2003a: 29)

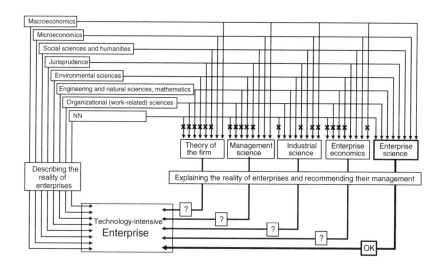

Figure 2.5 Concept enterprise science: a new basis for managing technology-based and innovation-driven enterprises

Source: Tschirky, 2000.

Technology strategies

According to Dodgson (2000: 134), for a technology-based[10] firm 'technology strategy comprises the definition, development, and use of those technological competencies that constitute their competitive advantage'. Tschirky (Tschirky and Koruna, 1998: 293) states that the purpose of technology strategies is twofold: on the one hand, technology strategies draw up a solid foundation for decision-making in order to enable the selection of technologies and strategic technology fields that are suitable for the creation and maintenance of an enterprise's competitive position.[11] This aspect is equivalent to the notion of a technology strategic goal or objective. On the other hand, technology strategies have to illustrate the appropriate paths leading to the mastery and deployment of the selected technologies. Figure 2.6 illustrates this 'goal' and 'path towards goal' perspective of technology strategy.[12]

Management should not design the enterprise's technology strategy as a self-contained assignment. Actually, on the contrary, management has to complete the task within the scope of overall business strategy development. Doing so will ensure that the technology strategy reflects an integrated part of a holistic business strategy, including a whole range of complementary perspectives, such as marketing, human resource and finance strategies.

Development of technology strategies: strategic technology planning

Strategy development is understood as a formalized planning procedure (see also this chapter, 'Strategy'). For the purpose of developing a technology strategy this procedure can be referred to as strategic technology planning. Defining strategic technology planning is surprisingly difficult; in fact, none

	Technology-strategic goals	Technology-strategic paths

Content	• Core technologies
	• Standard technologies
	• Support technologies
	• Obsolete technologies
	• Strategic technology fields
	  – Theories
	  – Core technologies
	  – Product/process technologies
	  – Support technologies
		• Leadership strategies
		• Follower strategies
		• Fusion strategies
		• Cooperation strategies
		• Make or buy strategies
		• Keep or sell strategies
		• Cost leadership strategies
		• Economy of scale strategies
		• Selective strategies

Method	• Technology monitoring • Technology intelligence • Technology assessment • Technology roadmapping	• Innovation audit • Market/product/technology analysis • Technology portfolios • Technology value analysis

Figure 2.6   Technology-strategic goals and paths
Source: Tschirky and Koruna, 1998: 294.

of the so-called state-of-the-art contributions of technology management literature provides a clear definition of this ubiquitous term. The approach of defining the general term of 'strategic planning' and then broadening it with the technology aspect has proven to be more successful. Mintzberg (1994: 12) has taken the task of going through the large body of strategic planning literature in order to provide a definition that has a good chance of winning approval from most strategy scholars. Building on his findings, the definition of strategic technology planning used in this book is: *Strategic technology planning* 'is a formalized procedure to produce an articulated result, in the form of an integrated system of strategic technological decisions' (Bucher, 2003: 69).

In the course of the above understanding (see this chapter, 'Basic functions of management in an integrated company context'), strategic technology planning must not be seen as an isolated activity but rather ought to occur within a joint and simultaneous collaboration between all parties involved in strategic planning. Tschirky (Tschirky and Koruna, 1998: 295) proposes a generic planning approach that consists of a stepwise and iterative integration of technology management issues into the typical steps of strategic planning such as setting strategic objectives, analyzing the environment, analyzing the company, elaborating strategic options, taking strategic decisions, implementing the strategy. Figure 2.7 illustrates this planning approach, emphasizing that it follows the distinction of strategy formulation and strategy implementation discussed in this chapter, 'Strategy formulation and strategy implementation'. The issues of technology management are regrouped into tasks, such as technology intelligence, technology

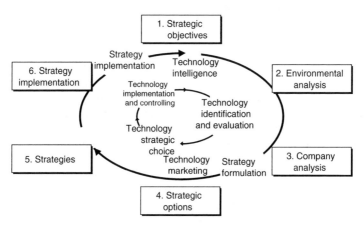

Figure 2.7   Integration of technology tasks into strategic planning
Source: Adapted from Tschirky and Koruna, 1998: 295.

identification and evaluation, technology strategic choice, technology implementation and controlling, technology marketing. These tasks can be associated with the typical steps of strategic planning. All these tasks together coordinated through strategic planning insure the three main functions of technology management (see this chapter, 'Technologies and technology management').

The next section describes each of the tasks of strategic technology planning and explains what kinds of technology issues are addressed. For the most part these issues elaborate the technology-strategic path step by step. Technology strategic goals were previously set in alignment with the other functional strategies and corporate strategy.

Technology intelligence

Technology intelligence is a task that cannot be assigned precisely to one or the other step of strategic management. It is a task that is on-going covering all steps of strategic management. The definition of technology intelligence in this book reflects well what task technology intelligence assumes in strategic planning. It is principally based on the definition from work conducted at the Center for Enterprise Science at the Swiss Federal Institute of Technology (ETH), Lichtenthaler (2000: 19) and Savioz (2002: 36): *technology intelligence* includes activities that support decision-making of technological and general management concerns by taking advantage of a well timed preparation of relevant information on technological facts and trends (opportunities and threats) of the organization's environment by means of collection, analysis and dissemination.

This definition shows that technology intelligence contributes considerably to fulfilling the first basic function of technology management: external acquisition of technologies (see this chapter, 'Technologies and technology management'). To further illustrate the definition, Savioz (2002: 32) highlights the following crucial elements:

- *Support decision-making of technological and general management concerns*: The purpose of technology intelligence is to promote and enable good technological decision-making rather than accurate forecasts.[13] This may not be consistent with one's typical expectations from forecasts; however, decision-making not only depends on the most reliable information, but also on intuition, traditions, resources, etc. Thus, technology intelligence is a supporting task, which can be pursued systematically or informally. Since decisions can be made within a planning process or spontaneously, technology intelligence has a reactive as well as proactive character. Technological trends may have an impact on any potential of the organization. Therefore, technology intelligence influences both technological and general management concerns.

- *Identify technological facts and trends (opportunity and threats)*: There is no restriction on the time focus or on the observation area. Facts and trends may emerge from weak signals and have a long-term scope. In turn, there may be established technologies solving a current problem. Thus, technology intelligence deals with strategic and operational questions. Whether facts and trends are opportunities or threats depend on their perception. In any case an integrated view comprising both technology and the market should be considered.

- *Well-timed preparation of relevant information*: Since today's information might have significance tomorrow because the organization's context is constantly changing, it is important to have this information well timed, not just as soon as possible. Otherwise there could be an information overload with the danger of misinterpretation and resource wasting.

The implementation of technology intelligence is described in literature through different processes. The process phases vary depending on the authors. For example, whereas Pfeiffer (1992) distinguishes only two different phases, Ashton *et al.* (1991) describe six different steps. Lichtenthaler (2000) has tried to combine various models and defines the following phases: (1) explicit or implicit formulation of information need; (2) information collection; (3) information analysis; and (4) information dissemination.[14] Associated with the process the authors describe various formal and informal sources of information and tools to analyze this information (e.g. patent analysis, literature analysis, etc.). Furthermore, the organizational integration of the technology intelligence into different company specific contexts is discussed (Lichtenthaler, 2000).

Technology intelligence plays a critical role in strategic planning with discontinuous technologies and radical innovation within the context of sustained innovation. It is especially important for companies to aim to anticipate discontinuities before they happen in order to assess consequences and prepare for them.

Technology identification and evaluation

Technology identification and evaluation is not clearly differentiated from technology intelligence. Some authors (Pfeiffer, 1992; Ashton and Stacy, 1995) assign technology identification and evaluation to technology intelligence. In this publication, technology identification and evaluation are considered as tasks collaborating closely with technology intelligence but following it in a sequential procedure.

Identification has the task of finding the technologies that will be attractive to the company in the future. What should be found are technologies that enable next generation products and services. Identification typically checks the company's internal strengths and weaknesses in order to find technologies that best fit the company. Evaluation assists identification to quantify or qualify why one technology should be preferred over another. Typical questions in technology evaluation are (Frauenfelder, 2000: 73):

- How much free cash flow (FCF) do the various technology decisions scenarios (best, real, worst case scenario) generate?
- What is the impact of the technology strategy in general when comparing alternatives?
- What is the financial return of each technology-related decision compared to its technology investment?
- Is there a strategic fit between the technology, business and product strategy?
- Are technology targets redundancy-free?

Technology evaluation most suffers from the uncertainty and complexity of technologies when its application is evaluated in the context of the company (Brodbeck *et al.*, 2003: 137). Especially with emerging technologies, most current evaluation approaches stumble as they are designed for specific projects.

Most of the identification and evaluation approaches in strategic planning are focused on assessing continuously evolving technologies. These approaches still have difficulties associating discontinuous technologies with a continuously evolving company context.

Technology strategic choice

In strategic technology planning there are three main strategic technology decisions to be taken into consideration, in alignment with the strategic goals: with regard to technology, Tschirky (Tschirky and Koruna, 1998: 296) describes three basically different but mutually complementary strategic decisions:

1. *Which technologies* originates from an extensive analysis of current and future products with respect to the major technologies determining the product performance and the process technologies required for product production and infrastructure operation. This analysis is based on technology intelligence activities, which include branch-overlapping searches of current technology, and technology evaluation. Based on this overview, a decision has then to be made as to which of the available and yet-to-be developed technologies are required for the continuous development of the enterprise.
2. *Make or buy* is concerned with the question as to whether the required technologies are to be made available through acquisition, collaboration with other companies or through in-house development.
3. *Keep or sell* deals with whether available technologies are to be applied exclusively for company purposes or can – or even must – be made available to other companies.

These three decisions are tightly interdependent and together represent the 'trilogy of strategic technology decisions'. (see Figure 2.8)

The multitude of options that can be composed from various forms of the 'make or buy' and 'keep or sell' implementation possibilities is enormous (Tschirky and Koruna, 1998). It provides a choice for every kind of technology, core, or support, process or product technology, an individual way of exploration and exploitation.

The trilogy of technology decisions, as well as the preparatory steps of identification and evaluation (see this chapter, 'Technology identification and evaluation') provide input for all three basic functions of technology management as seen in this chapter, 'Technologies and technology management'.

Technology strategy implementation and controlling

The implementation of technology strategy eventually creates and conducts organizational measures for the strategy to be executed in the organization, fulfilling one of the first basic functions of technology management: the internal acquisition and storage[15] of technology through R&D.

Organizational measures for the implementation of technology strategy are proposed by Tschirky (2003a: 73) through so-called strategic projects. Strategic projects are action-oriented instruments with a major strategic objective, for example, to establish a next-generation product technology. Being an instrument with project status – under competent project management – the deployment of resources is guaranteed and completion time is kept under control. Top management usually takes the responsibility for strategic projects.

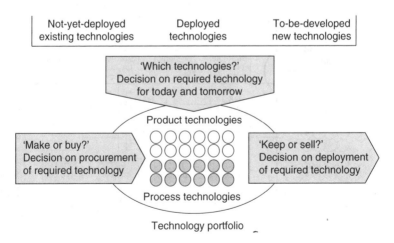

Figure 2.8   Trilogy of strategic technology decisions
Source: Following Brodbeck *et al.*, 1995: 108.

The approach of implementing strategy by means of strategic projects is illustrated in Figure 2.9. From a technology-management perspective, it is mainly a set of R&D projects that make a strategic project. Tschirky's approach provides a complete overview of all the current and planned R&D projects with their relevance for the various strategies defining the overall business strategy. Furthermore, it distinguishes between R&D projects that are directed towards developing product technologies, and projects that focus on developing or improving process technologies. This double aspect mirrors a basic principle of technology management, which strongly suggests the simultaneous development of product and process technologies. Finally, this overview allows crediting oneself with the proper and meaningful development of the company's technology potential consisting of the total of all product and process technologies to be mastered. It goes without saying that the notion 'R&D project' in this tool not only refers to in-house development but includes all other options of technology acquisition as well.

Once strategic projects have been initiated, strategic controlling checks whether the technology strategy is being implemented as planned and if the set strategic goals are going to be achieved. Hunger (Hunger and Wheelen, 2002: 10) defines control as 'the process by which corporate activities and performance results are monitored so that actual performance can be compared with desired performance'. As basic criteria for controlling the strategy and its action plan are taken (Schendel and Hofer, 1979: 18), supporting instruments can be milestone analysis, technology calendars and general

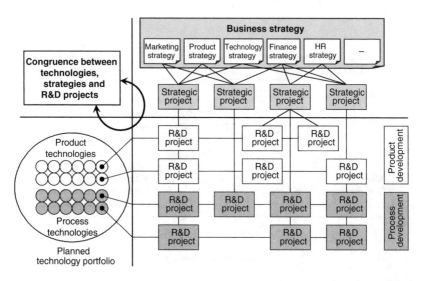

Figure 2.9   Strategy implementation using strategic projects
Source: Following Tschirky and Koruna, 1998: 341.

management control (Tschirky and Koruna, 1998: 346). For a more detailed review of strategic technology controlling refer to Jung (2003).

Current technology implementation approaches do not yet acknowledge the difference between continuous and discontinuous technology development projects. Thus, all projects are run through the same implementation approach despite the evidence that different kinds of projects need different kinds of implementation approaches. Furthermore, the presented implementation approach does not entirely support a sustained innovation mindset as it does not show how radical innovation and incremental innovation project are related to each other.

Technology marketing

The term technology marketing is being used in many different contexts that do not always coincide (Schaible and Hönig, 1991: 9). In the context of this publication technology marketing refers to applying 'technology strategically in the market place so that the firm gains competitive advantage' (Shaklin and Ryans Jr, 1984: 21). Although this definition is broad, it opens a new perspective on marketing. Technology marketing does not refer to marketing activities concerning technology-intensive products or services but directly to the technology as an immaterial good. Thus, it represents a second level of marketing activities trading with all kinds of knowledge associated with or generated from technologies. Figure 2.10 illustrates the traditional-level and the second-level trading of technologies.

From a technology-marketing perspective, the technology is conceived of as a product itself. This view on technology complies with the last of the three basic technology-management functions presented in this chapter, 'Technologies and technology management': the external exploitation of technologies. However, marketing technologies and technological knowledge prove to be significantly more difficult than marketing commodities or industrial goods (Koruna, 2001). In technology marketing, traditional assumptions

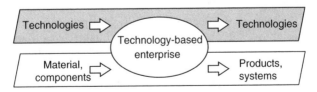

(Future) technology supply and sales markets

Technologies ⇨ | Technology-based enterprise | ⇨ Technologies

Material, components ⇨ | | ⇨ Products, systems

(Traditional) product supply and sales markets

Figure 2.10   Technology marketing as the second level of company trade activities
Source: Tschirky and Koruna, 1998: 303.

regarding markets cannot be upheld any longer as markets for technology are permanently challenged by the threat of market failure due to the character of (technological) knowledge. Due to the character of technological knowledge and the lack of transparency of markets for technologies, technology marketing – and especially sell-activities, meaning the external exploitation of technologies – is still largely underdeveloped in firms (Birkenmeier, 2003).

For the purpose of strategic planning with discontinuous technologies and radical innovation, technology marketing as an option for sourcing and reusing technologies is very interesting. Sourcing of discontinuous technologies from an external company, whether through acquisition, licensing or contract research can be very effective as the risk inherent with the internal development of discontinuous technologies and radical innovation can be reduced. Additionally, costs are easier to control and development time might be reduced as well. This might also be the case with successful joint development or strategic alliances. Besides sourcing, the sale of radical innovation, in terms of out-licensing, might multiply the application fields by revealing a whole new application. Thus, the ROI of the developed technology that initially was costly might be attained more quickly.

Innovation management

This section describes the basic understanding of innovation management underlying this publication. First, the term innovation with its different characteristics is explained, and then, in a second part, a brief overview of innovation management is given.

Innovation

Innovation has become a very common term in business administration. Commercial and business success is associated with it, as well as the image of a dynamic and well-run company. Accordingly, there are numerous definitions of innovation.[16] In this publication, innovation is referred to following Schaad (2001: 15): 'Innovation is a first successful commercial use of something new by an enterprise.'

Newness and types of innovation

There are differences in the degree of novelty in innovation. The difference in the degree of novelty is defined by the qualitative difference of an innovation compared to the previous state (Hauschildt, 1993a: 39). Innovation types can be differentiated as having a high or a low degree of novelty. Different authors define these so-called innovation types. The principal taxonomy of the innovation types is slightly different when comparing the authors' use of terminology.

The types of innovation representing a high degree of novelty are basically consistent. However, those referring to a low degree of novelty are not clearly delimited. Mensch's (1975: 54) definition points out that the innovation type referred to as 'pretended innovation' is at the limit of being a novelty and, thus, means that the limit of innovations is fluid. Tushman and Anderson (1997: 157) establish, the term 'architectural innovation',[17] which indicates a moderate degree of novelty. Summarizing the three main degrees of novelty, they can be described as follows:

A low degree of novelty is improvements or modifications of the actual performance.

A moderate degree of novelty is a new combination based on already existing elements.

A high degree of novelty is a completely new technological performance.

Within this publication the term 'radical innovation' is used to describe all innovation types of a high degree of novelty and 'incremental innovation' is used to describe all types of innovation with a low degree of novelty. For the middle degree of novelty the term 'architectural innovation' is used.

These interpretations of degree of novelty are basically formed through two subjectively differentiating viewpoints. Some authors are more influenced by a technology view, such as Rosenberg (1995: 180) and Tushman and Anderson (1997: 157). The author with a market-based viewpoint is Knight (1967: 484). Seibert (1998: 112) has a mixed viewpoint, in which he points out that innovations with a high degree of novelty are based on a 'technology push' and should be defined therefore by a technology point of view. The more frequent innovations with a low degree of novelty are mainly 'market pull' and their definition should be from a market point of view. These different viewpoints of a more technology-oriented view compared to a more market-oriented view can be elaborated with regard to the company. While the technology view is rather a company-internal consideration, the market view is more a company-external consideration of an innovation's degree of novelty.

Describing the degree of novelty from inside the company is a microeconomic[18] point of view. In doing so the degree of novelty is exclusively defined out of a subjective perspective of the considered company. A microeconomic innovation is therefore an innovation where a change for the specific company is new. For this reason imitations or adaptations of external developments are also considered as innovations. Therefore, the length of time the considered innovation has existed in other places is not important.

Regarded from outside the company the degree of novelty of an innovation follows a macroeconomic path (Kaplaner, 1986: 15). The degree of novelty is evaluated by comparing the innovation to the total offers available on the market. The degree of novelty in this case is highest when it is seen worldwide as a successful breakthrough. A more restricted macroeconomic view is proposed by Hausschildt (1993a: 15), the industry-economic view.

This view restricts the evaluation of the degree of novelty to the relevant environment. Therefore, a high degree of innovation can be reached, if in the same industry, there is no comparable innovation.

Figure 2.11 presents selected innovations according to their degree of novelty from micro- and macroeconomic points of view. This figure positions, in terms of conceptualization, the different types of innovations adapted from Booz *et al.* (1982). Figure 2.11 shows with which percentage companies are developing a tendency towards different types of innovation. It is obvious that from the microeconomic point of view, 30 per cent and from macro economic point of view, only 10 per cent of all the activities have a high degree of novelty. Therefore 70 per cent from a microeconomic and 90 per cent from a macroeconomic point of view indicated only a moderate to low degree of novelty in their innovation activities. Interpreting this result leads to the conclusion that companies more often develop innovations with a moderate or middle degree of novelty, regardless of the point of view from which this originates.

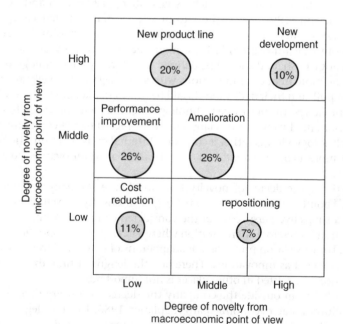

Figure 2.11 The degree of novelty of innovation from macro- and microeconomic points of view

Source: Adapted from Booz-Allen, 1982: 9.

Innovation management

Innovation management insures the planning purposes of innovation processes (Hauschildt, 1993b: 23). It handles all management tasks related to innovations including:

- Defining innovation strategy[19]
- Decision-making
- Establishing and influencing innovation-related information flows
- Creating and managing social relationships
- Interacting within these relationships in order to insure realization of decisions.

In an integrated view of innovation management these tasks do not exclusively apply to technological innovations for the benefit of new products, processes and services but also to organizational innovations and business innovations.

Worth mentioning is the explicit representation of technological knowledge, as the foundation of the enterprise's technological competence and source of product and process innovation.

Relation between technology management and innovation management

Technology management should not serve its own purpose, but should be regarded as an instrument to achieve a corporate goal (Tschirky and Koruna, 1998: 294). In innovation-driven companies such goals are a sustainable competitive advantage through innovation. Brockhoff (1997: 71) describes how technology management and innovation management interrelate. Technology management basically includes the three main tasks of acquisition, storage and use of new technological knowledge.

The acquisition of such new knowledge can be done company-internally as well as externally. There are many options for acquiring knowledge. Company internally the acquisition is made by R&D activities, but externally, for example, this is done through partnering or alliances. In this context R&D can be seen as part of technology management.

The storage of technological knowledge includes all activities relating to documenting and saving acquired knowledge. Saving knowledge is inevitably related to personnel management as a great deal of knowledge is stored in people's minds, coming from individual and personal experiences. Thus, technology management also includes tasks such as identifying knowledge carriers, securing knowledge transfer, and avoiding fading of knowledge related to personnel fluctuations.

The use of technological knowledge is probably the most obvious task of technology management which is related to innovation management.

However, without previous acquisition and a storage mechanism, the supply of technological knowledge to be managed during its deployment in R&D and innovation activities would rapidly disappear.

Innovation management carries on the activities started by the technology management by transforming the technological knowledge and knowledge from other fields such as marketing or production to marketable goods and services. Innovation management in the broad sense covers many different disciplines across the entire company, integrating this complete knowledge in order optimally to position the company's value-added profitably in the marketplace.

2   Research on discontinuous technology and radical innovation

Defining the phenomenon

There is a great variety of terms used to describe the *phenomenon* of technological discontinuity and radical innovation (Green *et al.*, 1995: 203; Garcia and Roger, 2002: 110). Both terms are often used synonymously with no differentiation (Lehmann, 1994: 10). Besides the terms radical innovation (North and Tucker, 1987: 11; Damanpour, 1988: 546; Leifer, 2000: 4; O'Connor and Veryzer, 2001: 233) and breakthrough innovation (Nayak and Ketteringham, 1986: 181; Mascitelli, 2000), authors speak of breakpoint (Strebel, 1995: 11) or revolutionary innovation (Abernathy and Clark, 1991: 61). Lately the term disruptive technology, promoted by Christensen (1997; 2003), has also gained popularity. The following will focus on the most popular terms in order to differentiate them; these terms are discontinuous technology, radical innovation and disruptive technology.

The following section attempts to more specifically define these three terms working from the current understanding of definitions and descriptions as well as identifying more carefully their individual characteristics. These differentiations are then analyzed critically according to their suitability in strategic management. Finally, a new set of definitions will be stated that represent the understanding for this research.

Current understanding

A *discontinuous technology* is a technology that is the result of a scientific breakthrough achieved through a long-term research effort. It builds on newly acquired scientific knowledge that usually does not follow the expected evolution of existing technologies. It is the deviation from what was expected by forecasting experience that makes the technology discontinuous (Lehmann, 1994: 8ff.). Thus, it represents a breakpoint within a given technological paradigm[20] that initiates a change to a new technology trajectory (Dosi, 1982: 152).[21] Tushman and Anderson (1997: 5) point out that technological discontinuities can be competence enhancing as well as competence-destroying.[22] As a consequence, not all discontinuities affect companies in the same way. For some companies the same technological discontinuity might be helpful to sustain competitive advantage as the discontinuity enhances its existing competencies, while for the other company it might mean the debasement and destruction of its competencies (McKelvey, 1996: 108ff.). As a consequence, this company has to substitute the greater part of its technological knowledge in order to follow the discontinuity. Thus, there are discontinuities that affect only a few companies while other discontinuities affect a whole industry.

From a market perspective discontinuous technologies often provide the basis for a new product with an order of magnitude improvement (actual or potential) in price/performance[23] ratio, caused by a substantially changed technology[24] base (Anderson and Tushman, 1990: 604; Ehrnberg and Jacobsson, 1993: 28).

The successful commercialization of a discontinuous technology can lead to either a *radical innovation* or to an incremental innovation (Brodbeck *et al.*, 2003: 137). Radical innovation can be defined by its degree of novelty (see this chapter, 'Newness and types of innovation'). Concretely speaking it involves (1) the application of significant new technologies often emerging from a discontinuity or (2) significant new combinations of existing technologies and new market opportunities (Tushman and Nadler, 1986: 74f.). Radical innovation 'departs dramatically from the norm' (Anderson and Tushman, 1990: 604) and 'transforms the relationship between customers and suppliers, restructures marketplace economics, displaces current products, and often creates entirely new product categories' (Leifer *et al.*, 2000: 2). It can lead to either a new product-class lifecycle, or a discontinuity in an existing lifecycle, following the substitution of a new product or process for an old one (Lambe and Spekman, 1997: 102). Radical innovations bring forth whole product lines that are not only new for the companies that create them but that are also new for the marketplace. Often this addresses an urgent customer need that had yet not been articulated, or it noticeably improves the price/performance ratio of existing products (O'Connor, 1998: 151).

Beside these definitions of radical innovations that are primarily focused on a market perspective, a few authors only give definitions, or rather descriptions, of radical innovations from a company perspective. Green *et al.* (1995: 203ff.) for example, consider innovations radical if the four following dimensions apply: (1) technological uncertainty; (2) technical inexperience; (3) business inexperience; and (4) high technology cost. Shenhar *et al.* (1995: 179) classify technologies according to their uncertainty at the time the project is initiated at the company. With regard to the fact that most technological projects employ a mixture of technologies, some emergent and highly uncertain and some more mature and less uncertain, they suggest defining four types of innovations according to the overall uncertainty of the project: *low* technological uncertainty over *medium* to *high* up to *super-high* technology uncertainty.

Similarly to radical innovations, *disruptive technologies* address the *commercialization* of a discontinuous technology. As a matter of fact technological discontinuities are considered a subset of technological disruptions (Ehrnberg and Jacobsson, 1993: 44). A discontinuity is considered a disruption if it has a restructuring effect on an established industry (Christensen, 1997: 13ff.; Porter, 1998: 253; Rafii and Kampas, 2002: 116; Vojak and Chambers, 2004: 123). Ehrenberg and Jacobsson (1993: 44) hypothesize three causes that might play a role when a discontinuity turns into a disruption. As a first cause they suggest the destructive character of the technology. The more the discontinuity destructs or renders obsolete existing technological knowledge, the more it might have a disruptive effect on the industry. Second, the more new technologies from a distinct generic area are added to the existing technology base of the industry, the higher the probability for a disruption. As a third cause, these authors name the rate of diffusion of the technology. It is stated that the faster the diffusion of the discontinuity the more disruptive its effect will be. This is due to the fact that the time companies have at their disposal to detect and to react to a discontinuity is determined by the speed of diffusion of that technology between users.

Although disruptive technologies are seen to be a threat to an established industry they usually create growth in those industries they penetrate. They might even create entirely new industries by introducing new products and services (Kostoff *et al.*, 2004: 141). Typically, disruptive technologies emerge in industries different from the ones they finally disrupt. In their initial industry they first appear in niche markets from which they grow to penetrate other industries with more attractive markets in terms of margin and volume (Christensen, 1997: xv ff.; Gilbert, 2003: 28).

Critics of the current understanding

The above-mentioned definitions of disruptive technologies and discontinuous technology focus mainly on changes and the consequences of these phenomena from a product, market and customer view within the industry as a whole.[25] In sum, a discontinuous technology or a radical innovation initiates major changes within a given structure of an industry while a disruptive technology triggers changes that restructure a whole industry. Descriptions and definitions of radical innovations are also considered from a market view, based on their degree of newness (see also this chapter, 'Newness and types of innovation') compared to existing products or through their price/performance competitiveness. This most common understanding of discontinuous and disruptive technologies and radical innovation is emphasized in Table 2.2 adapted from Kassicieh *et al.* (2002: 385). It shows from which most common perspectives the different authors define the three terms. These perspectives are change perspectives – (1) change in technology; (2) change in technology and products; (3) change in markets; and (4) change in benefit of the customer – through which authors define discontinuous/disruptive technology or radical innovation. It is apparent from Table 2.2 that most authors focus on perspectives 2, 3 and 4: the technology and product, market and customer benefit change perspectives. These perspectives as a basis for definitions represent a very basic deficiency for their application in successful management. According to these considerations, a discontinuous or disruptive technology or a radical innovation can only be recognized by management as such in hindsight (Kostoff *et al.*, 2004: 142). Only if a technology has proven to have a continuous successful and changing impact on products, on markets, or a significant benefit to the customer, may it be qualified as discontinuous or disruptive. Radical innovation can only be qualified as such innovation after

Table 2.2 Four perspectives of defining discontinuous/disruptive technologies and radical innovations

	Carroad and Carroad (1982)	Abernathy and Clark (1985)	Foster (1986)	Meyers and Tucker (1989)	Moore (1999)	McKee (1992)	Bower and Christensen (1995)	Ehrenberg (1995)	Lynn et al. (1996)	Walsh (1996)	Lambe and Spekman (1997)	Veryzer (1998b)	Rice et al. (1998)	Leifer et al. (2000)	McDermott and O'Connor (2002)	Clark (2002)
Perspective 1: Change in technology																
Change in technology base										■						
Technology learning curve					■											
Perspective 2: Change in technology and products																
Technology/product paradigm					■											
New industry architectural technology/product paradigm		■														
New industry revolution technology/product paradigm		■														
New product families								■						■		
Perspective 3: Change in markets																
Newness of technology/product/market	■							■				■			■	■
New firm technology/product/market paradigm						■										
Perspective 4: Change in customer benefits																
Change in customer benefits				■										■		
Order of magnitude improvement in cost or performance									■				■			
Increase in user benefits			■									■				
Competitive advantage		■														

having proven to be more competitive than the existing products. These descriptions represent a *macroeconomic*[26] view towards discontinuous/disruptive technologies and radical innovation. This view may be helpful to understand implications of different technologies for a given industry; however, considering the difficulties that companies encounter with discontinuous/disruptive technologies and radical innovations it might not be the optimal approach.

How should a company that only recognizes technologies as discontinuous/disruptive and innovations as radical in hindsight manage such technologies and innovations differently from incremental innovations and continuously evolving technologies? These definitions that only apply ex post on an *absolute* market situation contradict the mindset of strategic planning, namely to be anticipative in positioning the company relative to a certain market situation.

To be concise: there is a need for a set of definitions that allows (1) an anticipative rather that an ex post consideration that is not only focused on (2) the macroeconomic view of the industry and the market, but also on the microeconomic view of the company, while taking a strategic management perspective which is (3) relative rather than an absolute consideration of the company towards the market.

A set of clear definitions

Based on the current understanding (see this chapter, 'Current understanding') and bearing their critics (see this chapter, 'Critics of the current understanding') in mind, this section will elaborate a set of definitions that clarify the limitations and interdependencies of the terms discontinuous technology, disruptive technology and radical innovation for the purpose of this research work.

In the previous two chapters a differentiation of the three terms has been achieved through distinctly assigned descriptive elements found in literature. It can be observed in this same literature that some definitions mix up or ignore one or more of these specific descriptive elements causing confusion when trying to differentiate the three terms: discontinuous technologies, disruptive technologies and radical innovations. Bearing these specific descriptive elements in mind, the definitions to elaborate should also follow the criticism made of the current definitions and descriptions. Table 2.3 summarizes the main descriptive elements as well as the main criticisms that have to be addressed in the definitions. The definitions should be designed in a way that they consider these descriptive elements without mixing them up or ignoring any of them.

With regard to the requirement of Table 2.3, definitions for the purpose of this research are formulated as follows:

- *Discontinuous technology at the company level*   A technology is considered discontinuous at the company level if it triggers major changes in a company's set of core technologies.

Table 2.3   Key elements and criticism of discontinuous/disruptive technologies and radical innovations

Current definition of	Main descriptive elements of those definitions
a discontinuous technology	Is competence-enhancing or competence-destroying Can affect distinct companies or an industry as a whole Can generate incremental and/or radical innovation Is discontinuous relative to an existing technology
a radical innovation	Is a commercialization of a discontinuous technology
a disruptive technology	Is a commercialization of a discontinuous technology Always affects a whole industry
Three main three criticisms of current definitions	**Specifications**
Criticism 1	Anticipative perspective instead of ex post perspective
Criticism 2	Microeconomic and macroeconomic view instead of only macroeconomic view
Criticism 3	Relative rather than absolute perspective of the market

- *Discontinuous technology at the industry level*   A technology is considered discontinuous at the industry level if a great number of company-level discontinuities trigger a run for a new dominant design in the industry.
- *Radical innovation at industry and company level*   An innovation is considered radical if the technology underlying its commercialization is discontinuous at the industry level.
- *Disruptive technology at industry and company level*   A technology is considered disruptive if its commercialization is discontinuous at the industry level and if it is competence-destroying at the company level.

Management implications

The current presents the *implications* of the above-described phenomenon for the management of a company. The implications shown in this chapter represent the common understanding within the whole community of researchers investigating in this field.

There is a broad agreement among researchers that management usually handles the emergence of discontinuous technologies and radical innovation with a low sense of urgency (Lambe and Spekman, 1997; Rafii and Kampas, 2002: 102). This is due to the long-term perspective of the research and development projects of these technologies. Generally such projects last up to ten years and more (Rice *et al.*, 1998: 58), which makes it difficult for managers to see the applicable outcome of these efforts right from the beginning. Thus, such projects are often run with low priority having a minor sense of urgency. However, these projects require a great deal of resources and management attention (McDermott and O'Connor, 2002: 425) before they can eventually be transferred into marketable products. These contradictory characteristics – low priority and minor sense of urgency compared to the high degree of resource and management requirement – result in conflicts. Furthermore, the progression of radical innovation projects starting from basic research via development to the first stages of commercialization is an endeavor accompanied by a high level of uncertainty (Abernathy and Utterback, 1978: 45; Rice *et al.*, 1998: 58; Veryzer, 1998a: 318). Such uncertainty is of multiple dimensions (Milliken, 1990; Leifer, 2000: 18ff.). For instance, it is due to a lack of technological and market knowledge as no previous technological or reliable market insight exists in the company (Christensen, 1997: 209; Jolly, 1997: 7ff.). Market data is seldom available and customer requirements are often vague (Wieandt, 1995: 450; Song and Montoya-Weiss, 1998: 132; Veryzer, 1998b: 149).[27] Veryzer (1998b: 147) brings it to the point: 'for discontinuous new products customer input may not necessarily be relied upon as heavily to guide the product development process as it is in developing incremental new products'. All of this lack of information leads to uncertainty making strategic planning of radical innovation projects very difficult.

It is the people within the existing organization, meaning managers, that are most concerned by the uncertainty inherent to a discontinuous technology or radical innovation project. Often managers have difficulties seeing the business opportunity targeted by such projects as they do not fit in their existing mindset formed through the present portfolio of projects. Many companies view business opportunities too narrowly through the lens of their existing assets and capabilities (Kim and Mauborgne, 1997: 106). This cognitive filter is referred to as dominant logic. It is the set of biases, beliefs and assumptions – about the markets to enter, technologies to use, competitors to watch, people to hire and businesses to run – that is rooted within an organization (Afuah, 1998: 97ff.). Dominant logic is defined as 'a mind set or a world view or conceptualization of the business and the administrative tools to accomplish goals and make decisions in that business. It is stored as a shared cognitive map (or set of schemas) among the dominant coalition' (Prahalad and Bettis, 1986: 491). The dominant logic of an existing company hinders organizations from recognizing the opportunity behind a totally new technology. Thus, it may provide at least a partial explanation for the uncertainty organizations encounter when confronted with discontinuous technology or radical innovation.

In addition to the existing organizational hurdles described above there are resource uncertainties that complicate the decision for and the implementation of radical innovation projects. Resource uncertainties are the result of the probability of a major loss of funding because of an overall decrease in corporate performance or a change in senior management sponsorship (Leifer, 2000: 23). In sum many of these uncertainties coupled with a high level of resource assignment make discontinuous technology and radical innovation projects very risky. This is why many organizations are reluctant to engage in such projects (McDermott and O'Connor, 2002: 425) and tend rather to further develop their competencies within a relatively narrow scope and range (McKelvey, 1996: 109) focusing on short-term revenues. Thus, once a discontinuous technology is ready for the market, it is often commercialized by outsider companies instead of established industry leaders (Utterback, 1994: 160; Strebel, 1995: 11; Christensen, 1997: 85).

In general, there is broad agreement between scholars that discontinuous technologies and radical innovations have a very specific character that is distinct from continuously evolving technologies and incremental innovation (Lynn *et al.*, 1996: 11; O'Connor, 1998: 162; Rice *et al.*, 1998: 57; Song and Montoya-Weiss, 1998: 132; Kessler and Chakrabarti, 1999: 231). This distinction of technologies and innovations asks for different styles of management including differentiated types of strategic actions and organizational capabilities (Kessler and Chakrabarti, 1999: 235). Thus, conventional management techniques are not suitable until the technological innovation has reached a certain maturity level so that it can fit the pattern of incremental innovation (Abernathy and Clark, 1985: 20; Rice *et al.*, 1998: 58; Veryzer, 1998a: 319; Kessler and Chakrabarti, 1999: 231; Leifer *et al.*, 2000: 11). Authors (Tushman and Anderson, 1986; Tushman and O'Reilly, 1996; McDermott and O'Connor, 2002) agree that sustainable growth requires specific management skills for both types of innovation – incremental and radical – at the same time. Thus, Tushman and Anderson claim (1986: 734) that companies have to overcome the dilemma to master 'evolutionary and revolutionary change' simultaneously. Tushman and O'Reilly (1998: 40) emphasize that, on the one hand, companies have to plan and align their activities along a relatively stable and evolutionary change. On the other hand, they have to eliminate these achievements once the competitive environment changes radically, knowing that new technologies will substitute the foundations underlying their present products.

These understandings that reflect the very different nature of radical versus incremental innovation represent the initial positions. *Due to the inherent uncertainty and risk of radical innovation a management distinct from the one used for less uncertain and risky incremental innovation is needed. However important this distinction is, scholars agree that the dilemma lies in the necessity for the simultaneous management of both types of innovations, as sustained innovation is the combination of changes initiated by radical innovation and followed by continuous incremental improvement innovation.* The dilemma is initiated by the condition to fulfill conflictive requirements in one and the same innovation management concept. The resolution of the conflictive requirements needs management to fulfill the following major capabilities:

1. The capability to simultaneously manage long-term and short-term issues in differentiated ways.
2. The capability to simultaneously manage issues with different levels of risk in differentiated ways.
3. The capability to align management issues of long-term and short-term character, as well as management issues with different risk levels to one single strategic planning purpose.

These capabilities can be considered as major criteria to be fulfilled in order to resolve the dilemma caused by the management of sustained innovation.

Management solutions in current literature

This section will analyze which solution approaches already exist in literature, which contribute to successful management of discontinuous/disruptive technologies and radical innovation according to the criteria for sustained innovation management.

Solutions from industry-level focused research

Research focused on the industry level aims to describe, analyze and give solutions for the consequences of a technological discontinuity on the macroeconomic level within a given industry structure. Thus, scholars collect empirical data over long periods of time within one or more specific industries. Analyzing this data, they look for patterns that emerge whenever a discontinuity happens. The benefit of this research is twofold: on the one hand, it allows the dynamics of the phenomenon of discontinuous technologies to be studied and, on the other hand, modeling and generalizing observed patterns helps to develop planning approaches for the management of future discontinuities.

The major findings representing successful management solutions for sustained innovation can be summarized in seven points.

1. Create an organization separated from the core business and cultivate outside perspectives for the management of discontinuous technologies and radical innovation

Research findings (Clark and Bower, 2002: 6ff.) prove that independent organizations perform better in the implementation projects of a discontinuous technology than projects conducted in the regular parent company. Organizations separated from the core business are usually more innovative and score higher market-penetration rates.

Cultivate outside perspectives: the creation of an independent organization is the first right step in providing the initial position for a successful implementation of a strategic discontinuous technology project. However, it does not guarantee that the organization will be managed as an independent one. Crucial for this to happen is the choice of people selected to carry out the project. Relying exclusively on people from the core organization might, thus, be the wrong approach as their work processes, decision-making pattern and focus might be too strongly attached to the core business of the parent organization. Thus, it is suggested that one include managers with an outside perspective and a certain distance from the core organization in the project team.

2. Differentiate the management of technology development and the management of product development

Kusunoki's (1997: 381) findings suggest that different problem-solving approaches are appropriate within organizations depending on the type of project. In improvement types of projects that rely on evolutionary patterns of technology a product problem-solving approach should be applied. However, when targeting radical innovation through a discontinuous technology-type project, a technology problem-solving approach should be applied. In a nutshell, Kusunoki proposes that organizations carefully separate product development from technology development in order to generate radical innovation.

3. Manage early endeavors with discontinuous technology and radical innovation as a portfolio of strategic options with the aim of long-term competence learning

Floyd (1996: 15ff.) and Strebel (1992: 203ff.) both handle the problem of uncertainty inherent in the anticipation of discontinuities in the context of creating strategic options. Bearing in mind that forecasting is imprecise and that detected discontinuities might influence the business in a way other than was predicted, it is important to think in options. This means, first, that besides *investing effort in more than just one* of the predicted discontinuities it is recommended, second, *to maintain business as usual*. Investing in more than one emerging technology is what Floyd calls 'placing side bets'. It is the approach of building up competencies and learning what effect specific technologies might have on the existing and future business of the company. This procedure allows a company to react quickly once one of the technologies has demonstrated advantages over an existing one. The required reaction is twofold: first, the company must change internally from one technology to another as a basis for its products and services and, second, it has to bring these new products and services to the market. There is usually not a lot of time for both of these activities. Experience shows that once a technology is accepted and acknowledged as a challenger in the market, 80 per cent of the market can switch within five years, provided that there are no regulatory barriers (Floyd, 1996: 17).

4. Build and foster firm internal and cross-firm boundary-spanning networks to (1) eliminate uncertainty and (2) influence emerging industry standards

Tidd (1995: 308ff.) points out that the development of complex product systems is likely to require managing across traditional product-division boundaries and inside the company. Outside the company strong interfirm networks are supportive as they can offset missing internal competencies.

5. Let the organization perceive a discontinuous technology as a threat. Let the organization implement a discontinuous technology as an opportunity

Clark and Bower (2002: 4ff.), note that, in order to direct the necessary management attention to an upcoming discontinuity or radical innovation, it is best framed *first* as a threat. Their findings indicate that the way a challenge is perceived – in this case a discontinuous technological innovation – influences an organization's behavior when approaching it. When a radical innovation is only seen as an opportunity, resources are allocated too scarcely. 'Framing the innovation as a threat will generate a serious commitment in the form of funding and other resources because managers, worried that the innovation will weaken their position in the marketplace, will suspend traditional investment screening criteria' (Clark and Bower, 2002: 4). Once the initial resource allocation is secured and the innovation acknowledged as being important, it is then, in a *second* step, time to reframe the innovation from a threat to an opportunity. This is typically the time when a new business model needs to be created and the identification of the demand for the radical innovation should be evaluated. According to Clark and Bower, it is important to reframe the innovation because now managers need to find new and unique applications associated with the innovation. This is best done under the assumption of dealing with an opportunity. If at this moment in time the innovation was still perceived as a threat, managers would react rigidly and apply old models and approaches because comparison and benchmarking to existing innovations has been done.

6. Enter the competition with a discontinuous technology in a predominant design phase to ensure higher success rate in the market

Suarez and Utterback (1995) suggest that strategies to enter an industry are most successful in the period of pre-dominant design. The probability of failure for companies entering a number of years before a dominant design is established in an industry, is clearly lower than when entering in the post-dominant design period (Suarez and Utterback, 1995: 428). The authors explain the success of the early-entering companies by the time they have had to learn and experiment with the new products during a period when demand changes were rapid.

7. Master the interplay between both strategies: deliberate and emergent, according to the lifecycle of the discontinuous technology

Christensen and Raynor (2003) describe the need to master two fundamentally different strategy processes simultaneously when coping with discontinuous technologies. This twofold approach is based on the concept of strategy-making involving a coexistence of a deliberate and emergent strategy process. This approach was originally described by Mintzberg and Waters (1985). The deliberate strategy aims to organize actions in an organization. It represents a top-down, forward-directed strategic approach that fixes goals and coordinates their implementation within the collective interest and intention of the company. The emergent strategy represents a bottom-up approach that emerges from within the working organization doing its daily job. The nature of emerging strategy is more tactical and operational than strategic. Together both approaches eventually determine how a company is going to act strategically, which is finally the realized strategy.

Depending on the stage in the lifecycle of a discontinuous technology, one specific approach might lead to success while another to failure. At the emerging stage of a discontinuous technology, a deliberate strategy is the approach to avoid. Companies that try to manage their organization according to deliberate strategies in this stage will eventually fail. All the resources spent to find and implement the right strategy will be in vain as the right strategy cannot be known at this stage. In the early stage of a nascent technology, it is the emerging-strategy approach that applies best, as the whole dynamics around the technology is discovery-driven.

However, once the market for the technology and its applications become clear, companies should change their approach to a deliberate strategy. This change is critical because in this stage companies have to focus their resources on one common goal, enter and position themselves in the newly opened market. 'The switch from an emergent to a deliberate strategy mode is crucial to success in a corporation's initial disruptive business' (Christensen and Raynor, 2003: 222).

Solutions from the company-level focused research

Research focusing on the company level analyzes and gives solutions for the consequences of technological discontinuity on the microeconomical level affecting one or more companies. Thus, scholars collect within one or more company case studies empirical data over a short or longer period of time. The benefit of this research is that it observes pattern within a concrete company within given structures, methods and processes. Its conclusions are thus generally more specific. A drawback is the limited generalization of findings except if a considerable number of cases is used as sample.

The major findings representing successful management solutions for sustained innovation can be summarized in seven points.

1. Ambidextrous leadership

Kessler and Chakrabarti (1999: 239) found that the long development time of radical innovation projects can be shortened considerably by setting clear goals for such projects, in contrast to incremental innovation projects, where the reverse was observed. These and other fundamental differences in the management of radical and incremental innovation are the initial position for O'Reilly and Tushman (2004: 80) who make a claim for an ambidextrous leadership. This approach is based on the heritage of the research conducted since the late 1980s by a group of researchers from Stanford and Harvard University. This leadership focuses its strategic goals on two types of businesses – those concerned with exploiting existing capabilities for profit (incremental innovations) and those concerned with exploring new opportunities for growth (radical innovations). Table 2.4 summarizes the essence of this leadership approach from different management aspects that need to be directed despite the twofold focus.

2. Design imagining and visioning processes to facilitate the link between discontinuous technology and its potential market application

In order to bring clarity to a uncertain market situation where neither quantitative assessments nor customer insight is available O'Connor and Veryzer (2001: 232) suggest a process of market visioning. Analogous to the innovation management step 'imagining' proposed by Jolly (1997: 3),

Table 2.4 Ambidextrous leadership

Alignment of:	Exploitative business	Explorative business
Strategic intent	Cost profit	Innovation, growth
Critical tasks	Operators, efficiency, incremental innovation	Adaptability, new products, breakthrough innovation
Competencies	Operational	Entrepreneurial
Structures	Formal, mechanistic	Adaptive, loose
Controls, rewards	Margins, productivity	Milestones, growth
Culture	Efficiency, low risk, quality, customers	Risk-taking, speed, flexibility, experimentation
Leadership role	Authoritative, top down	Visionary, involved

Source: O'Reilly and Tushman, 2004: 80.

visioning aims to mentally relate a discontinuous technology to a potentially attractive market opportunity.

3. Involve a high number of champions in projects who are willing to promote high risk and high potential projects

According to the findings of O'Connor and Veryzer (2001: 234ff.) there are a number of drivers that initiate and sustain vision (see 2. above), such as: the participation of senior management as a promoter of a company-wide focus for innovation and as a communicator of goals, or scientists with an understanding for business that could act as opportunity recognizers. The process is best conducted when champions, 'implementers' and 'ruminators' are involved. Champions are people that 'are entrepreneurial in accessing resources to accomplish a mission, and are action oriented and focused' (O'Connor and Veryzer, 2001: 239). Implementers are people that enjoy participating in projects and have the potential to trigger major changes in the organization, while ruminators are contemplative and experienced people who spend their time thinking about the future and that have the ability to break with the bounded company view.

4. Assign highly positioned project leaders with short company tenure, and experienced team members with long-term tenure in the company

Kessler and Chakrabarti (1999: 241) show a relationship between the speed of radical innovation development and the choice of the project leader and project members. For a radical innovation project, speed increases the higher the project manger is positioned and the shorter his tenure. For project members, however, longer tenure most speeds up the development of the project.

5. Realize early prototypes, process pilots and market tests, probe and learn within a set strategic context with a long-term competence building perspective

Once the link between a discontinuous technology and a potentially attractive market application is found, Lynn *et al.* (1996) suggest proceeding according to the 'probe and learn process'. 'Probe' means experimenting with prototypes and introducing early versions of products into the market. However, probing only makes sense if it is done with a higher strategic goal. The goal is typically to 'learn' in order to enter into or to build up a market that is new for the company. It has nothing in common with a trial and error approach as it is done within a strategic context with defined corporate goals. It can rather be compared with an online and stepwise learning procedure as the feedback generated from a first 'probe' or attempt can instantly be used for a second one. Doing so, the discontinuous technology is usually first commercialized in applications other than the finally targeted one and in a market still familiar to the company. The idea behind this procedure is to apply the technology in products that do not yet require a performance as high as the final one and to learn how the market will react. Instead of merely developing the technology's performance until it has reached the final level required in order to enter an unfamiliar market, it is better to commercialize it first in familiar markets with lower performance requirements as early as possible in order to learn about its acceptance and technological possibilities step by step and then to approach an unfamiliar market. This way the technology is commercialized as soon as its performance level fits to a first application. Besides reducing the total risk of a new market entry in manageable risk entities, this procedure is also favorable to the approach of 'fast failure'. Fast failure describes the approach of companies that try to stop projects immediately as soon as their failures become visible. The 'probe and learn' approach allows failure to become visible much faster than if a technology is held back from its eventual customers until it reaches the level of performance necessary to enter its finally targeted market.

The 'probe and learn' process, however, bears one disadvantage not to be underestimated: it is the risk of commercializing a technology in a stage that is too early to be already enough well developed or known. Such a technology might reveal side effects or have consequences unpredictable in an early commercialization. At a later moment in time these undesired effects could have been relieved and patched. Thus, the probe and learn process bears the inherent risk of scattering a potential future market before it has even been created.

6. Collaborate through strategic alliances with industry and academia in order to eliminate uncertainty and influence industry standards, leverage credibility and reduce risks

The most common form of collaboration to respond to a discontinuity or to radical innovations is a strategic alliance (Lambe and Spekman, 1997: 108). Such strategic alliances are especially attractive as they require much lower overall investment and pose considerably less risk when trying to eliminate technical or market uncertainties. The dynamics created by strategic alliances further enables companies to combine technological capabilities with the opportunity to shape inter-organizational networks and coalitions to influence the development of industry standards.

7. Ensure that front-line managers are charged with opportunity recognition of discontinuous technology and radical innovation

Veryzer (1998a: 319) suggests that before going into a detailed environmental and market analysis, it is especially important in the case of discontinuous technology and radical innovation to formulate beforehand initial applications of the technology. The explanation of this procedure is due to the nature of such technologies and innovations; they tend to be further removed from the market and are more technology rather than market driven. Thus, it is good to have a target application before going into market research for opportunity recognition. According to Rice *et al.* (1998: 57) and Strebel (1995: 19) this opportunity recognition is best done by first line or front line managers – not by senior managers. In his study it was first line managers that were most successful in initially identifying future market opportunities. These are people with entrepreneurial character, who are leading improvement teams. Aided by an informal network operating between R&D and business units and between R&D and outside constituents like customers, suppliers and governmental agencies they can eliminate uncertainty inherent to radical innovation and discontinuous technology can be eliminated (Rice, 1996: 531).

3 Summary and conclusion – gaps and implications

Gaps in management theory

Although the insights found in literature are valuable for the strategic management of discontinuous technologies and radical innovation, it shows two major shortcomings with regards to practitioner-oriented sustained innovation management:

1. However some authors describe hands-on management tools and methods, only very few are straightforward enough so that practitioners could apply them in their daily jobs. Furthermore, these tools and methods are described as a single piece within a management framework. The framework, however, showing the whole image is only fragmentally described, which makes it difficult to understand the management context. Practitioners wanting to apply these tools and methods are left on their own to put all the bits and pieces together in order to create their own planning processes.
2. None of them describe how to integrate the management of discontinuous technologies with one of continuously evolving technologies. Although most authors acknowledge the need to separately manage radical innovation from incremental innovation and to structure and manage them side by side in differentiating manner, there is not one author that shows how such an integrated and holistically sustained innovation approach could be designed. All authors merely focus on handing the strategic management of discontinuous technology and radical innovation in an isolated way. There is no description of how the interaction of both approaches could be integrated in one single concept in order to enhance sustained innovation management.

To conclude, it can be said that present management solutions do not yet support the concept for sustained innovation management. This is the gap in current management theory; it can be formulated as follows:

Gap in management solutions: Existing management literature fails to provide satisfactory solutions to foster sustained innovation: existing solutions lack integrated and holistic systematical concepts that refer to both incremental and radical innovation.

The gap in management solutions is generalized and described in detail by the gaps 1–3 in theory:

Gap 1 in theory: Systematic approaches for the holistic and integrated strategic management of discontinuous technologies are missing.

Gap 2 in theory: Only fragmental solution approaches are presented. Processes are not integrated and do not systematically cover the entire strategy formulation or include enabling structures and supportive methods.

Gap 3 in theory: Only single-edged approaches are presented. Existing management approaches focus either on continuous technologies and incremental innovation or on discontinuous technologies and radical innovation. Holistic approaches considering sustainable innovation through the management of both kinds of technologies and innovation do not exist.

Gaps in understanding

As a consequence of a lack of solutions enhancing sustained innovation management there are no studies examining how today's management solutions would prevail when challenged under the assumption of this management. Thus little is known about which effects are initiated in a company by which management causes.

Without this understanding it is difficult to realize the redesign of today's management processes, methods and structures for sustained innovation management.[28]

Gap in understanding: Literature lacks concrete descriptions of how today's management approaches prevail in the challenge of sustained innovation. The understanding on causes and effects of today's management approaches is missing.

The gap in understanding is generalized and described in detail by the gaps 4–6 in theory:

Gap 4 in theory: The understanding of the implications of today's management approaches is missing.

Gap 5 in theory: Implications of today's management approaches cannot be assigned to causes of its own management.

Gap 6 in theory: Weaknesses of today's processes, methods and structures are not detected.

3
Managing Radical Innovation – Corporate Case Studies

Today it is no longer sufficient for companies to merely concentrate on continuous improvement of existing technologies by following proven incremental innovation patterns (see Chapter 1). Henceforth, it is more and more necessary for companies to also master discontinuous technological evolution and radical innovation in addition to the more common incremental innovation. Thus, this book provides answers to understanding the processes, structures and methods required for the successful management of both radical and incremental innovation and how these processes, structures and methods can be implemented.

Analysis conducted of current literature (see Chapter 2) shows, however, that there are only fragmental approaches that handle the management of discontinuous technologies and radical innovation. Existing approaches are incomplete without the same focus and depth as the goal of this research. The main gaps in the existing published research are twofold. First, systematic and holistic approaches are missing and, second, there is no understanding of the implications of today's management approaches, making the redesign of the latter practically impossible.

Although literature could not provide a satisfactory answer, through its gaps it focuses the orientation of this chapter on analyzing state of art management with discontinuous technologies and radical innovation. This chapter has two specific goals:

- To show how current state-of-the-art management performs with discontinuous technologies and radical innovation and discuss this performance related to issues of processes, structures and methods of strategic management. This discussion will identify the gaps in practice in state-of-the-art management with discontinuous technologies and radical innovation.
- Based on the discussions described above, as well as on insights from the literature review, a further goal of this chapter is to formulate propositions for the requirements of processes, structures and methods designed for the strategic planning of sustained innovation.

These goals correspond to gaps 4, 5 and 6 (see Chapter 2, 'Gaps in understanding') in theories and partially contribute to answering the question on how processes, structures and methods should be designed.

This chapter is structured in five sections. The first briefly introduces the cases conducted in practice and describes the research methodology applied. The second section is an in-depth description of three cases. In the third, a cross-case comparison is conducted discussing the cases from a process, structure and methodological perspective formulating the gap in practice. The fourth elaborates the propositions of a strategic-planning concept for sustained innovation management that simultaneously manages incremental and radical innovations. The last part summarizes and concludes this state of the art in practice.

1   Introduction to the cases

This research follows the case study methodology as described by Yin (1994).

According to Yin's method, as an initial position a theoretical model on the research topic has to be developed. This model is represented by the framework of aspects relevant to the management of discontinuous technology and radical innovation derived from literature (see Chapter 2). This framework shows that current management approaches are still fragmented and incomplete with regard to coherence in process design, methods and structures for discontinuous technology and radical innovation within a sustained innovation perspective. This incompleteness and fragmentation is under investigation in the following case studies.

In order to collect data that apply to the theoretical model and help to reach the goals of this chapter, the company cases were selected according to the following criteria:

- *The company chosen for a case study must be regarded as established in its industry.* The previous two chapters always referred to management problems with discontinuous technologies and radical innovation in relation to established companies. A company is regarded as established if it existed prior to the emergence of the discontinuous technology or the radical innovation that is the object of the case's analysis (Christensen, 1997: 9). This means that the company either used another less advanced technology prior to the emergence of the discontinuous technology or that the discontinuous technology allowed the company to create a new business that it did not have prior to the emergence of the technology in question.

  Established companies are especially vulnerable to discontinuous technology change and also show greater difficulties in generating radical innovation (see Chapter 1). This is due to the fact that established companies are trying to stay with the traditional technologies that have brought them success in the past. They tend to remain stuck in established albeit proven routines, technologies and innovation patterns so that every business opportunity either initiated by a discontinuous technology or by an attempted radical innovation has a hard time being acknowledged within the organization.

- *The company must be part of a technology/innovation-driven industry.* As described in the first chapter, discontinuous technology change and radical innovation are absolutely crucial for companies competing on the basis of technology and innovation. Thus, the objective of successfully mastering discontinuous technology and radical innovation primarily affects companies competing in innovation- and technology-driven industries. Innovation-driven industries, within this publication, are understood as industries where the competitiveness of its players is significantly determined by their innovativeness.[1]
- *The company must have a specific size in terms of employees.* The management challenge to respond to a technological discontinuity or to autonomously generate radical innovations seems especially hard for large companies as these tend to be run according to strict routines and processes that are meant to reduce complexity in business. Compared to a small enterprise with few employees run with informal structures and by highly dynamic management, a large company is rather inert and slow in reacting to or initiating in changes such as the ones triggered by a discontinuity or needed for radical innovation. Thus, in this research no company is analyzed that has fewer than 500 employees.
- *The discontinuity or radical innovation must be relevant for the core business of the company.* The technological discontinuities or radical innovations that are the object of analysis in the cases must be directly relevant to the company's competitiveness in one or more of its core businesses. Management must not ignore the discontinuities that this research will analyze because the consequences can be significant long-term losses in market share or return on investment.

Following these criteria three case studies were selected for this publication. All cases studies were conducted between April and October 2003 and lasted between twelve and sixteen weeks. These cases were conducted as projects that were part of the Swiss Federal Research Program by the Commission for Technology and Innovation (CTI) on nanotechnology.[2] CTI is the Swiss innovation promotion agency that aims to accelerate the conversion of state-of-the-art laboratory findings to marketable products. The nanotechnology-oriented program called TopNano21 was run between 2000 and 2003. It was funded by CTI with CHF 62 million in order to achieve the following goals:[3]

- To consolidate the Swiss economy by implementing new, nanometer-based technologies.

- To expand the scientific horizon of Swiss universities and other academic institutions with a view to applying the nanometer in industry.
- To teach nanometer technology in order to promote young scientists, researchers, engineers and other specialists.
- To support start-ups.

The three cases studies presented in this research on managing discontinuous technology and radical innovation were conducted in the course of the TopNano21 program. Nanotechnology seemed to be a suitable technology for this purpose. Relatively new to the broad industry, it represents great potential for technological discontinuity in many industries. Specialists (Holister, 2002: 4ff.) promote this technology as a main source of radical innovations in the decade to come.

The case studies basically investigated ex post four main technology and innovation management aspects of the companies that were engaged in nanotechnology; first, how the company got involved in nanotechnology was reconstructed; second, how the technology that was new to the organization was selected; third, what strategic decisions the technology caused; and, fourth, what the eventual outcome was, or what the decision taken was on the subject of nanotechnology. This investigation was conducted through a great number of interviews and workshops in the companies. Those companies wished anonymity, therefore they have been given imaginary names and logos, as well as only a basic description of their field of activity (see the following section).

2   Cases from reality

In the following section, three case studies will be presented in order to investigate state-of-the-art management with discontinuous technologies and radical innovation. Table 3.1 provides the overview of the three cases.

Case 1: Quali-Chem-Tech

In late 2001 the emergence of a nanotechnology-based titan oxide with a UV protecting effect was reported to represent a potential substitution threat for Quali-Chem-Tech's own technologies in one of its main businesses. This report triggered a series of investigations and strategic decisions in the course of the following year. At the end of this period the situation seemed to be clear for Quali-Chem-Tech. A number of measures, such as monitoring and intelligence activities, as well as a competence network on nanotechnology were established. The chronological course of the Quali-Chem-Tech case is illustrated in Figure 3.1.

Quali-Chem-Tech

Table 3.1 Case study overview[4]

Case	Industry	Company / unit	Company logo	Year	Sales CHF million	Number of employees	% R&D investment of Sales
1	Chemical	Quali-Chem-Tech	Quali-Chem-Tech	2003	6500	15000	4.2
2	Manufacturing	Inject-Tech	Inject-Tech	2003	200	1000	Not published
3	Chemical	Pro-Chem-Tech	Pro-Chem-Tech	2003	2800	6000	8

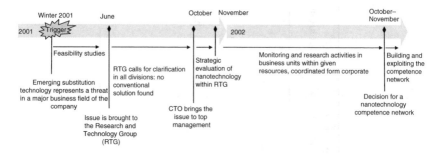

Figure 3.1   Chronology of Case 1

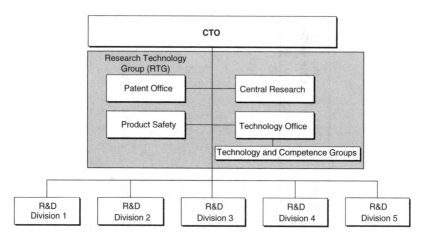

Figure 3.2   Business unit and technology and innovation management structures at Quali-Chem-Tech

Initial situation

Quali-Chem-Tech is active in the production of industrial chemicals. It covers five market fields by its five distinct divisions. These divisions provide products for markets in Asia, Europe and America. The market orientation of Quali-Chem-Tech is reflected in its division and technology and innovation management structures (see Figure 3.2).

The biggest parts of R&D activities are decentralized and market-oriented in the five divisions of Quali-Chem-Tech. Beside these activities, Central Research is a unit that functions as a competence center for special issues and for the design of new products. All these technology and innovation management activities are headed by the CTO, who is a member of the board of Quali-Chem-Tech. He is assisted by the Technology Office, responsible for open questions in technology and innovation management on behalf of the CTO. He is also responsible for coordinating and managing the activities of Quali-Chem-Tech's Technology and Competence groups. These groups, composed of technical experts from different divisions of the company, represent a strong instrument for the investigation of issues that have been requested for clearance by the CTO. Usually these issues of technology and innovation affect the company strategically as a whole.

The responsible managers, of all the divisions (mostly R&D heads), together with the members of the Technology Office, the Central Research unit, the Patents Office and the Product Safety unit – form the Research and Technology Group (RTG). The RTG, led by the CTO, is a structure that is responsible for the implementation of the technology and innovation strategy and for controlling issues of the latter. In addition to this, it is the drop-in center for all kinds of innovation proposals, especially for those coming from the divisions. It also governs an extra innovation fund of several million Swiss francs which finances those research proposals that are not supported by the division's R&D budgets.

However technology- and innovation-driven the chemical industry can be, it is nonetheless regarded more as a conservative rather than a highly innovative industry. Thus, Quali-Chem-Tech has focused its biggest proportion of R&D activities towards the market. The company has excellent innovation-management and new product development-processes targeting, in the first place, market driven incremental innovations. These processes are harmonized over the divisions and managed independently by each one. Thus, divisions are responsible for their own technology intelligence activities and the choice for new technologies is strongly directed towards enhancing the existing businesses. Beside their probability of technical and commercial success, these technologies are evaluated according to their projected return, their business-strategic fit and their ability to leverage existing resources and skills.

This strong focus on incremental innovation represented an unfavorable initial position for Quali-Chem-Tech when it was confronted with nanotechnology for the first time in late 2001.

Nanotechnology at Quali-Chem-Tech

As a chemical company Quali-Chem-Tech is, of course, not totally unfamiliar with the effects nanoscale particles cause; however, it never approached these effects systematically from a nanotechnology perspective. Therefore the effects based on nanotechnology that were registered as a potential substitution technology for conventional UV absorber substances used in many products of Quali-Chem-Tech represented a discontinuous technology for the company. Because nanotechnology as a science was unfamiliar to Quali-Chem-Tech, it represented a discontinuity but it also did so because of the totally different technological approach of nanoparticles that provide an even higher UV protection than the conventional technology.

Quali-Chem-Tech uses state-of-the-art technology to provide UV protection in many of its products from paint to sun lotion. This technology consists of organic substances such as Oxybenzon, which is used, for example, in sun lotion. This substance protects skin from the sun by absorbing and scattering UV radiation and finally turning it into heat. While absorbing radiation the organic molecules in these sun lotions degrade bit by bit and lose their protecting effect. The technical approach of such a substance is to chemically filter UV light. Instead of a chemical filter, nanotechnologically produced inert substances such as titan oxide, or zinc oxide use a physical filter. These substances do not absorb radiation but they reflect it (see Figure 3.3). The reflecting effect is dependent on the size of the particles; the smaller the particles the better the reflection. Thus, by using nanoparticles, the protection out-performs the conventional protection technology with organic substances. A major advantage of this technology in sun lotions is that the UV protection lasts longer than with the conventional scattering technology, as the degradation of the reflecting nanoparticles is much slower.

The first considerations for a nanotechnology approach rose from the bottom up, out of one of the company's divisions in 2001. This awareness initiated several technological feasibility studies that were conducted within that same division. A trainee was hired whose main job was to gather information, investigate patents and review scientific literature. Besides the technical feasibility, the goal of this study was to find out which opportunities and threats nanotechnology represented for Quali-Chem-Tech and whether the company should extend its portfolio with nanotechnology-based products. Although the feasibility studies could shed light on many aspects of the nanotechnology approach, one major technical problem connected directly with the nanoparticles could not be solved: the particles could not be kept separated. They stuck together inhibiting the targeted UV-protecting effect. These agglomerated nanoparticles formed macroscopic particles that did not show radiation-reflecting properties. By June 2001 the study indicated that the agglomeration problem could not be solved within the division. Thus, it turned to the RTG with a request for a company-wide inquiry aiming to acquire solutions internally. The Technology Office processed the request using its connections and networks all over the company. It made a general

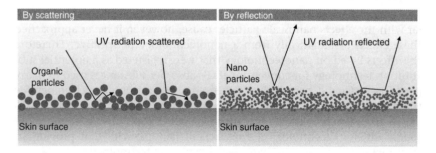

Figure 3.3   UV protection technologies, by scattering and by reflection

request for solutions within all divisions. The outcome of this call showed that the problem with agglomerated nanoparticles was a generally unsolved problem in the company. Most divisions that were active in the field of nano-technology research had encountered the same problems for which the RTG and Technology Office had been requesting solutions.

As a result of this unsettling outcome, the CTO as head of the RTG took the initiative. In October 2001 he informed top management of the unfor-tunate situation concerning nanotechnology. In reply, top management demanded that the Technology Office clarify the strategic relevance of nanotechnology for the company. One month later, in November, the RTG presented its statements to top management. It reported that all divisions saw great potential in nanotechnology and that research and development activities in the company in this area were generally quite advanced. All divi-sions had already started projects related to nanotechnology. Nevertheless nanotechnology still represented a fairly unknown field for the company. With this information, top management instructed the RTG to coordinate nanotechnology monitoring activities in all the divisions and to secure efforts that would allow the company to follow future opportunities that would be triggered by nanotechnology. Besides setting up monitoring activities the RTG recommended that the divisions go on with their present projects in a first phase.

In a second phase, which started one year later in autumn 2002, the RTG introduced a concept that focused nanotechnology research activities all over the company in order to use synergetic effects across the divisions: a knowledge network called Technology and Competence group for effects based on nano-materials was established. The following goals were defined for the network: (1) coordinate research and knowledge sharing in nanotechnology research over all divisions; (2) extend existing competencies in nanotechnology and build up core competencies in nanotechnology; (3) identify new company-internal and external approaches in the field of nanotechnology; (4) promote project requests in the field of nanotechnology. The activities conducted in the field of nanotechnology were financed by the innovation fund of the RTG.

Discussion and conclusion

The initial position for Quali-Chem-Tech to achieve with discontinuous technologies and radical innovation is not a very fortunate one. As the industry is rather conservative and slowly developing, discontinuities are uncommon. Thus, Quali-Chem-Tech's experience with this issue is quite limited. Additionally, the sense of urgency originating from the emergence of nanotechnology in the industry is somewhat limited. There are two main reasons for this, among others: first, Quali-Chem-Tech is not a supplier to the consumer market where successful radical innovations might experience a great speed of market diffusion, which would bring about a strong sense of urgency for management to react. The market Quali-Chem-Tech provides products for is a rather stable and slowly changing market of industrial customers. Thus, radical innovations and discontinuous technologies usually need a long period of time to be acknowledged in the industry. Second, the revolution that nanotechnology was going to trigger in all industries and in all markets still does not seem to be happening. The benefit of nanotechnology is believed to be more on a longer-term basis. There is no talk yet of how nanotechnology is invading market after market, making known products better, cheaper and higher performing, not to mention the radical new products and markets that should have been created by now.

The combination of these factors creates an initial competitive environment that is best challenged by processes, methods and structures that are market-focused, targeting incremental innovation. As a matter of fact, Quali-Chem-Tech does have state-of-the-art innovation processes in its divisions. Although these processes perform well and contribute to the development of new products, they are mainly directed towards an operational innovation management. They check technical and commercial feasibilities rather than strategic implications of innovations. The main concerns in this process are, for example, the availability of raw material or the ease of chemical synthesis, along with some infrequent attempts at strategic analysis, which examine market positioning and competitive issues. The divisions are explicitly focused towards the exploitation of the existing business, and their lack of strategic focus makes it hard for discontinuous technologies and radical innovations to be assessed adequately in the divisions. The main drawback of this management is that divisions might not recognize all of the opportunities that are behind certain technologies, if they are not directly relevant to their present business, and thus they are not forwarded to the corporate structures for further assessment. However, these corporate structures are explicitly responsible for promoting out-of-the-box innovations with a more radical character. They are highly dependent on innovation ideas coming from the divisions because they do not have their own technology intelligence. This approach to promoting radical innovation is unfavorable for two reasons: on the one hand, corporate management has no technology intelligence system of its own in order to independently collect innovation ideas; on the other hand, divisions from which radical innovation ideas are expected are not designed to recognize the latter.

A further point that attracted attention is that however well corporate structures are developed, interconnected and disposed over a financial instrument, the innovation fund, which finances out-of-the-box ideas, there is neither a systematic process nor methods that are designed for the strategic evaluation and assessment of discontinuous technologies and radical innovation. The lack of processes and methods for the evaluation of such ideas makes it difficult for managers at the corporate level to allocate resources objectively out of the innovation fund. Interviews with these managers showed that one of their biggest problems, which was seen as an effect of a missing radical innovation evaluation process, is that they have difficulty justifying their portfolio choice of radical innovation projects in front of the members of the board of directors.

As a final point it can be suggested that a closer cooperation and coordination between strategically focused corporate technology and innovation management units and rather operationally focused divisional innovation management units could accelerate and improve the discontinuous technologies and radical innovation decision process in the company. A closer collaboration would allow better alignment of the different views, strategic and operational, to common long-term goals.

From this description it can be concluded that appropriate practice concepts within the strategic management of discontinuous technologies and radical innovations in this company are missing. Thus, there is a lack of concepts that support:

- Processes in the market-oriented units that distinguish between incremental and radical innovation opportunities in order to promote the latter to a differentiated more strategic rather than operational evaluation.
- Intelligence systems that are coordinated between structures focusing on both incremental innovation and radical innovation.
- Systematic processes and methods designed especially with an emphasis on evaluating strategic issues on radical innovation and discontinuous technologies.
- Balanced and coordinated views and actions of innovation processes between the operational and the strategic level.

These gaps will be addressed within the solution concept of this publication.

Case 2: Inject-Tech

Inject-Tech

In the beginning of 1994 Inject-Tech, active in the field of injection molding, created a research group in order to build up a new business in a so far unfamiliar high-tech plastic market. Initial technical and commercial investigations focused the group on a micro- and nanotechnology-based injection molding technology for the production of ultra-fine structures in plastics. This technology was to form the basis of the new business. By 1995, after several internal research projects and collaborations with customers, the new business had grown to an independent unit. However, the expected return did not come and orders were scarce. Today, a decade after the kick off in 1994, the technology is well mastered; however, customers interested in mass-produced products based on the

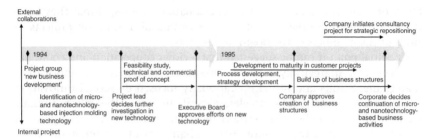

Figure 3.4   Chronology of Case 2

technology are still hard to find. The chronological course of Inject-Tech case is illustrated in Figure 3.4.

Initial situation

Inject-Tech is a globally active company producing injection molding devices for a variety of industries such as automotive, plumbing, sensory and medical, using a range of innovative and mature technologies. They manufacture products such as bumper bars, showerheads, cassettes and cartridges for medical sample testing machines etc.

Through its long experience in this field Inject-Tech has advanced to being a leading innovator in its industry. The company has branches in Europe and the American continent. The main market of the company is Europe generating 80 per cent of sales, to equal parts; USA and Latin America are covered with 10 per cent each.

Inject-Tech specializes in customized injection-molded products and is highly focused on key accounts in its industries. Thus, the company is organized along a matrix organization with business structures, which are focused on its main industries and are crossed by functional supporting units. There are no explicit R&D structures either in the businesses or on the corporate level. Customization in the well-matured injection molding technology demands more high-level engineering and quality-management competencies than R&D insight. Innovations generated within the customer projects are most often of an incremental nature, enhancing existing technologies.

The trigger to initiate efforts, which would build up an additional business field based on a new technology, emerged out of distress in two of Inject-Tech's businesses. In the first business, the company saw the necessity to generally stimulate the performance. By 1994 this business was lacking a clear strategic differentiation compared to its competitors in the market. It was not clearly positioned in the market and it was not committed to a unique selling proposition. It was managed rather like a general store manufacturing all kinds of products for all kinds of customers. The business operating in a very price-sensitive and competitive market was run according to an excessively diversified strategy so that it could accept all kinds of orders. The second business in distress was run as OEM business to the automotive industry. The increasing price pressure from the automotive industry towards its OEMs kept rising so that continuous growth in this business was more and more questioned. In order to respond to these circumstances, Inject- Tech was looking for a new business that would provide a clear position in the market and a strong unique selling proposition. Entering a high-tech plastic market based on a new injection molding technology seemed to be the right choice for establishing a strong business with high margins. Thus, in 1994, a small project team called the 'new business development group' was created.

Nano- and microtechnology at Inject-Tech

At the beginning, the new business development group worked mainly on customer projects with conventional injection molding technologies. Rapidly, however, the idea arose to build up a strong business around a specific technology that could bring the company a long-term unique selling proposition in the targeted high-tech plastic market. In spring 1994 some of the customer projects began to indicate an increased need for high-tech plastic with ultra-fine structures enabled through a micro- and nanotechnology-based injection molding process technology. Further customer inquiries confirmed this impression. As a result, the project team created a small research sub-team, which would investigate feasibility aspects of the new technology, check the patent situation and study state-of-the-art literature. Market analysis turned out to be difficult at the beginning.

The technology development began with initial pilot tests in summer 1994, but soon the need for more sophisticated process instruments required more funding. The project group began to detail market analyses in order to present commercial and technical proof of concepts to the Executive Board. After new means were freed with the approval of the Executive Board in winter 1994, the technology could rapidly be developed so that it could be presented to potential customers.

In the meantime, the technological advances in development narrowed the application range of the technology, so that a preliminary strategy for the emerging new business could be drafted. This strategy planned to establish the new business development group as a specific customer solution-providing business in the segment of high-tech plastics. One newly developed product based on the new technology is a laboratory analysis instrument. It is an injection-molded disc used for drug delivery and as an instrument for screening chemicals. It allows substances to be identified and appointed in liquids. Thus, the liquid to be analyzed is first injected into the center of the disc. Then, using centrifugal forces, the liquid is driven through micro-channels to the edge of the disc, where it reacts with indicating substances in detection cuvettes.

The market barriers in the field of such high-tech plastics are great due to very demanding quality requirements. Newcomers such as Inject-Tech can only beat already-established competitors by using new and superior technology. Thus, the market entrance was planned to be prepared through the intensification of R&D activities and through the exploitation of existing customer contacts. Additionally, research alliances with international institutes and universities were to be established, both to provide an image of a cutting-edge research company and to gain insight into the latest technology and market trends.

In spring 1995 the first customers were attracted to collaborate on the development of the new technology. While these collaborations financed the biggest part of development, the customers received their own tailor-made prototypes. This level of knowledge resulted in the development of a business plan including the enabling business structures in summer 1995, which was approved by the Board of Directors in late summer the same year.

At that time the project group was operating on two complementary levels, focused on the consequent development of the new technology and actively seeking contract projects with conventional technologies. Many of the latter projects were acquired thanks to the new research project, which turned out to have a fairly good advertising effect and allowed the company to differentiate itself from its competitors as an innovator in the industry.

Under these favorable conditions, with secured cash flow through projects with conventional technologies, the structures enabling the new business were continuously extended. In the meantime, the collaborative research development projects with customers allowed the technology to take shape for mass production. Some of the customer projects were followed by promising projects for the production of single-use products.

By the end of 1995 the new business had grown to an independent unit. But before this process was completed, it became clear that the turnover calculated in the initial business plans could certainly not be achieved. Especially in the new technology based business, only a few projects turned into attractive orders. Thus, the Board of Directors decided in the third quarter of 1995 to initiate a consulting project in order to verify the market position of the new business. At the end of 1995, the Board of Directors decided to carry on with the business after the consulting company determined that the business was still attractive.

This new technology has still never been in mass production. At the end of the case study in October 2003 only one product based on it was in production and, contrary to initial assumptions, it sells only a small number of pieces with disappointing margins.

Discussion and conclusion

There are a number of initial factors that at first sight make continuously evolving technologies and incremental innovations much more attractive for Inject-Tech than the challenge of discontinuous technologies and radical innovation. One factor is the company's business model; besides a number of mass-produced products, Inject-Tech is strongly focused on the design and production of customized injection molding products. First, in their custom business, most products are characterized by strict requirements and concrete data of exactly how the customer wants his products. Such specific orders do not leave a lot of space for radical innovation. Second, the injection molding technology is a rather mature technology. Thus, the innovation potential of the technology is more or less exhausted so the company has to focus on incremental innovation. A second factor that does not promote Inject-Tech's routine with radical innovation is due, on the one hand, to the clientele the company is producing for and, on the other hand, to the management of the latter. Inject-Tech's clientele mainly comes from mature industries that themselves have difficulties with radical innovation. For example the automotive or the plumbing industries which are main customers of Inject-Tech are rather conservative industries that do not challenge their suppliers with innovative concepts and visionary new requirements. The management of such customers as key accounts is the typical consequence for a supplier of mature industries. Key accounts focus mainly on mass production, on price and on quality, all three attributes that are best served with incremental innovation and continuous improvement. Inject-Tech managed incremental innovation and continuous improvement by excellent engineering competencies carried out by outstandingly qualified employees. Thus, there was no need for explicit R&D structures so that the company could efficiently build up insights to diversify its technologies or to enter into new market areas. Mainly the marketing people that are also all highly skilled engineers or technicians ran small R&D activities.

The company seemed perfectly adapted to the product-market strategy it was following. However, in 1994 when the business felt its first distress, strategic processes, methods and structures to manage innovation in general, not to mention radical innovation, were missing. Today this situation is still unchanged. Innovation is still done as part of customer projects and managed according to solid project and quality-management rules rather than according to state-of-the-art innovation management.

The lack of explicit innovation-oriented structures makes it hard for the people from marketing, who are only unofficially charged with this task. They are often in conflict about how to manage their time; the question is how much time to dedicate to daily business and how much to dedicate to innovation. Asked in interviews, people almost always answered that most often more time was spent working on daily business to the detriment of the planned innovation activities. Even if people had been explicitly assigned time to work on innovative projects, it was difficult to use this time, as daily tasks were not reduced significantly. As a result, innovation was done rather as under-cover work, without informing the division or unit manager, not to mention top management. At Inject-Tech this was the case above all at the beginning of the project, just after the new technology was identified as a potentially interesting technology.

The most obvious methods and tools that were found to be missing were the ones that allowed strategic evaluation of radical innovations and discontinuous technologies. These projects were different from most familiar projects and thus uncertain and risky to the company and existing tools and methods for evaluation could only be applied in limited ways. Furthermore, as is typical for a discontinuous technology, the market situation was uncertain at the beginning of the new business development project, so that engineers had difficulty systematically elaborating a consistent and fact-based argument to present the project to the board. Interviewed managers felt that the main problem in generating radical innovations was, first, to systematically select the really good business ideas from all the propositions in a period of high uncertainty and, second, to systematically work out good arguments in order to promote risky projects to superiors.

This case shows how a company can be faced with difficulties once it decides to change the strategy in one or more businesses through the introduction of a discontinuous technology. Again, a number of gaps can be derived from this case; it can be concluded that strategic management with discontinuous technologies and radical innovation needs concepts, which include:

- Explicit structures enabling innovation activities that do not focus exclusively on the existing businesses. These structures should be designed so that they do not interfere with daily business.
- A systematic process supporting the evaluation of strategic innovation targets.
- Methods that support the systematic elaboration of a consistent argumentation justifying choices of uncertain and risky technologies and innovations.

These gaps will be addressed within the solution concept of this book.

Case 3: Pro-Chem-Tech

A Pro-Chem-Tech researcher had the idea to use nanotechnology for the optimization of chemical ingredients delivered for consumer products (see Figure 3.5). Research activities initiated for the investigation of this idea were conducted for almost the next one and a half years without the official approval of the research project evaluation team. During this period of time, the research carried out was mainly done in alliance, first with an external research lab,

Pro-Chem-Tech

then with a main customer who was interested in the technology. After the official start of the project in the first quarter of the second year since the beginning of the project, the involvement of the customer had already grown so strong that Pro-Chem-Tech had a hard time directing the research according to their own ideas. After four years of research, the project was concluded successfully from a technical point of view. However, there were still no orders from the collaborating customer who had exclusivity rights on the products based on the new technology.

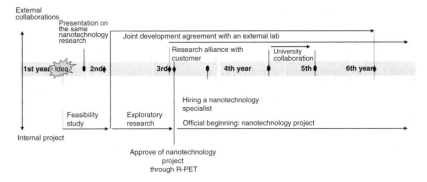

Figure 3.5   Chronology of Case 3

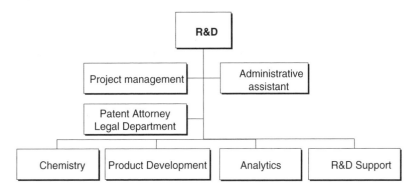

Figure 3.6   Structure of Pro-Chem-Tech

Initial situation

This case was conducted in a chemical company that produces ingredients for consumer goods. The analysis was conducted in a division of Pro-Chem-Tech that is divided into three market-oriented business units, a research unit and an operation unit. The business-focused units are subdivided into customer units. Each one of these customer units has their own sales department.

The research unit is structured in the four areas: Chemistry, Product Development, Analytics and R&D Support (see Figure 3.6). These areas are run as independent units without being assigned to a specific business unit or sales department. However, business units finance the budgets of the research unit. These payments are proportional to sales of each unit and delivered as a lump sum independent of the number of projects made by a unit.

The alignment of the research structure according to different areas and not according to the business unit's market focus requires a procedure that evaluates, approves and assigns research projects proposals from the business units to specific areas of the research unit. This procedure is covered by phase I of the Research Project Evaluation Team (R-PET) process. This process describes the phases from the creation of a new idea to the commercialization of the project (see Figure 3.7).

In phase I, a possible innovation idea has to be submitted as a document project proposal through a technical project sheet together with a separate business contract. These two documents contain, on the one hand, a technical description of the project and, on the other hand, an estimated market potential of the targeted business. These documents are presented to the R-PET committee, which grants approval of the project proposals and establishes their priority. If priority is high and enough resources are available, the project is added to the portfolio. If not, it is added to the prioritized pipeline.

The R-PET is the active body of the research project evaluation process. It reviews project proposals, allocates resources to projects, starts and controls them. The R-PET is composed of people from different units and functions from all over Pro-Chem-Tech's division: it includes people from the sales units, from the Product Development unit and people from the R&D and Operations unit. The R-PET reports to the president of the division and its management committee.

Nanotechnology at Pro-Chem-Tech

The idea using nanotechnology to improve the performance of Pro-Chem-Tech's chemicals that are designed for consumer products was triggered by

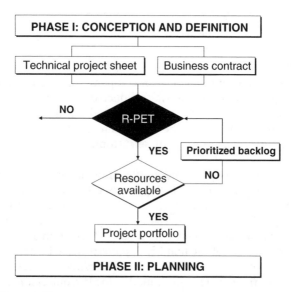

Figure 3.7 Phase I of Research Project Evaluation Team (R-PET) process

a researcher in the R&D unit at the end of year one. This person, who had joined Pro-Chem-Tech from another industry, merely transferred a technology, which was classically established in the area he was leaving, and brought it to a new area, where this technology was unknown. The new target application constituted the novelty of the idea. Soon after the idea was born, small, preliminary tests were run. At that stage, the work was conducted informally and outside of the R-PET context, i.e. there was no formal approval of the project management structure. The success of these tests was limited at the beginning, but they sufficed to show an initial feasibility. A few months later in the same year, a third, independent research laboratory published a paper on that same research subject. This confirmed the need to continue the so far limited and loosely connected research efforts at Pro-Chem-Tech. This led additionally to the initiation of a joint development agreement with the external laboratory in the spring of the project's second year.

The goal of the collaboration was, in the first place, to extend the present research activities without having to apply internally for a new product development project from R-PET. The signed cooperation indeed accelerated the acquisition of knowledge and furthered the feasibility phase with a clearly appreciable financial commitment. The possibility to benefit from the knowledge and the resources of the collaborating partner were especially valuable, as the research activities within the company had barely been intensified even after this partnership.

Internally, however, the nanotechnology project still had only low priority. This can be explained by the brief initial enthusiasm of product developers that rapidly turned into marked skepticism, as the new nanotechnology-based technology showed unfamiliar properties in the delivery of its effect, which implicated a discontinuity with the traditional technology-based effects. The properties of the effect delivered by the nanotechnology-based technology were completely different from that of classic technologies. In order to assess the effect delivered by the new technology, product developers had to learn the properties of each effect based on nanotechnology ingredients. The motivation to learn these changes was limited so that the priority of R&D projects was laid on other short-term projects.

In the beginning of year three, the collaboration delivered its first results. However, they mainly came because of the research partner. Results were estimated to be good enough to apply for project status at the R-PET to finally convince engineers in product development to undertake a new product-development project based on the new technology. At that time, there were still no official activities in the nanotechnology project within the company. This was due to a lack of resources and to the unchanged low priority classification of the project.

But before the proposal could be presented to the R-PET in spring of year three, a product-focused research alliance with a main customer of

Pro-Chem-Tech was signed. Through this alliance, the nanotechnology project finally succeeded in attaining higher priority. As a consequence, the project was soon presented to the R-PET. By that time the R-PET had few options, as the customer's influence was quite strong. The project was accepted. This was finally the official start of the nanotechnology project, and in October of year three a nanotechnology specialist was hired as the project manager.

Even though the contract with the customer gave the project a higher status at Pro-Chem-Tech, the company lost a great deal of its autonomy in the research project as the power of this big customer collaborating with Pro-Chem-Tech on the nanotechnology project was immense. At the end, anchoring the project to this customer slowed down the general pace of research. This was due mainly to two reasons: first, some parts of the project moved back to basic research instead of being transferred to more application-oriented analysis and, second, the status of the project did not have a high priority for the customer, and in particular there were no clear requirements from the business side.

Pro-Chem-Tech financed an academic post-doctoral position from year four to year five, aiming to visualize the effect delivered by the new technology in the products that used it. An experimental set-up was developed and built. But as a consequence of new budget restrictions, this work was stopped just before the experimental set-up could be systematically operated.

In spring of the same year, the research collaboration with the external lab was also stopped, as the main goals of the projects had been achieved and a new level of knowledge did not seem to be emerging.

In the sixth year, the nanotechnology project was finished from the technical side. The feasibility was proven and the scale-up had been carried out successfully. Product-specific work and application was being run. The final concept had to be presented to the collaborating customer, but by the end of the case study there was still no guarantee from the customer that the benefit from the nanotechnology project was going to be used commercially.

Discussion and conclusion

The initial position for Pro-Chem-Tech to excel in the management of radical innovation and discontinuous technologies is a challenging one. Pro-Chem-Tech is operating in a quite conservative industry dominated by mature and proven technologies. Although this industry is technology- and innovation-driven, most of the innovations are incremental by nature, focusing on cost reduction. Costs are one main argument in a mature industry; this is also very strongly the case in the chemical industry delivering ingredients for consumer products. Thus, radical innovations that usually require costly R&D expenditures are not common, as these expenditures need to be shifted to the product price. Unless the customer benefit is very high and obvious, innovation does not legitimate higher costs.

Another difficult aspect typical of a chemical industry producing ingredients for consumer goods is the ever-changing strategies and interests of the industry's customers, coupled with a strong dependence on the latter. Frequent strategy changes of this segment of the chemical industry's customers are due to the high-level competition and instability of these companies' markets. A large segment of Pro-Chem-Tech's customers are companies producing a wide variety of consumer products for the retail market. These markets are highly marked by changing competitive rules and dynamically altering customer trends. In addition to these frequent changes of the industry's customers, customers are scarce in general. Pro-Chem-Tech has quite a limited number of customers; however, their size gives them a great deal of power. Thus, Pro-Chem-Tech is obliged to follow the changes of its customers as quickly as they occur. At Pro-Chem-Tech, therefore, a project that initially had a high prioritization can be stopped abruptly because the strategy of the customer has changed. The inverse is possible as well. A project or even a proposal for a project queued in a backlog list can become very important from one day to the next, simply because a customer indicates an interest in it.

This change of priorities leads to a very short-term focus in processes, methods and structures of project planning and prioritization. In such short-term thinking it is difficult to create an innovation culture that allows discontinuous technologies to grow into radical innovations. The result is that evaluation structures like the Research Project Evaluation Team (R-PET) are fully committed to incremental innovation targeting projects promising quick returns. As a matter of fact, the R-PET decision process does not differentiate in the evaluation of different types of projects according to their newness to the company or the risk that they represent. Furthermore, members of the R-PET showed high-risk aversion when deciding on innovation projects that changed traditional production methods. In particular, during the nanotechnology project it was difficult to convince some product-developing engineers, partly chairing the R-PET, to adopt the changes implicit in the product-development processes.

Under the conditions described above, it is very difficult for radical innovation ideas to not be eliminated at the R-PET. One reason for this is that radical innovation ideas are evaluated with the same methods and tools, and from the same perspective, as incremental innovation proposals, although there is a fundamental difference in the characteristics of both types of innovations (see Chapter 2). Another reason for this too narrow evaluation focusing on incremental innovation is that the Research Project Evaluation Team, as the name reveals, is mainly a project management unit rather than a strategic planning unit. The strategic focus is missing in this unit, as it has only a weak focus on positioning the company in a competitive environment. It is more concerned with selecting and prioritizing projects according to merely financial criteria than with comparing them one by one in a strategic context.

The evaluation process in Figure 3.7 represents a guideline in order to explain how decisions are taken; however, it does not represent an integrative and systematized method of elaborating decision criteria for the evaluation of the projects. An integrative process would require that information processing in different functional areas of the company would produce a harmonized and coordinated set of evaluation criteria that would serve as a basis for consensus decision-taking.

Generally, the decision-takers showed a low level of commitment to the nanotechnology project, which finally led to a critical loss of time at the moment of decision-taking. This lack of commitment was also visible in the implementation of the project where, at the beginning, there was no explicit project organization. The organization that had started as 'skunk' work grew organically during the project. Many interfaces between unhomogeneous groups of people working on this project blocked free-flowing information within the company. This could be a consequence of the fact that there was no project manager responsible for both the market and technological aspects. On the research side of the organization it was not optimal that a project manager be named relatively late after the start of the project; this was, again, a consequence of low initial prioritization. Furthermore, there were budget restrictions leading to the premature discontinuation of the post-doctoral project at the university, at a point where relevant data were just starting to be collected, and a sign of insufficient consensus between the management and the research department. With this decision, all of the money that had been invested in this student's work was more or less lost.

This case shows that technology-management concepts for the practical management of discontinuous technologies and radical innovations are still missing. Gaps derived from this case can be formulated as follows:

- There is no fundamental understanding of the evaluation processes and methods of innovations. Radical innovations are still evaluated and assessed in the same way as incremental innovations.
- A strategic perspective in the assessment of project proposals is missing. There are limited strategic analyses that elaborate criteria for decision-taking.
- The decision-taking process is trivially designed. Although the R-PET process provides guidelines for the decision on innovation proposals, it is not an integrative process that coordinates the elaboration and processing information out of different functional units in a systematized way as a basis for decision-making.

These gaps will be addressed within the solution concept of this book.

3   Cross-case comparison

Analyzing and comparing these cases led to the identification of a number of issues related to processes, methods and structures. These issues address the implications of state-of-the-art management with discontinuous technologies and radical innovation.

Process-related issues

*Dominant activities not systematized – lacking **systematic process***

The three cases show that none of the companies had a systematic strategy-formulation process tailored for discontinuous technologies and radical innovation. As there were no existing NPD processes that could handle the uncertainty and risk inherent with project ideas, it took the ideas much longer to be evaluated, and managers said that they did not know how to proceed in order to be sure that the ideas had been assessed in the best possible way. Thus, all of the projects were assessed in an ad hoc process. Comparing this process across the three cases, four main activities turned out to be dominant. These activities were the (1) initiation of the process itself, (2) the evaluation, (3) the decision and (4) the realization of the innovation idea. However, the activities were not defined as such, thus it was not clear what their focus was. Furthermore, the activities were not aligned along a process that provided guidelines in order to efficiently and systematically assess the innovation opportunity. They were, on the contrary, found to be uncoordinated and loosely related.

*Difficulties in reliable strategic decision-making – **lacking evaluative activities on a strategic level***

Analyzing the various ad hoc process activities in more detail, a critical pattern emerged in all three cases. The evaluation of the innovation ideas was carried out almost exclusively on an operational level, and evaluation on the strategic level was very rare. Thus, an innovative idea that triggered the initiation of the process, independent from its originating level (strategic or operational), was always assigned to the operational level for evaluation. Such evaluations included efforts to prove technical feasibility as well as to examine preliminary market expectations. While these analyses were running, there was almost no activity that investigated the strategic implications of the innovation idea. Objectives connecting the strategic and the operational level for the evaluation were not given. This made it difficult for managers on the strategic level to decide on projects, since all decisions had to be made based on information elaborated exclusively from an operational perspective.

*Slow process lead times – **lacking coordination and interrelation between the strategic and operational levels***

This observation was generally made in all three cases and concerned most analyzed activities. Within the ad hoc process, the various activities from initiation of the process through evaluation, decision and implementation lacked coordination between the operational and strategic levels for the various project activities. Findings that had been worked out on the operational level in the course of the process could not be benchmarked with previously set strategic goals. An iterative and determined course of actions that narrowed the scope of analysis step by step with clear strategic goals was not explicitly visible in any of the cases. As a result, the analyses conducted in operational-level projects were executed with poor focus. Thus, all activities related to radical innovation idea analysis turned out to be time consuming and slow.

Method-related issues

Ineffective information processing – lacking **market and technology intelligence tools**

To gain a first-mover advantage, which is highly beneficial with radical innovation, it is critical to identify an innovation opportunity early. None of the companies systematically gathered information in order to discover weak technological and market signals leading to radical innovation. Only one company conducted some kind of monitoring activities; however, these were explicitly designed to follow the continuously evolving trends and therefore designed towards incremental innovation.

Once the reception and identification of such signals has succeeded, a company has to filter ideas, deciding which to analyze in more detail and which ones to eliminate. An initial evaluation needs to be quick in order to process as many ideas and related information as possible. Furthermore, such a process should guarantee an acceptable degree of accuracy. In the analyzed cases none of the companies applied such a quick assessment tool.

Eliminating potential radical innovation ideas by inappropriate evaluation – lacking **evaluation tools for decision management under high uncertainty and risk**

The analysis of the methods used to support evaluation and decision-making further showed that in all of the three cases, companies did not differentiate innovation opportunities with either incremental or discontinuous character. Managers used the same set of techniques for both types of innovation. Such methods relied heavily on the idea of quantitative assessment: for instance, return on investment, net present value, etc. Irrespective of this, the adequacy or accuracy of such methods for evaluating breakthrough projects in a very early stage and applying the same set of evaluation methods for all innovation projects in a company bears the danger that many radical ideas can be eliminated too early as a result of being seen as either too uncertain or too risky. A possible consequence of applying such evaluation procedures might be that it prevents companies from generating and tracking radical innovation ideas.

Structure-related issues

Emergence of skunk work – lacking clear **assignment of tasks and responsibility**

In none of the cases was there a designated person responsible for acting as a key or contact person, taking explicit care of radical innovation ideas that existed. Often such ideas just do not fit into a company's on-going business activities and thus it is not at all obvious who might be assigned to which tasks. This was the case in all three projects, and as a result it took project ideas much longer to receive attention compared to incremental innovation activities. In two cases, a consequence was that project evaluations had already been started before top management was informed. Leifer *et al.* (2000) call such hidden activities 'skunk' work. Although (skunk) work can sometimes be effective for generating radical innovation (Christensen, 1997), it is not part of a systematic process of promoting radical innovation throughout an organization.

Another issue concerning responsibility was the ownership of the project idea. It was observed that responsibilities on a strategic level were only assigned once the ideas had been evaluated and the decision had been taken that the idea was to be further investigated in a project. During the period, when ideas did not yet have project status, no responsibilities were assigned. The consequence was that the initiation of the evaluation and the drive of the latter were much slower than top management wished for in general. In addition, there was no standardized planning responsible for directing the operational evaluations or for formulating and reviewing evaluation deliverables.

Structural conflicts between daily business and radical innovation activities – lacking organizational alignment

In all three projects, ideas that were followed from birth until the decision confirming it as an official project hardly ever left their organizational home. Most of the activities registered were conducted beside the on-going business in the regular organization. This caused structural conflicts between the two kinds of projects. On the one hand, researchers complained that resources that had been granted for radical innovation purpose could not be used as daily business and on-going innovation had higher priority. On the other hand, managers who were under pressure to perform reported that their daily business suffered from radical innovation projects.

Comparing the issues described in the above sections – process-related issues, methods-related issues and structure-related issues – across the three cases, a cross-case comparison can be drawn. Its key findings are summarized in Table 3.2.

The analyses follow the categories described in this chapter (see Section 3, throughout). 'Non-existent' means that an approach towards this issue could not be found; 'partly existent' means that the company already had rudimentary approaches or considered this issue implicitly in one way or the other; 'existent' means that this issue was explicitly implemented and in use.

Gap in practice

The cross-case comparison (see Section 3) discussed the most frequently observed implications of state-of-the-art management from a process,

Table 3.2 Case comparison overview

	Case 1	Case 2	Case 3
Process related issues			
Systematic process	Non-existent	Non-existent	Partly existent
Evaluation activities on strategic level	Partly existent	Partly existent	Non-existent
Coordination and interrelation between strategic and operational level	Partly existent	Partly existent	Non-existent
Method related issues			
Market and technology intelligence tools	Partly existent	Non-existent	Non-existent
Tools for decision management under high degree of uncertainty and risk	Non-existent	Non-existent	Non-existent
Structure related issues			
Clear assignment of tasks and responsibility	Partly existent	Partly existent	Non-existent
Organizational alignment	Partly existent	Partly existent	Non-existent

○ Non-existent   ◑ Partly existent   ● Existent

method and structure perspective. These issues explained why most managers have difficulties planning for or reacting to discontinuous technology change or preparing their company for the strategic management of radical innovation.[5] In fact, they represent the gap in practice, which is, generally speaking, the lack of integrated concepts for the strategic planning of discontinuous technology and radical innovation. Formulating this lack according to the particular issues discussed in the previous chapter results in the following gaps:

Gap in current practical management approaches: Current management approaches applied in practice fail to address the challenge of sustained innovation: strategic planning processes lack a systematic and clear conception and the applied methods and structures lack a differentiated deployment for incremental and radical innovations.
The gap in current practical management approaches is generalized and described in detail by the gaps 1–3 in practice:
Gap 1 in practice: Systematized planning processes with a strategic focus strongly coordinating and aligning strategic and operational matters are missing.
Gap 2 in practice: Methods for systematized information gathering and for a differentiated evaluation of innovation opportunities according to their risk and uncertainty are missing.

Gap 3 in practice: Structures assigned for the management of discontinuous technologies and radical innovation while respecting the priority of daily business are missing.

The identified gaps in practice represent the last building block besides the insights from theory and the discussions of the cross-case comparison necessary for the formulation of the propositions for the concept (see following Section 4). They show that research in the field of managing discontinuous technologies and radical innovation is needed in order to close these gaps in practice.

4 Propositions for a concept

In the present section, a set of propositions is formulated as a guideline for a strategic planning concept with discontinuous technologies and radical innovations. They are synthesized out of the entire through process elaborated so far in this research and represent the quintessence of this work. Structured according to process propositions, structural and methodological propositions, they aim to capture in a concise way the requirements for the design of processes, structures and methods of an integrated strategic planning concept, following the mindset of sustained innovation.

Process propositions

Proposition 1: The design of the process, managing radical and incremental innovation ideas, should be structured systematically along the main tasks of strategy formulation: (1) identification, (2) evaluation, (3) decision and (4) implementation of innovation project ideas.

Proposition 2: The action of the process should be continuously extended in order to cover all major tasks referring to both strategic and operational levels.

Proposition 3: The process should include complementary assignments on the strategic and operational level and should be coordinated continuously by the strategic level.

Proposition 4: The process design should allow a simultaneous but differentiated management of radical and incremental innovation ideas according to their level of newness and risk.

Methodological propositions

Proposition 5: Methods should be used to support market and technology intelligence systematically during the identification phase.

Proposition 6: Methods should be used to quickly assess the relative newness and risk of innovation ideas for the company.

Proposition 7:   Methods should be designed to evaluate the strategic impact of innovation opportunity differently, according to their level of newness and risk.

Structural propositions

Generally, structures should be designed to enable execution of processes and methods. Additionally, keeping with the guidelines, two further propositions are suggested:

Proposition 8:   Structures should be created that provide a contact point and assume responsibility for the management of radical innovation ideas.

Proposition 9:   Structures should allow simultaneous and harmonized management of radical innovation beside daily business in order to insure organizational alignment.

5   Summary and conclusion

This chapter analyzed how state-of-the-art management performed when faced with discontinuous technologies and radical innovation. Generally speaking it can be stated that existing management concepts used in coping with discontinuous technologies and radical innovation showed weaknesses. The origin of these difficulties was analyzed and presented in a set of three gaps in practice that refer to processes, methods and structures used in practice. These gaps in practice together with the gaps in theory represent the necessity of research in the field of discontinuous technologies and radical innovation. Following the course of research conducted at the ETH Center of Enterprise Science these gaps represent the *twofold gap in management theory and in reality* calling for research action.

Although three new gaps have been uncovered in this chapter, the insights gained through the practical case studies in this research can be used, to close three gaps, 4, 5 and 6, in theory, shown in Chapter 2. They are closed by the insights gained in this chapter. These gaps provided the missing research, which analyzed the performance of existing practical management concepts for handling discontinuous technology and radical innovation. The gaps have been closed by the cases and their subsequent cross-comparison in this chapter (see section 3, cross case comparison). The overall performance of the existing strategic planning concepts is to be rated weak; it has been recorded in the three gaps in practice.

The question asks for the requirements of strategic planning with discontinuous technologies and radical innovation that will determine successful management and implementation of sustained technological innovation in innovation-driven enterprises could be closed by the present chapter. This question has already been worked out by reviewing the state of the art in theory. Together with these previous insights, the knowledge acquired through the cases in the present chapter provided a set of nine propositions, which have been formulated in Section 4 and represent the requirements for successful strategic management and implementation of discontinuous technologies and radical innovation. Structured according to processes, methods and structures of strategic management, they perfectly describe how the management concept for strategic planning should be designed.

4
Sustained Innovation Management

Insight gained in the previous two chapters, on state-of-the-art literature and state-of-the-art practice, delivered an answer to the question asking for requirements that determine successful strategic planning and implementation of sustained technological innovation management in innovation-driven enterprises. As already described in Chapter 1, sustained technological innovation management aims to simultaneously manage both incremental and radical innovations. The requirements for such management have been formulated in the form of nine propositions describing the design of processes, methods and structures of a sustained innovation management concept.

The investigation of literature and case studies, however, could not identify applicable concepts that show how the requirements could be put into action through concrete processes, methods and structures of strategic planning, in order to achieve implementation of a sustained innovation management concept. Thus, in this chapter, a concept is developed based on the nine propositions that suggest a possible design of processes, methods and structures that will enable a practitioner-oriented planning concept for sustained innovation management.

The concept aims to provide an applicable practitioner-oriented procedure for formulating a technology and innovation strategy for companies competing in innovation-driven industries. The concept should represent a systematic process that guides the manager step by step through all strategic analyses necessary to prepare a strategic decision and to finally take the decision. Guided by this process, the manager can be assured that all necessary analysis and information has been considered before the decision in question is taken. This allows him to prepare such a decision regardless of the uncertainty inherent in some decisions, as he knows at any time that the decision process has been run thoroughly, and all available, relevant information has been processed appropriately for the decision to be taken. Decisions taken in this way are fully comprehensible to everyone in the organization; they can be justified and their development traced back at any time. In this way, the process aims to follow the logic of sustained innovation management; this means that strategies worked out with this process not only focus on short- to medium-term competitive strategic issues, but also on long-term development strategic issues. Thus the manager can, on the one hand, go on exploiting and strengthening existing businesses while, on the other hand, simultaneously exploring new businesses in order to prepare the company to be more prominent or better prepared for major changes in the environment. It is the goal of the concept to connect long-term strategic goals and short- to medium-term strategic goals in a balanced way. The concept is designed to provide a guided procedure, which continuously converts company development strategies into competitive strategies.

1   Development of the concept

This section aims to provide the basic understanding of the concept. Thus, the concept is developed step by step, first by explaining how the suggested process model in this chapter responds to the requirements set in the previous chapters. Additionally the holistic perspective as well as the integrative nature of the concept is explained. These explanations help to understand the *rationale* of the process in order to provide in a second step, an *overview* of the concept's process. This overview explains the choice of the methods supporting the process. In a last step *structures* are suggested that enable the process as a whole. In subsequent sections (see Sections 2–5), the process will be explained in more detail. Each process phase will be presented including the details of each method and their corresponding structures supporting the latter.

During the development of the concept as well as during the more detailed elaboration of its phases, practical examples and best practice examples from industry will be presented.

Rationale

As defined in Chapter 2, a concept for strategic planning following the course of sustained innovation management comprises a strategic process supported by methods and enabled by structures. Although the concept is mainly focused on the strategic level, it has to be considered as a part of a holistic management concept interacting with normative and operational management (see also Chapter 2, 'Integrated technology management'). Furthermore, it has to be regarded similarly to a business strategy as an integrative part of a corporate strategy. Thus, it should provide strategic goals and paths from a technology and innovation management perspective as an integrative part of an overall corporate strategy.

The rationale of the concept will be explained by using its main guiding element that is the strategic planning process. Methods and structures supporting and enabling the process, and particularly the design of the process, are what is most essential for shaping the rationale of the concept. The design of the process is determined according to the four process propositions, as stated in Chapter 3, Section 4. Figure 4.1 shows the fundamental design of the process. The following paragraphs explain this fundamental design.

The process design follows a holistic management view: The holistic management of this process is insured by the interaction between the normative, strategic and operational levels. As an initial position for the strategic planning process, *the normative level* provides the guidelines through a corporate vision,[1] a company policy[2] and an innovation policy. These three elements provide a raw but focused direction to the innovation activities on the strategic level. The direction indicated by the normative level influences the whole strategic process, affecting all the phases of the strategy formulation and strategy implementation.

Once the strategic process is initiated, it works in close relation with the operational level. The relation between the strategic and operational level can be seen similarly to the relation between the normative and strategic level. However, the directives given by the strategic level to the operational one are much less broad than the ones directed from the normative to the operational level. As a matter of fact, the strategic level steers and decides which actions have to be carried out, in which way, by the operational level.

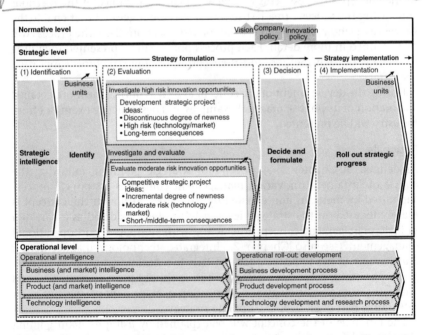

Figure 4.1   Basic design model of the strategic planning process for sustained innovation management

For example, the very first process phase of the strategic level – the strategic intelligence – fixes first which technology-related information has to be gathered, then the operational level is charged with collecting this information.

The process design provides an integrated process. The process designed in Figure 4.1 is an integrated part of the corporate strategy run by different business units as well as by the corporate unit. The process phases run by different business units are symbolized in Figure 4.1 by process symbols that are doubled, as for example in the case of the 'Identify' process phase. When the symbols are not doubled, such as for the process phases 'Decide and formulate', they have to be run merely by the corporate unit. The actual integration of all strategic decisions from different units to one corporate strategy takes place in the process phase 'Decide and formulate', where all the information elaborated during the process flows together.

On the strategic level the concept is structured along process phases' successive process steps differentiating between strategy formulation and strategy implementation. The concept is designed in four phases: (1) identification, (2) evaluation, (3) decision and (4) implementation. These concept phases are symbolized by the four dotted boxes, and within each of these boxes the typical process arrows symbolize the process steps. The following paragraph describes as an overview the content of each of these four phases referring to Figure 4.3:

1. The 'Identification' concept phase comprises the process phase 'Strategic intelligence Identification (1)' and Identify. 'Strategic intelligence' comprises all strategic activities related to gathering information relevant for the best possible decision to be made.[3] 'Identify' is charged with detecting innovation opportunities out of the information gathered.
2. The 'Evaluate (2)' concept phase comprises the process phases 'Investigate high risk innovation opportunities' and 'Evaluate moderate risk innovation opportunities'. The upper process phase limb in Figure 4.1 handles high risk innovation opportunities. These opportunities formulated in the form of project ideas are of the discontinuous degree of newness with long-term consequences for the company. These project ideas, if realized, are of a development-strategic nature for a company. They enable the company to evolve as an organization by developing its future new strategic competencies. These competencies are meant to be deployed in products of the second next generation. Thus, in the company, such projects ideas intend to initiate learning about technologies that will allow future competencies to be developed. This initiation is based on the 'Investigate high risk innovation opportunities' process arm. Therefore, its ultimate task is to assess and eventually to select those new technologies' project ideas that will lay the foundation for the company's changing competencies. As project ideas are often very uncertain and difficult to assess, they are handled differently from so-called competitive strategic innovation

opportunities. Such opportunities are analyzed in the process called 'Evaluate moderate risk innovation opportunities' shown in the lower process arm of the concept phase 'Evaluate (2)' in Figure 4.1 The innovation opportunities analyzed in this process are of an incremental degree of newness, usually enhancing familiar applications and businesses of the company. The primary goal of this process is more straightforward; it is not about developing new competencies for the future of the company but to yield next-generation products that sell and that allow an existing market position to be expanded or strengthened. Project ideas at the basis of such goals should be of moderate risk and have rather short- to mid-term consequences for the company. The differentiation in dealing with innovation project ideas according to their level of risk or newness is illustrated in the Best practice case 4.1 of BASF.

3. The 'Decision (3)' concept phase comprises the process phases which review all the analysis done in the previous phase in order to formulate the innovation strategy.

4. The 'Implementation (4)' concept phase is focused towards the successful implementation of the strategy. It redesigns the organizational corporate structures and optimizes the implementation.

For the description of the design of a strategic planning concept following the course of sustained innovation, the focus is laid on the three first phases: identification, evaluation and decision. The implementation phase, which is outside the focus of this publication, is a standard procedure that is not specifically adapted to sustained innovation management.[4]

On the operational level there are two major process blocks, 'Operational intelligence' and 'Operational roll-out', grouping operational processes for the simultaneous and differentiated management of radical and incremental innovation. In the 'Operational intelligence' process block, technology intelligence, product intelligence and business intelligence are handled separately. The separation has the main purpose of appropriately managing the different management contents and their various time horizons, priorities and strategic steering structures.

As a matter of fact the technology intelligence process in operational intelligence is mandated in the first place by strategic intelligence, identification and strategic evaluation structures in charge of high risk innovation opportunities. This operational intelligence process collects technological information above all from radical innovation opportunities. For these kinds of innovation opportunities, technical feasibility and the assessment of technical risk are most important, while product and market information are still scarce. In alignment with the strategic level, this information is forwarded to the 'Technology development and research process' step in the 'Operational roll-out' process block. In this step which is initiated after the strategic level has passed its 'Decide and formulate' process step, the

BASF classifies innovation activities according to different levels of technology and market newness.

Technology platform research and development refers to R&D activities focusing on technologies and markets that are established within BASF. The three technology platforms in the fields of specialty chemicals, chemicals and engineering, and polymers, perform research and development activities in order to strengthen and extend the core competencies of the company.

Exploratory research is a strategic instrument to secure BASF's technological and methodological competence in the long term. With that, the potentials from scientific and technical progress for the existing portfolio as well as for new attractive business areas are exploited. Basic research activities are left up to universities with which BASF's research units have good contacts. Most of the BASF exploratory research is carried out in Germany.

New business development is conducted in the operating divisions of BASF. It aims to identify new markets outside the current businesses that are based on existing and already mastered technologies. The focus lies on the development of new partnerships with customers, start-ups or universities, utilizing the expertise available in-house.

Plant biotechnology research is conducted within BASF Plant Science GmbH, a spin-off company of BASF founded in 1998. It focuses on 'young' technology in the area of consumer-oriented and value-adding development of plants.

Corporate innovation scouting is conducted within Strategic Planning, a unit with tasks in product area strategy definition, mergers and acquisitions, strategic controlling, competitive intelligence and macroeconomic analysis. They cooperate with Corporate Research Planningon planning and reporting on corporate-financed research as well as division-based R&D. Innovation scouting is a global platform for the entire BASF group used to identify new cross-divisional business opportunities, evaluate those and propose an appropriate model of how to address these new opportunities. The understanding of the term 'innovation' is not limited to new products, but also to new business models based on existing products from more than one division. So-called 'innovation scouts' will trigger and support the idea creation process, work on business opportunities, leverage existing and develop the future product portfolio, as well as create innovative business solutions.BASF Future Business GmbH is a 100 per cent BASF subsidiary with the task of identifying and developing new business areas for BASF group.

Best practice case 4.1   BASF, adapting R&D activity to level of market and technology newness

Source: Interview at BASF, 2005, M. Reisel, T. Jäger, G. Trauffler.

intention is to develop the technology to a level where it is technically mastered. The time horizon of such technology development projects is rather mid- to long-term, as it often takes five years and more as a result of being only of moderate priority.

As a contrast, the horizon of product development projects, and its corresponding product and market intelligence, is usually of a short-term horizon with a high priority. Such projects are driven by a time to market pressure built up by the competitive environment of the company (Petrick and Echols, 2004: 85). In order for a company to be successful in this competition, the company should master the technology underlying the products, just as the risks and uncertainty of both a technical and market nature must also be mastered.

Best practice case 4.2 shows how IBM clusters innovation projects in different time horizons according to their level of uncertainty.

For the above reasons of uncertainty and risk, the operational processes of 'Product intelligence' and 'Market intelligence' (as well as the 'Product development' processes) should be mandated by the strategic evaluation structures for moderate risk innovation opportunities, and only be fed with incremental innovation opportunities based on mastered technologies. Once the technology is mastered and the products are on their way to development, operational business and market intelligence processes and business development processes can be run. These processes develop the business model for the product that is close to being fully developed. Best practice case 4.3 illustrates how Heidelberg first pre-develops technologies, and then in a second stage develops products. At the same time a sophisticated employee rotation system secures the knowledge transfer between pre-development and development.

Table 4.1 summarizes what strategic process is in charge of steering which operational-level process. Furthermore, it shows the differences in the management content: the various characters of the technologies and innovation opportunities that are managed according to various time horizons and levels of priority.

The different strategic processes in charge of steering different operational processes with various foci fulfill the requirement for a simultaneous and differentiated management of discontinuous technologies and radical innovation versus continuous technologies and incremental innovation. The illustration in Figure 4.2 shows the rationale of Table 4.1 in the given process design. This figure shows that the relation between the strategic and operational level is not a unidirectional steering relation from the strategic level to the operation level: it is rather an iterative exchange between the two levels. Although the strategic level directs the action in the operational level processes, its directives are continuously adapted to the feedback from the operational level.

Table 4.1 Strategic processes in charge of corresponding operational-level processes

Strategic-level process	Corresponding operational-level process	Character of technologies and innovation opportunity-managed	Time horizon/level of priority, goal of the process
• Strategic intelligence/identify high risk innovations opportunity	1. Technology intelligence	1. Discontinuous technology/radical innovation	• Mid- to long term/moderate priority • Goal: find technologies to build up future competencies and core competencies
• Strategic intelligence/identify moderate risk innovation opportunity	1. Product intelligence 2. Business intelligence	1. Continuous or mastered technology/incremental innovation 2. Mastered product/incremental innovation	• Short term/priority driven by time to market pressure • Goal: find technologies to enhance existing products, strengthen existing markets
• Decide and formulate • Strategic roll-out	1. Technological development and research 2. Product development 3. Business development	1. Discontinuous technology/radical innovation 2. Continuous or mastered technology/incremental innovation 3. Mastered product/incremental innovation	1. Mid- to long term/moderate priority 2. & 3. Short term/priority driven by time to market pressure

The simultaneous but still differentiated management of radical and incremental innovation has been found to be realized at IBM. The differentiation is done according to their level of newness and risk. IBM chose to differentiate innovation opportunities according to time until commercialization and level of uncertainty involved with the opportunities. For this differentiation, three 'horizons' have been defined that are drawn against the growth potential of innovation project ideas: innovation project ideas are clustered in these horizons depending, on the one hand, on the time and level of uncertainty they represent for the company and, on the other hand, on the level of their growth potential.

Ideas that are well defined concerning time to market and uncertainty are assigned to Horizon 1 (H1). The realization of these project ideas target the extension and defense of core business.

Ideas with moderate time to market and uncertainty are assigned to Horizon 2 (H2); these project ideas should already be based on scale-proven business models. Their goal is to increase market share and growth opportunities.

Finally, distant time to market and highly uncertain project ideas called emerging business opportunities (EBO) at IBM are regrouped in the Horizon 3 (H3) cluster. In this third horizon business models of project ideas are developed and tested. Viability and values of the ideas are proven.

All three clusters are managed differently from each other.

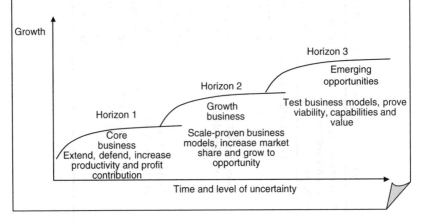

Best practice case 4.2   IBM, managing the portfolio of innovation ideas according to three distinct horizons

Source: Interviews and presentation material at IBM, 2003, G. Trauffler.

Overview

In the previous section, the rationale of the concept has been presented by explaining how normative, strategic and operational levels communicate and interact. The choice as well as the arrangement of the process steps has been explained.

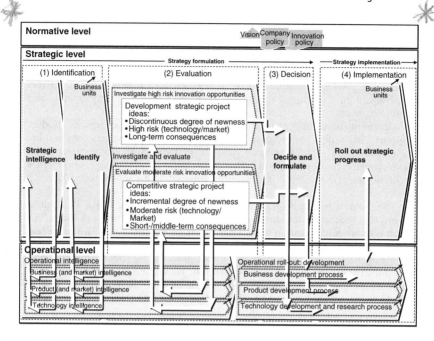

Figure 4.2 Rationale of the strategic planning process model: iterative interaction between the strategic and operational level

Based on this understanding, the present section aims to present the fully developed process, including all its main tasks, its supporting methods and, finally, the structures proposed to enable the process as a whole in an organization.

First an overview of the process and methods will be given and then, in a subsequent section, structures will be shown.

Process and methods overview

The process is presented in Figure 4.3. It is composed of five main phases, enumerated from 1–5 on the strategic level, and of six operational level processes, enumerated from a–f.

The strategic process starts with phase 'Strategic intelligence (1.1)' (for details see this chapter, 'Strategic intelligence'). Its function is to coordinate and direct all tasks related to technology intelligence. It defines which information should be collected and subsequently analyzes the information that has been delivered in collaboration with operational processes. The method supporting this strategic process is the opportunity landscape, which structures and visualizes the technology search fields and the issues of interest within this search field for intelligence purposes (for details see this chapter, 'Strategic intelligence').

The entire spectrum of Heidelberg's R&D activities can be roughly divided into the chronological process stages of pre-development and development.

Pre-development is in charge of research topics not directly or not yet relevant to existing products. Examples of such research are examinations of surfaces with regard to their applicability for Heidelberg products; sensors and laser technologies etc.

Development comprises product relevant development as well as product support. In order to increase the innovation effectiveness of product development, on a regular basis Heidelberg transfers researchers from pre-development to development. This way implicit knowledge about new technologies and concepts is constantly brought in to product development projects.

The human resource vacancies in pre-development are filled, if possible, mainly by technical staff from the development entities of Heidelberg. The result is a sort of job rotation within Heidelberg's R&D structures. This procedure is supposed to prevent the emergence of mismatches and maladjustments along the whole R&D process. Additionally unilateral recruiting streams from outside, e.g. universities, can be avoided. As a result, all researchers acquire a holistic understanding of the challenges in research, on the one hand, and product development, on the other hand. This understanding provides the basic premise for sustainable innovation according to Heidelberg.

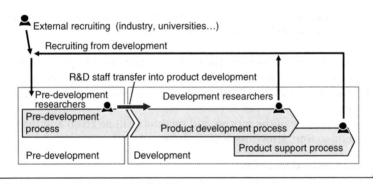

Best practice case 4.3   Heidelberger Druckmaschinen, a holistic understanding of research and development

Source: Interview at Heidelberger Druckmaschinen, 2005, T. Jäger, M. Reisel, G. Trauffler.

In addition to these traditional intelligence tasks, this process phase hosts a corporate venture approach (for details see this chapter, 'Back-end intelligence aided by corporate venturing'). This strategic process is in charge of collecting information about the technology-oriented start-up scene and small companies; it further handles typical venturing tasks that emerge within the company. A tool that is at the disposal of corporate venture is the Technology Watch List (for details see this chapter, 'Back-end intelligence aided by corporate venturing'). This list supports the systematic monitoring of a number of start-up companies and small companies whose technology could be of interest to the established company's business.

The second phase 'Identify all innovation opportunities (1.2)' is the step that initiates the proper strategic planning process (see this chapter, 'Identify all innovation opportunities'). It is split into two parts: it starts by (1) revising the initial position of the company, then out of the information collected from strategic intelligence new innovation opportunity fields are (2) identified and further (3) detailed. The initiating three steps of this phase are supported by the method called 'Innovation architecture' (see this chapter, 'Kick-off'). It is a method that creates transparency across the company, showing the relation between, on the one hand, technologies used in the company and, on the other hand, the products delivered and markets addressed. Doing so guides a process of structured creativity helping to identify new opportunity fields from a technology and business perspective. The innovation architecture can be used simultaneously in order to assess the newness of a technology or business field for the company.

Once innovation opportunities are identified and their newness is roughly assessed in the second part of the identification phase, the risks of the innovation opportunity are analyzed. Thus, the CTO sits together with business unit (BU) heads to assess the identified opportunities in the risk portfolio (see this chapter, 'Quick assessment').

According to the results of this risk assessment, including the consideration of the degree of newness done in the previous step, innovation opportunities that are formulated as project ideas are directed to either phase 'Investigate high risk innovation opportunities (process phase 2.1)' or 'Evaluate moderate risk innovation opportunities (process phase 2.2)'. Usually the newer and the more risky the project idea, the less related it is to the existing business of the company.

The strategic process phase (2.1) investigating high risk innovations opportunities is designed to analyze innovation ideas that are considered new and risky to the company. Often these ideas are the source for radical innovations that are based on the development of discontinuous technologies.

The process phase (2.1) is composed of two steps, 'Acknowledge' and 'Investigate', collaborating in the first place with the operational level technology intelligence process (see Figure 4.3).

In the 'Acknowledge' step, the attention of the persons in charge of assessing the project ideas should be directed towards acknowledging ideas that are at first sight not related to or are unfamiliar to the existing business, and cannot obviously be recognized as potentially valuable in the future and strategically important in the long run. The 'Acknowledge' step has been integrated into the process model as, (in line with the interviews conducted for this research), one big concern of engineers and researchers was the challenge of finding, among the many novel ideas unrelated to the familiar business of the company, the ones that were actually beneficial for the company's

92

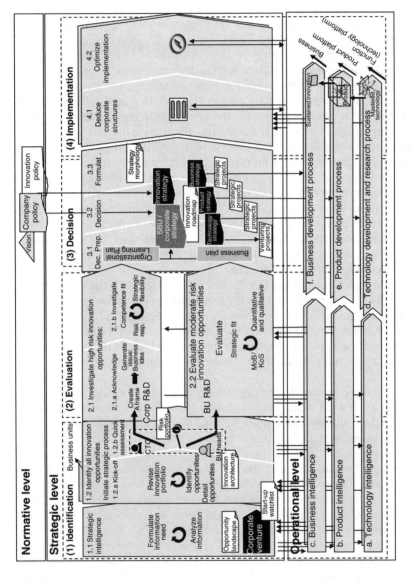

Figure 4.3 Overall strategic planning process model for sustained innovation, including main methods

future. Most of the interviewees indicated that the problem was not missing innovative ideas for projects but, on the contrary, usually they were too numerous, making it difficult to distinguish the good and valuable ideas worth further investigation from the ones that were less worthy. Thus, 'Acknowledge' creates, in a first step, an assessment framework that forms a reference for evaluating the project ideas from many different perspectives. These perspectives emphasize the assessment of innovation project ideas in relation to the company's external competitive environment.

In a second step, the innovation ideas that fit into this evaluation frame are then looked at for their market application potential. Business ideas based on the technology are imagined and sketched. These business ideas do not need to be concrete; however, they indicate a rough direction of the research that could be involved with this idea. Those project ideas that still seem to warrant further analysis after 'Acknowledge' are forwarded to the 'Investigate' step.

'Investigate high risk innovation opportunities' in process phase (2.1) deepens the analysis of the selected innovation project ideas; its analysis emphasizes a more company-internal perspective, looking at the competencies that the innovation ideas can bring to the company. Furthermore, it assesses the strategic flexibility a project idea provides to the company and, finally, measures are developed that can respond to the risk that has been assessed earlier. The outcome of the process 'Investigate high risk innovation opportunities (2.1)' is an 'organizational learning plan'. This plan records, in a nutshell, which radical innovation project ideas should be worth considering for realization. It is a strategic document that contains the list of strategic arguments justifying why and how an uncertain and risky project should be implemented, even if the return of the project can only be vaguely estimated. Thus, the 'organizational learning plan' describes the development of strategic projects or venturing projects that are important for the company to evolve in the long run, even if in the short term this projects will, above all, generate costs. As already mentioned earlier in this chapter, the technologies that are suggested in this learning plan are suggested with the goal to become the basis for products of the second next generation.

The process phase 'Evaluate moderate risk innovation opportunities (2.2)' is conducted in each business unit having an R&D unit. It is run in collaboration with operational product and business intelligence processes (b and c). This evaluation comprises the usual strategic analysis, as implemented in most companies, and is designed for incremental innovation opportunities: a strategic fit analysis, some qualitative and some financially quantitative analysis, eventually followed by some make or buy/keep or sell considerations (MoB/KoS). The outcome of this phase is a 'business plan' that includes financial arguments justifying why and how a project should be realized. The 'business plan' describes competitive strategic projects that are important for the company on the short-term horizon because they would generate and strengthen return in existing business fields. Thus, as already described earlier in this chapter, the business plan contains those innovation project ideas that are suggested as innovations for the next generation of products.

The differentiated evaluation of innovation opportunities described here through the two process phases for high risk opportunities (process phase 2.1) and moderate risk opportunities (process phase 2.2) is illustrated by the Best practice case 4.4 for IBM.

In concept phase 'Decision (3)', both the organizational learning plan and the business plans from different business units are presented for decision on a corporate level. In alignment with the corporate strategy, an innovation strategy is deduced from the presented plans. As a supporting method for the formulation of the strategy, the so-called 'strategy morphology' is suggested (for details see Section 4). This method promotes a systematic procedure of combining several strategic goals and paths in order to evaluate strategic

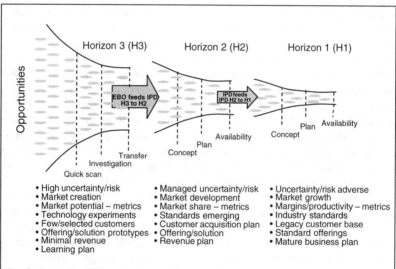

Similarly to the differentiating analysis in the sub-processes 'Investigation' and 'Evaluation' of the suggested strategic planning model in this research, IBM uses different types of measures to assess different types of innovation project ideas. After having clustered project ideas according to three different horizons (see Best practice case 4.1), IBM uses differentiating priorities according to various horizons. Using an integrated portfolio development (IPD), the ultimate goals is to filter an initially great number of emerging business opportunities (EBO) step by step from H3 to H1 and to build up new core businesses managed in H1.

Best practice case 4.4 IBM, differentiated evaluation according to three different horizons

Source: Interviews and presentation material at IBM, 2003, G. Trauffler.

options for the company. Once the strategy is formulated, the 'innovation roadmap' is used to schedule the technical and market projects along a strategic time line. The realization of the formulated strategy is implemented through the definition of strategic projects (for details see this chapter, 'Formulation'). These projects are of high priority and realized on the operational level. Depending on their goals, they are managed according to technology development and research processes (d), product development (e) or business development processes (f), or using a combination of the three types of operational processes. The execution of these processes is steered and rolled out by the strategic concept process phase called 'Implementation (4)'. It comprises a redesign of the deduction of corporate structures and optimizes the implementation.

The principle of inter-subjectivity

The success of the strategic planning process described in the previous sections depends on the accuracy and correctness of the strategic decisions made in it. However, in management it is hard to tell which decision is the most accurate and correct decision with regard to a company's internal and external situation. It is especially hard, in the case of uncertainty, when the information underlying a decision is not complete. In such a situation objectivity in decision-taking is practically impossible, as missing information has to be replaced by speculation and individual assumptions, which are, however, tainted by individual subjectivity.

Objectivity not being possible and individual subjectivity not being satisfactory for decision-taking, a trade-off of both is suggested; it is called inter-subjectivity. Inter-subjectivity describes consensus-driven decision-taking that involves, as a basis for decision preparation, a variety of expertise from persons with different backgrounds, and a variety of data from different sources. Thus, inter-subjectivity is determined by consensus between qualified subjective appraisals, such as carriers of original information for taking decisions, carriers of responsibility for decisions and main representatives affected by decisions (Tschirky, 2005).

In order to enable a consolidation of different people's expertise and a consolidation of different sources of data, in this publication the procedure of inter-subjective opinion blending is suggested to increase accuracy in the strategic planning process. This procedure coordinates the collaboration of different groups of experts while working with diverse and independent sources of data. The data is related to specific management tools and evaluated by a by a group of experts. Thus, inter-subjective opinion-blending encourages experts to work together in collaboration with other experts, using a multitude of management tools during the strategic planning process. It is a way to substitute speculation and individually subjective assumptions by a collective inter-subjective opinion that has been reached by a consensus based on the knowledge and experience of all participants.

The matrix manages the collaboration between experts and the tools (see Figure 4.4). The axes of the matrix are provided, on the one hand, by the tools deployed and, on the other hand, by the groups of experts using them during the strategic planning process. Every expert group is composed of people with different backgrounds but with a specific expertise about one of the tools. This group is responsible for this specific tool, in that, for this tool, it represents the main contact point for support when other people or expert groups apply it. Additionally, the responsible group updates and further develops its tool according to the latest insights from management theory, and continuously adapts it to the company and industry-specific situation. In the matrix shown in Figure 4.4, expert group 1 is responsible for tool 1; expert group 2 is responsible for tool 2, one expert group is led by a leading R&D person in the company, for example (the R&D division head).

The matrix is the initial position to begin to manage the principle of inter-subjective opinion-blending while preparing the decision for an innovation project idea. The matrix is managed by the CTO in collaboration with the R&D heads of the divisions. These people assign all the project ideas that have to be evaluated for a strategic decision to different fields in the matrix. This way each project idea is assigned to *at least* one field in the matrix. Thus, the group of experts using their tool corresponding to this field will evaluate each project idea.

Once the assignment of projects is done (this is the situation displayed in Figure 4.4), the principle of the inter-subjective opinion-blending can be applied. It is a twofold consensus-forming procedure: *first*, there is *group*

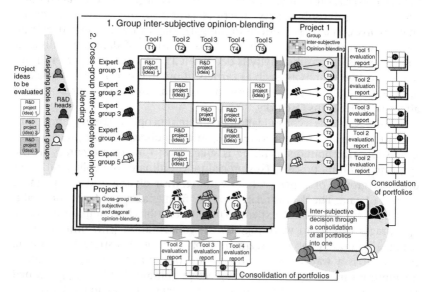

Figure 4.4   Inter-subjective opinion-blending

inter-subjective opinion-blending (horizontal procedure through the matrix), which promotes the exchange of opinions within one and the same expert group applying a range of different management tools. Doing so within one horizontal row of the matrix, one innovation project idea is evaluated by the same expert group using different tools. With these first evaluations made in every group, the *second* consensus-forming iteration can be done: the *cross-group inter-subjective opinion-blending* (vertical procedure through the matrix). Here different expert groups exchange their opinions applying one and the same tool. Then, within one vertical column of the matrix, all the groups assigned to the same project meet for a workshop to elaborate an evaluation. The expert group that is responsible for the corresponding tool leads the workshop.

From group inter-subjective opinion-blending, as well as from cross-group inter-subjective opinion-blending, evaluation reports are elaborated along the strategic planning process. Once an evaluation report is elaborated for all project ideas, persons from the expert groups come together to cross-compare the projects and write proposals for the interesting projects to be chosen in the 'Decide and formulate' phase.

Structures overview

The structures designed to enable the process in Figure 4.3 are meant for a technology- and innovation-driven company with a strong market orientation. The suggested organization, displayed in Figure 4.5, is composed of two types of structures: a business unit-oriented structure and a corporate unit structure.[5] Although both types of structures have distinguished competence areas, they still work closely together. The distinction in their competence areas is specified by the distinction of various processes that they host along the management process, as displayed in Figure 4.3.

An example of how corporate units and business units can work together is given by the Practice example 4.1, the Swisscom case.

Starting with strategic intelligence, this process is hosted by the corporate unit. It is the corporate R&D department that decides which technology fields should be investigated. Researchers and engineers in the business unit do the actual collecting of the information in the selected fields. Therefore, a network of gatekeepers has to be built up that gathers information across the whole company and outside of it in different fields. Additionally, the corporate unit also hosts all venture activities.

The 'Identify' process is hosted in all the business units and the corporate unit. Each of the units is responsible for finding the innovation opportunities which are most interesting for their own business. In this way all innovation opportunities that are interesting in short- as well as long-term perspectives should be registered. In a subsequent consensus-seeking step, a responsible corporate manager (in collaboration with a business unit manager), assesses the risk of these innovation opportunities. According to the risk assessed, the opportunity is directed either towards a corporate or a business unit for assessment.

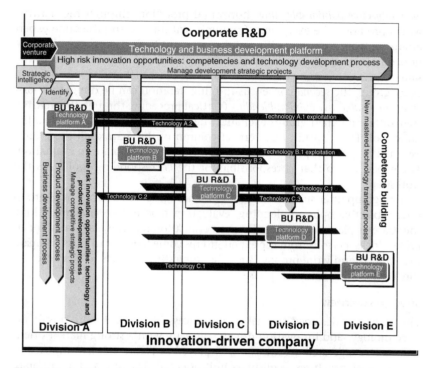

Figure 4.5   Enabling structures hosting the strategic planning process model

The 'Investigate high risk innovation opportunity' process is hosted by the corporate R&D unit and led by the CTO. The corporate unit, not being as strictly market-driven, is in charge of exploring new technologies in order to estimate their strategic and future market potential. These technologies do not necessarily have to be related to the company's familiar businesses; on the contrary, research done on the corporate level should open the existing technological and business horizons of the company to enable it to enter into new and unexplored fields. Thus, the main competence of corporate R&D has to be to develop new technologies and businesses.

The Best practice case 4.5 of Degussa shows how different organizational units are assigned to different competence-building and innovation-management tasks.

This competence can be regrouped in a virtual organizational structure called a platform. A platform on the corporate level represents a collection of competencies serving one common purpose. In the present case, the platform regroups all the competencies necessary to develop new technologies and to build up new businesses. It includes skills from basic research to new business development and venturing. The generated technological and/or market knowledge are not meant for internal use at the corporate level but,

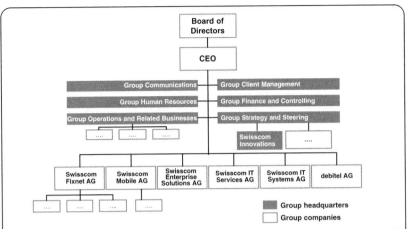

Swisscom, the Swiss telecommunication company that unifies a number of independently operating companies, has founded on a corporate level the company 'Swisscom Innovations'. Operating independently, this company has the task of fostering innovation within the group of Swisscom companies and consulting the Strategy and Steering group. As a telecommunication provider, the group is not aiming to develop new telecommunication technologies itself, it is but interested in using the latter as a basis to enable new communication services. Thus the main goal of 'Swisscom Innovations' is not R&D; it is rather to evaluate, to find, to compare and test available or emerging telecommunication technologies that enable the group companies to develop innovative telecommunication services. Although 'Swisscom Innovations' is not to be understood as a typical corporate R&D department that develops technologies, the fact that it is run as an independent business on the corporate level and that it is attached to 'Strategy and Steering' follows the mindset of this research: being run as an independent unit on the corporate level it is financed 30 per cent by the group. The other 70 per cent has to be gained with projects with the group's companies. This way 'Swisscom Innovations' is forced to run attractive and innovative technology and market evaluations that can be sold as projects to the group's companies. This again is beneficial for the group's companies, as they can stay in touch with cutting edge telecommunication technologies when collaborating with 'Swisscom Innovations' without having to neglect their own businesses. Furthermore, being attached at the corporate level to 'Strategy and Steering', 'Swisscom Innovations' can directly influence the strategic attention to more long-term company development strategic issues.

Practice example 4.1   Swisscom Innovations, fostering innovation from the corporate level

Source: Interviews at Swisscom, 2004, G. Trauffler.

in the first place, to extend the knowledge of existing business units or to create new businesses. It has to be emphasized here that the deliverables of the corporate R&D unit are new knowledge that is meant to be beneficial for the business unit R&D.

Practice example 4.2 shows how manifold platform structures can be interpreted by different companies.

The Best practice case 4.6 of Clariant shows how such an exchange of knowledge between the various units of a company can be managed.

In Novartis terms, a platform represents a number of different but somewhat related research areas, which are managed together in order to increase efficiency in research and generate synergies.

In pharmaceutical research, such potential areas of synergies occur quite frequently, as chemical structures and substances often have similar characteristics. Reasons can be found in evolutionary processes: proteins, for example, occur in families with structural similarities. This fact in some cases allows different proteins of the same protein family to be explored together in an early phase, specialization of research on individual proteins being necessary only in subsequent phases of R&D. Thus, research in early phases can focus on protein family-specific phenomena.

At Bayer the core processes providing solutions and services along the lifecycle of processes, facilities and products, both for the business subgroups of the company as well as for external customers, are referred to as technology platforms. Within these platforms typically R&D projects are positioned that are attractive at the same time for several business subgroups.

Bayer has created a distinct internal organization which is responsible for fostering the technological evolution of those platforms: Bayer Technology Services.

Syngenta refers to a technology platform as a non-product-specific field of competence that is used across all businesses of the company. Thus, the technology platforms align the company-spanning research activities, which are handled on a corporate level. Insights gained in technology platforms provide the basis for inventions, new products and new markets.

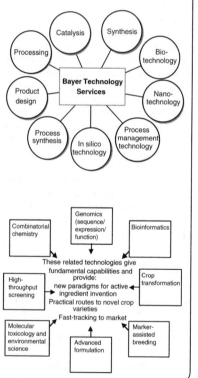

Practice example 4.2   Different interpretations of platforms

Source: Interviews at Novartis, Bayer and Syngenta, 2005, M. Reisel, T. Jäger, G. Trauffler.

The 'Evaluate moderate risk innovation opportunity' process is conducted in every business unit and is led by the R&D responsible for that business unit. The innovation opportunities evaluated in these business-oriented structures have to be easily related to the unit's existing business and activities. Ideally these innovation opportunities have to be used to enhance existing products and markets by improving the technology incrementally. Such incremental innovations should fit into the competencies accumulated in a specific business unit's technology platform. Similarly to the platform described earlier on the corporate level, the platforms on the business unit level should be regarded as centers of competence in a specific technological field.

The innovations generated in these business unit platforms can be twofold: on the one hand, their new products and services are developed to be delivered to the markets of the business unit; on the other hand, the technological

---

R&D responsibilities at Degussa are assigned to three different organizational structures according to their innovation management focus: business units' R&D, corporate innovation management and Creavis.

Innovation management in Degussa's business units pursue low risk technology development and enhancement of existing core competencies following the business unit strategies.

The corporate innovation management unit leads research coordination and strategy at Degussa. It diffuses best-practice management processes elaborated in business units, directs communication among researchers and coordinates collaborative projects.

Creavis Technologies and Innovation is run as a unit within Degussa that is in charge of Degussa's strategic research and development and a corporate venturing. It manages moderate and high risk innovation projects.

Business unit innovation management
- Allocation of BU's R&D budgets according to BU strategy
- R&D portfolio management
- R&D project management

Corporate innovation management
- Corporate guidelines (best practice)
- Allocation of corporate R&D funds according to corporate strategy
- Check and balance process of BU´s technology positions
- Support of BU innovation through coordination of internal/external R&D-networks and R&D-information systems

Creavis technologies and innovation
- Strategic radar, technology watch
- Idea management
- New business development (outside existing portfolio)

Best practice case 4.5   Degussa, innovation management responsibilities adapted to foci
Source: Interview and presentation at Degussa, 2003, G. Trauffler.

In order to secure knowledge transfer across the company, Clariant has created the corporate entity R&D Knowledge Management.

Aiming to reveal what kind of technology knowledge is available in which company area R&D Knowledge Management has defined interdivisional competence fields grouped intechnology platforms. To be hosted by a platform, technology fields have to represent a core competence of the company, which is relevant to more than one single division.

For each competence field, representative experts from across all divisions are identified and brought together within so-called technology teams.

The transfer of knowledge across these technology teams is achieved through competence-specific exchange meetings, where the technology teams present their on-going divisional projects and discuss problems and experiences. Meetings for each of the technology teams are held at least twice a year.

As a result of those meetings a company-wide expert organization is built up that can be used as a gate keeper network.

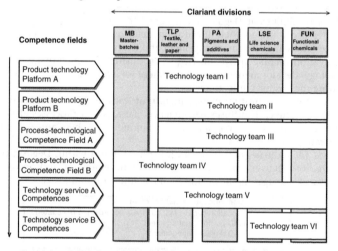

The benefit arising from this expert organization is threefold.

First, on an interdivisional level, synergies can be leveraged while at the same time redundancies in development activities are avoided.

Second, greater transparency is created in R&D-related decision-making; a broader information base for those decisions is provided.

Third, there is a more effective intellectual property management. Discussing the range of applicability and interests of a technology in the technology team meetings helps determine the extent to which technologies should be legally protected.

Best practice case 4.6 Clariant, knowledge exchange through platform structures
Source: Interview at Clariant, 2005, T. Jäger, M. Reisel, G. Trauffler.

knowledge arising from these activities can be cross-used in other business units and/or integrated into their products and services. The main purpose of this technology cross-use is to exploit the technology as broadly as possible, using it in many different fields. This allows a company to use technological synergies across different businesses.

Practice example 4.3 shows how ABB structures its research and development activities depending on the focus of innovation: product development and research in technology are organized in differentiated ways.

ABB basically structures its R&D activities on the divisional as well as on the corporate level according to their two main segments: (1) automation technologies and (2) power technologies.

The divisional R&D activities in these two main segments are further structured according to business areas such as automation products, manufacturing automation, etc., in segment automation technologies and power systems, medium voltage products, high voltage products, etc. in the segment power technologies. Each of these business areas has a business area R&D manager who focuses and coordinates activities for the development of *present and next-generation products*. They define their own product and systems strategies. Local R&D representations of the business area R&D in countries are business area units (BA-U. R&D).

The corporate R&D activities led by the CTO are conducted in ABB's two global labs: one focusing on automation technologies, the other on power technologies. These labs, locally represented in research centers around the world, develop the technologies for the *second next and beyond product generations*. Those technologies are explored within interdisciplinary research programs that cover areas of emerging technologies.

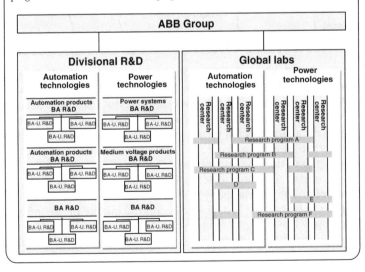

Practice example 4.3   ABB, product generation-focused R&D structures

Source: Interview at ABB, 2005, M. Reisel, T. Jäger, G. Trauffler.

2   Identification (concept phase 1)

The overview on process, methods and structures was given in the previous section; this section will now describe in full detail each step of the process shown in Figure 4.3. Methods and structures corresponding to each process step will also be explained in detail. The descriptions in the following sections will be primarily focused on the strategic level.

Strategic intelligence (process phase 1.1)

The goal of the 'Strategic Intelligence' process is to manage all kinds of information-gathering activities relevant to the strategic purpose of the company. Information needed for this purpose is meant to help when assessing the competitive environment of the company. The process of 'Strategic intelligence' is a continuous process that should be managed centrally from a corporate level in cooperation with a tight network of people all across the company. Its task is to 'Formulate the information need' and then to 'Analyze information.'[6]

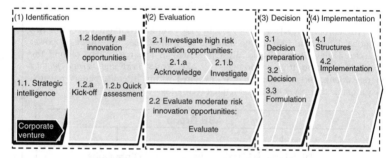

The formulation of the information need may be explicitly formulated, (for example, from the top down, as a demand or a request for clarification), or implicitly (for example, as the result of a previous strategic decision). It aims to define the scope of the information needed. Following the saying 'if you don't have a target, you'll miss it every time' (Basalla, 1988: 141), it limits the observation area focusing the gathering activities. This limitation is done according to the strategic intent of the company. Strategic intent is an 'animating dream' or 'sense of direction, discovery, and destiny', that is meant to determine the company's future (Basalla, 1988: 141). The analysis of information is then needed depending on the quality of the information to be interpreted, as the goal of analysis is to give the information a meaning. Some information already comes to the company in a form that can instantly be interpreted, but there may also be fragmented pieces of information which require a great deal of effort for analysis.

The Best practice case 4.7 shows how Infineon organizes its technology intelligence and how much weight it puts on it.

At Infineon, technology intelligence is conducted as part of the corporate function 'strategy, investor relation and mergers and acquisitions'.This function handles matters related to corporate strategy, mergers and acquisitions and innovation management.

Technology intelligence is responsible for screening scientific literature etc., with regard to the following main questions:

- Which new technologies are interesting or represent an opportunity for Infineon?
- What technologies does the competition focus on?
- Which technologies of Infineon intellectual property assets are used (licensed) by whom and to what extent?
- Which manufacturing technologies have to be mastered in the near future? Interesting technologies and business opportunities are further assessed and tested for compatibility with the company.

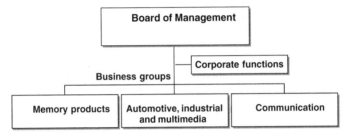

Technology intelligence has a consulting function within the company. The information gathered and assessed is forwarded in the form of proposals to corporate research and to the business groups. Within the business groups the technology innovation officers are the recipients of the proposals. It is their responsibility, together with their corresponding business group's experts, to draw conclusions and make decisions, based on technology intelligence information.

For special cases technology intelligence can access top management to consult regarding its decisions. Its task is to provide the management board regularly with technology intelligence data as well as with information on all research and development activities at Infineon.

Best practice case 4.7   Infineon: technology intelligence organization
Source: Interview at Infineon, 2005, M. Reisel, T. Jäger, G. Trauffler.

Front-end intelligence aided by the opportunity landscape

Front-end intelligence aims to anticipate activities in the early stage of innovation opportunities, also called the 'fuzzy front end'[7] of innovation. A tool to support front-end strategic intelligence is suggested by Savioz (2002: 123ff.; 2003: 193ff.), the opportunity landscape (OL). The OL is used with the aim of managing the fields of information according to the strategic intent of the company. These information fields are managed in a competency-based manner. The OL is based on the gatekeeper approach (Allen, 1986) and constitutes an organizational knowledge base of facts and trends in a company's environment. Measures for the management of these competencies can then be derived from this knowledge base. The concept of the OL will be presented step by step in the following, based on Savioz's (2003) descriptions.

First, an inventory of the present knowledge domains has to be created. This should be complemented with domains that could be relevant in the future. The determination of the current and additional domains can be performed basically in two ways: top down and bottom up. In the top-down approach one derives, to the degree possible, the strategic knowledge areas and the constituent knowledge domains from the company strategy that are typically formulated by top management. In the bottom-up approach, employees from different departments (research and development, marketing, production, etc.) and from different management levels are brought together in workshops, where, via brainstorming, they determine, consolidate and approve possible relevant knowledge domains. The knowledge domains are then broken down into knowledge fields.

The Best practice case 4.8 shows how Novartis has designed the top-down and bottom-up approaches by establishing intelligence collaborations between the operational and strategic level.

The knowledge domains correspond to the competencies that should be built up in the future and the ones that should be maintained and further developed. Because at any given time not all knowledge domains are of the same level of importance, observation depths should be determined. This implies that knowledge domains, whose relevance is already quite high, should be observed more intently than the ones whose importance is only presumed. The OL foresees three observation depths, with a decreasing degree of intensity: the game field, the substitute bank and the offspring.

Visualization gives the OL a face that promotes transparency and hence communication. A good visualization has three characteristics: completeness, simplicity and sustainability. A possible visualization of the OL is shown in Figure 4.6, where the domains are introduced as 'issues'.

The OL is based on what is inside the heads of the participants. Therefore, for each defined knowledge domain, a gatekeeper is defined; the gatekeeper is responsible for having the most current state of knowledge about his or her issue at any given time. Thus, responsibilities are assigned. The designated gatekeeper is ideally an expert in his own field; otherwise, personnel with the necessary potential have to be developed. Together, the gatekeepers form the so-called gatekeeper network. The gatekeeper has the responsibility of observing facts and trends in his knowledge domain. The following three aspects should be covered in this respect: technology, market and competition. What exactly should be observed and how precisely this observation should be made is determined by the gatekeeper, because this person has the best knowledge to decide and to know the strategic direction of the company as

At Novartis general R&D activities are staged in three phases: pre-clinical phase, clinical testing and market-entry phase. Throughout these three phases, the driving forces and involvements change first from non-direct product-oriented research to product focused development and finally to product registration and marketing.

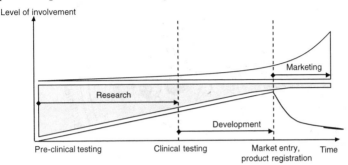

The different intelligence and R&D management activities conducted at Novartis are aligned with the above described R&D activities: the Novartis Institute for Biomedical Research Strategic Alliances (NIBR) together with the Translation Research and Development Board is in charge of intelligence and R&D management activities in the pre-clinical testing phase. They accept and evaluate research opportunities and external project offerings with or without direct product reference. Further, they manage the portfolios of those research projects. Additionally the Pharma Business Development and Licensing Group (Pharma BD & L), together with the Innovation Management Board, handle intelligence and R&D management of the clinical testing phase. They collect and assess product-relevant development opportunities and external offerings and manage the portfolios of product development projects.

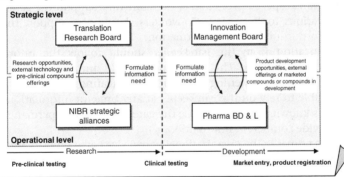

Best practice case 4.8   Novartis, activity-focused intelligence and portfolio management

Source: Interviews at Novartis, 2005, M. Reisel, T. Jäger, G. Trauffler.

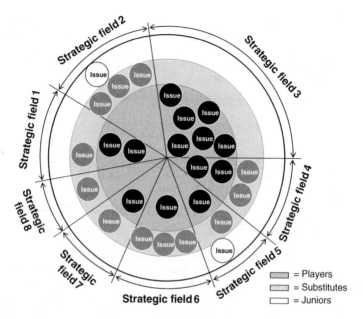

Figure 4.6   Visualization of the opportunity landscape

well as the areas in which it needs to act. In particular, the gatekeeper must define his information sources (e.g. journals, databanks, internet, formal and informal networks, etc.), build them up and maintain them. Naturally, the gatekeepers should be supported. A person, for example the CTO, can coordinate the gatekeeper network and at the same time support the gatekeepers with the various tools needed. Co-workers should also support the gatekeeper by forwarding relevant information.

Communication from the gatekeeper should follow the information push-and-pull principle. The gatekeeper should inform the concerned decision-makers of threatening or opportunity-creating events, and anyone should be able to rely on the gatekeeper at any time for information in the gatekeeper's knowledge area, because the gatekeeper should permanently be able to provide competent information.

The OL is primarily the organizational knowledge based on facts and trends in the company's environment. Actions, however, should be derived from this knowledge base. The first action could be the initiation of development projects, which should be initiated on the basis of the gatekeeper findings. Thus, the OL supports the idea generation in the early phases of the innovation process (Savioz *et al.*, 2002). The second action of the OL can be the support during the innovation process, since this organizational knowledge base can offer expert knowledge for problems in projects. The third action concerns the interaction with the strategy process. The knowledge from the OL can influence or update strategic decisions or the company strategy as a whole. The OL can in turn be updated through a new strategy: for example, by observing and developing new technology fields in order to cover new market performance. This shows that the OL is a dynamic process, which should be properly managed. As a fourth action, one needs to mention the alarm function of the OL. The gatekeeper can recognize important developments (e.g. a discontinuity) in the company's environment and they can, depending on the extent of the development, react, for example, by informing those concerned.

Concluding, the opportunity landscape is an organizational knowledge base of facts and trends in the company's environment, it is an alarm system for discontinuities and it is a pro-active idea generator. Therefore, the OL is a basic strategic intelligence tool that summarizes trends, internal ideas, customer needs, strategic requirements and competitor activities in the form of specific issues. It supports classical front-end intelligence work. The structural implementation of the OL through a working gatekeeper's network can be coordinated within the organization by so-called 'Communities of Practice' (CoPs). Generally, a CoP is composed of a group of members interested in a common domain. These people can be regarded as experts in their domain and use the CoP for knowledge exchange with the goal of further developing their expertise. Within these communities that meet regularly, their own work methods and a common language are developed. After a CoP has been established successfully in a company, they are considered as a contact point for all kinds of challenges concerning their knowledge domain.

Best practice case 4.9 shows how Heidelberg collects (rather like CoPs) information by a network of technology scouts. The collected information is evaluated locally by a technology team.

The concept of CoP[8] is a suitable way to establish and manage a gatekeeper's network across a company. Projected on the structures suggested in this research, each technology platform can be regarded as a host for one or more CoP, which grow and share expertise related to the technology of that platform (see Figure 4.7). The sum of all CoPs hosted in one platform virtually represents the platform. As a platform was described as a competence center (see this chapter, 'Structures overview') for a technology, it is the actual members of its CoP that are the carriers of the knowledge of this platform.

Besides working for the purpose of strategic intelligence guided by the OL, the CoP can be regarded as interface between knowledge generated in the corporate R&D unit and their business unit platform. As described in 'Overview' (this chapter), corporate R&D takes care of risky, uncertain and new technological and market issues and explores the possibilities of the latter. Once this exploration is finished, the generated knowledge is transferred to one or more business units for exploitation of the technologies through their integration in products and services that can be sold in that same or another unit's market. It is this transfer of knowledge from corporate R&D to business unit R&D and later its integration in marketable goods that has to be facilitated by members of CoP. These people have a network across the

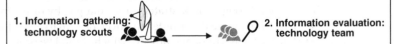

1. Information gathering: technology scouts → **2. Information evaluation:** technology team

At Heidelberg, technology intelligence is operated by scouts that report to a technology team. The scouts conduct broad screenings for emerging technologies and their potential applicability for Heidelberg, together with a preliminary evaluation. The technology scout attempts to incorporate as many technologies as possible from a wide range of different industries. In periodic meetings, the most promising information about technology and innovation is formulated as proposals and suggested to the so-called technology team.

The technology team consists of selected employees from the R&D units, leading representatives of production, representatives from the corporate strategy teams and the technology scout himself.

The tasks of the technology team and its members are to assess and select technologies and conceptual ideas, as well as to promote them to top-level management, based on a strategic rationale.

Best practice case 4.9 Heidelberger Druckmaschinen, operationalization of technology intelligence through technology scouts and technology teams

Source: Interview at Heidelberger Druckmaschinen, 2005, T. Jäger, M. Reisel, G. Trauffler.

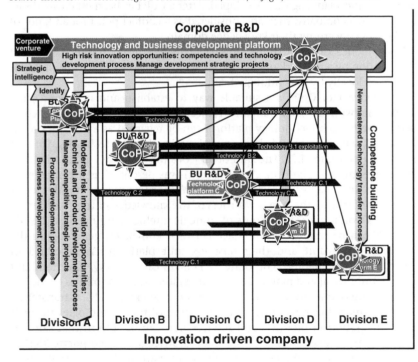

Figure 4.7 Communities of Practice (COP) supporting the internal network of technology intelligence

company that enables the exchange of knowledge necessary to successfully realize the vertical knowledge transfer from corporate R&D, as well as the horizontal transfer of knowledge to and from other business units.

Back-end intelligence aided by corporate venturing

Besides focusing on the classical front-end intelligence, as supported by the opportunity landscape and the concept of CoP described above, there is a second form of intelligence work that seems to have become more and more popular in practice. In this research it is called back-end intelligence, as the intelligence efforts are concentrated at the back end of what a company considers as innovation opportunity.

The back end of an innovation opportunity represents that moment in time where the innovation opportunity has already been developed by a third party to the point that it can soon be commercialized. The technical and market proof of the concept of such innovation opportunities is almost concluded and it is only a few steps away from market entry. From an established company's point of view such opportunities are most interesting to track when the developing company is a small company and/or very young company and when the technology is discontinuous and quite risky. The ultimate goal of the established company is to recognize the innovation opportunity before the younger company enters the market itself, and to get involved with it in order to acquire the generated knowledge. This procedure is also known in external corporate venturing practice (Sharma and Chrisman, 1999: 19). This practice has become necessary for established companies after the observation that small companies or newly established companies will be generating a growing part of the innovations in the future (see Figure 4.8).

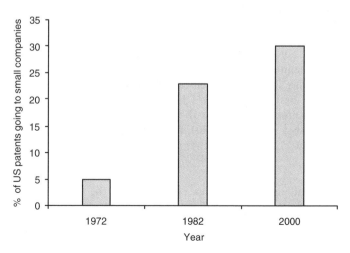

Figure 4.8   Growing small companies' share of innovation
Source: Research & Technology Executive Council, 2001.

For the established company, getting involved with a small third-party company generating the innovation opportunity is very convenient for two reasons: first the smaller the company is, the easier it is for a large company to get involved or to acquire it, because the resources of the newer and smaller company are usually quite limited. In this way, the established company can easily act as sponsor and, second, the younger company that has developed a highly innovative product or service often does not have the market expertise necessary to commercialize the innovation successfully. In this case an established company can easily get involved by offering its own market outlets.

This kind of intelligence work, looking for opportunities already under development in small companies, has two advantages for established companies: first, established companies are known to have difficulties developing radical innovations even if their front-end intelligence identifies an innovation opportunity as interesting, as the formulation and implementation of a project developing the opportunity can be far from being initialized and realized. Thus, letting small, younger companies develop this kind of innovation, and get involved at a later period in time, is very attractive. Second, the established company getting involved with the opportunity as the proof of the concept is more or less concluded minimizes the investment risk in an opportunity right from the start at a moment in time when uncertainty and the risk of completely loosing the investments is high.

One back-end intelligence method is to systematically have an eye on interesting new companies by means of a watch list. This list comprises a number of companies, that are to be monitored in order to observe their innovation activities, which are potentially interesting for the business of the more established company.

However, identifying, recognizing and running such a watch list is not yet enough when the goal is to get involved with the knowledge generated from one of these companies at a specific moment in time. Thus, expertise on how to get involved with these companies or how to acquire such companies is also necessary. For this expertise, a venturing unit is suggested that is put in charge of managing all activities related to the back-end intelligence. Some large companies like Nokia, Siemens, BASF (see Best practice case 4.10) and DSM (see Best practice case 4.11) run their own venture units, called corporate ventures. Additionally, the venture unit of the German chemical company Degussa runs a watch list, monitoring some several hundred companies from the chemical and other industries.

Creativity

Besides the intelligence activities conducted in the identification phase, creativity is also a driver for generating innovation opportunities. The best-known methods of inspiring creative thinking include brainstorming, mind-mapping, discussion 66, method 635, bionic, Delphi method and the morphology method (Biedermann, 2002: 54). These methods encourage

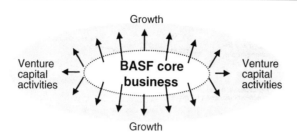

BASF Future Business GmbH is a 100 per cent BASF subsidiary with the task to identify and develop new business areas for BASF group.

Within BASF Future Business a subsidiary called BASF Venture Capital GmbH hosts all venture capital activities of BASF. BASF Future Business's small and flexible structure provides a similar-sized contact point for start-up companies that intend to work with BASF, as well as for any cooperation partner. A main focus is on activities in the fields of energy management, communication, information and entertainment and quality of life that are all located outside the core business of BASF. Both companies assume a crucial technology and business intelligence task through screening the flow of business proposals circulating in the network spanned by start-up companies and investors (deal flow). The close contact to this network allows BASF Future Business and BASF Venture Capital to sense the latest trends and research activities and to have a look at latest business plans in the start-up scene.

Best practice case 4.10   BASF, venture capital activities with technology and business intelligence interests

Source: Interview at BASF, 2005, M. Reisel, T. Jäger, G. Trauffler.

12 to 12 o'clock meetings are meant to elaborate solutions for management and research problems within a short period of time. These meetings are held outside the company, regrouping a team of people wanting to find answers to a number of open questions. The meetings start at 12 o'clock noon and last till 12 o'clock the following day. In the first day, after lunch, one or several problems are presented to the attendees. Till the evening of that same day solutions are elaborated in groups. These solutions are synthesized and presented the following day by the project manager in charge.

Practice example 4.4   Topsoe's 12 to 12 o'clock meetings

Source: Interview at Topsoe, 2004, G. Trauffler.

thinking out of the classical box of a company. Traditionally the basic question for these methods has been: 'What will the opportunities be in the future?'

Practice example 4.4 show how Topsoe tries to foster its employees' creativity.

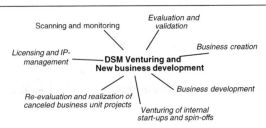

DSM's Venturing and Business (V&BD) development organization is a best practice example showing which variety of functions such an organization can cover in order to foster innovation, especially radical innovation in an established company. It is run similarly to a business unit as an autonomous entity of 100–150 people within the company. The following describes the main activities of this unit.

- *Scanning and monitoring*: V&BD support intelligence work by gathering information in wider fields than the ones covered by the business units. This information originally comes from three main sources: first, from participations in external venture funds that have young technology-driven start-up companies in their portfolio. Second, from all kinds external technology and business ideas proposed by entrepreneurial people as V&BD is positioned in DSM as a drop-in center for external ideas. Third, by recognizing company-internal ideas that are interesting but do not fit into the existing businesses of DSM.
- *Evaluation and validation*: Ideas that have been captured by the scanning and monitoring routines are evaluated and validated for their business potential by feasibility projects conducted within V&BD. Technology and market feasibility studies are conducted with the goal of checking the proof of concept for emerging technologies and novel business ideas. For such analysis business unit specialists are contracted to V&DB.
- *Business creation*: V&DB supports the elaboration of business plans for ideas with a high business potential.
- *Business development*: Once the business plan is approved, V&BD support the implementation of the first steps of business development. For this purpose projects are launched, for example for the elaboration of prototypes.
- *Venturing of internal start-ups and spin-offs*: After a successful business development phase, projects are transferred into an independent organizational form for their realization. This is done by founding internal start-ups for company-related opportunities or spin-offs for less related opportunities. Additionally, venturing is involved in external venture funds and external start-ups.
- *Licensing and IP-management*: Selling internal knowledge from business units that is available for externalization as well as procuring knowledge that is needed in the company.
- *Re-evaluation and realization of canceled business unit projects*: Projects that have been dismantled in the business units are picked up by V&DB for a second re-evaluation and a possible realization.

With all these activities, V&BD represents a unit within DSM that embodies technology change. It not only procures and develops radically new technologies and business ideas for the company by scanning, monitoring, assessing and finally developing them for their deployment in existing and new businesses. It also helps the company to 'get rid of' technologies and businesses by externalizing them through licensing and selling them.

Best practice case 4.11 Venturing and business development at DSM

Source: Interview at DSM, 2004, G. Trauffler.

Identify all innovation opportunities (process phase 1.2)

The second phase in the strategic planning process is 'Identify all innovation opportunities' (see Figure 4.3). Unlike 'Strategic intelligence', this step is not an on-going continuously conducted activity but it is run at a defined moment in time. It is considered as an initiating step of the strategic planning process and run as the starting point for every strategy development. It aims to identify – out of the information delivered by strategic intelligence – those innovation opportunities that are of strategic importance for the company.

'Identify' is composed of two sub-processes: the first sub-process (1.2.a),[9] called Kick-off, comprises the tasks: (1) to revise the innovation portfolio, (2) to identify the actual innovation opportunity and (3) to detail the latter.

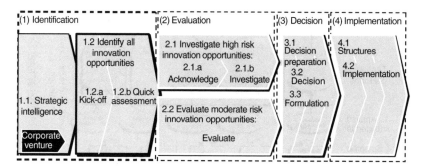

These three tasks have to be processed in each business unit. The second sub-process (1.2.b), called 'Quick assessment', is a quick check of the identified innovation opportunities assessing their degree of newness for the company and the level of risk that it represents. This assessment is done on a corporate level, analyzing all the identified innovation opportunities coming from the different business units.

Kick-off (process phase 1.2.a)

The execution of the three tasks from the first sub-process is aided by a method suggested by Sauber (2004: 98ff.): the 'Innovation architecture' (IA). It is a tool that visualizes, in a transparent way, how different types of knowledge are interrelated in a company.[10] For example, it shows how knowledge about business fields, markets, products, modules and strategic technology platforms interact, and which knowledge[11] has thus far been mastered, which knowledge still needs to be mastered and which knowledge is not yet well mastered (Figure 4.9).

From the top down, the IA shows markets and the corresponding customer needs and products, technologies, applied knowledge and scientific knowledge. From the bottom up it shows which knowledge is at the foundation of the company, enabling it to develop those technologies, products

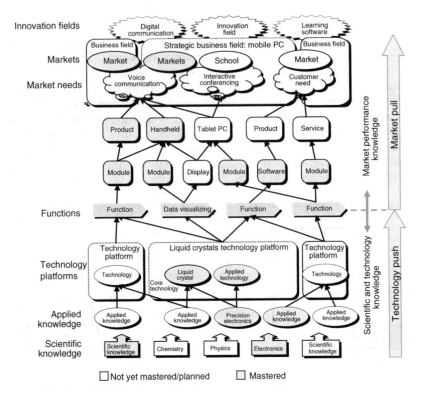

Innovation fields

Markets

Market needs

Functions

Technology platforms

Applied knowledge

Scientific knowledge

☐ Not yet mastered/planned   ☐ Mastered

Figure 4.9   Innovation architecture
Source: Sauber, 2004.

and modules, and to deliver them in markets to best satisfy customer needs. These two directions, top down from the market and bottom up from the company's knowledge, correspond to what is called 'market pull' or 'technology push'. However, they seem to point in opposite directions: on the one hand, market starting from performance knowledge and, on the other hand, starting from science and technology knowledge, technology push as well as market pull have common goals: to generate a value added for the company by serving the market. Thus, in Figure 4.9 the arrows for both market pull and technology push are directed towards the market.

The level in the IA establishing the connection between technology push and market pull, respectively science and technology knowledge and market performance knowledge, is the level of 'functions'. A 'function' is a description of a solution-neutral operation of variable inputs and outputs (Meier, 2002: 6). A 'function' describes in a very abstract way how an input is transformed into an output without constraining the technological knowledge inputs and market knowledge outputs of the transformation process.[12] This way, in the innovation architecture for one and the same function, there is a variety of technological solutions that can be used as input, and a variety of product solutions that can be seen as output.

'Revise innovation portfolio' as a first step in the process 'Kick-off' basically consists of understanding and drafting the initial company position in order to start the strategic planning process. Thus, this task draws a first sketch of the IA by only using the insight generated in the previous process step, strategic intelligence. Issues from the opportunity landscape, which represent ideas of concrete knowledge to develop, have to be arranged according to the structure of the innovation architecture. Based on this first draft, the IA can be completed with functions, innovation fields, business fields and technology platforms that have to be defined. The choice of these elements is critical as, to a high degree, they influence further investigations when identifying new technology platforms or business fields.

Once the basic structure of the IA is set up, it can be used as initial position of the next step: 'Identify opportunity fields'. This second step is a creative one; here new business fields and technology platforms are identified. Contrary to strategic intelligence, it is not the goal of this step to identify specific technologies or products; it is rather the intention to find a potential activity field for the company to enter into in the future. This field, called the opportunity field, should provide a competitive advantage to the company and is therefore strategically important.

Finding such opportunity fields is best done in workshops regrouping the gatekeepers supported by creativity methods. The newly found opportunity fields should subsequently be integrated in the visualization of the innovation architecture. This integration will certainly result in a nonhomogeneous and still incomplete architecture. This is the moment in time to go on to the third step, 'Detail opportunity fields', in order to achieve a similar level of detail across the whole innovation architecture. The process of detailing is done by finding markets and customers' needs in order to further describe business fields and by finding product and process technologies with the aim of detailing technology platforms. All these objects that have been added have to be linked to each other and to the existing elements in the IA according to their relation. Missing elements have to be identified and integrated in order to create a consistent structure that makes sense when tracking the elements from the top down as well as from the bottom up.

Detailing the opportunity fields closes the first sub-process in the 'Identify' phase and delivers an innovation architecture that reflects a first draft of the strategic innovation intentions of the company. This IA comprises all new innovation opportunities for the company. An innovation opportunity is the sum of all elements in the architecture necessary to detail an innovation field. It is a constellation including elements of all levels of the architecture for the purpose of enabling an innovation field.

Quick assessment (process phase 1.2.b)

The purpose of this step is to roughly, but rapidly assess the innovation opportunities that have been identified and chosen to be integrated into the innovation architecture for further evaluation. This assessment comprises two analyses: the first is the assessment of the level of newness of the innovation opportunities for the company, and the second is the assessment of the level of risk for the company. Depending on both of these levels, newness and risk of innovation project ideas are further evaluated according to different processes methods and structures. Both analyses of this sub-process are best conducted in a workshop bringing together the business unit heads and their corresponding responsible colleagues from R&D. These persons represent their business unit by introducing all the innovation opportunities that have been identified in their own business unit in a workshop. This group of people should be led by the CTO of the company.

Newness of an innovation opportunity

The development of the IA, as presented in the previous section, is suitable especially for young companies that do not yet have a strong technology and innovation identity. In companies without such an identity Sauber's (2004) descriptions enable IA to be developed from scratch using only the content delivered by the opportunity landscape. Legacy technology and innovation management systems do not have to be addressed.

This research aims to develop a strategic planning process for established companies which already have a strong technology and innovation management identity and a legacy system that needs to be taken care of in the IA. Thus, in established companies it is suggested that an IA be used as an initial position to visualize the existing legacy technology and innovation management system. New innovation fields, technologies, products and markets provided by the OL complete this architecture. At this moment the question is how the new elements fit with the existing innovation architecture and how easily they can be integrated in the legacy system. Generally, there are two possibilities: the first is that the integration of these new elements is no problem, as the search fields defined in the OL have been chosen to suit the existing strategic direction of the company. In this case they contain, for the most part, innovation issues that enhance the given structure of the IA. The benefit of such elements fitting the innovation architecture can be considered as incrementally innovative. The second possibility is that some or more search fields in the opportunity have not been chosen in alignment with the company's existing strategy. One reason for this might be weak management skills; another reason might be a deliberately planned strategic shift from the existing strategy. For the initiation of a strategic shift it can be very effective to define search fields in the OL that direct the business into a different and new direction. The newness of the search field will show that the issues collected in the OL will differ considerably from the issues to which the company is accustomed. Planned innovation fields, and their corresponding new elements meant to be integrated in the IA, like products, markets and technologies, can be unfamiliar to company activities so far. In this case it might be difficult to fit these new elements with existing elements of the IA.

A difficult fit of new innovation project ideas into the IA is an excellent indicator of the level of newness or familiarity of these ideas, especially for the technologies and markets fields of the company. Newness and familiarity can be defined as follows (Roberts and Berry, 1985: 4):

- Newness of a technology or service: the degree to which the technology or service has not previously been embodied within the products of the company.
- Newness of a market: the degree to which the products of the company have not been targeted in that particular market.
- Familiarity with a technology: the degree to which knowledge of the technology exists within the company, but is not necessarily embodied in the products.
- Familiarity with a market: the degree to which the characteristics and business patterns of a market are understood within the company, but not necessarily as a result of participation in the market.

Pursuing Sauber's (2004) theoretical understanding of the IA, the above definitions of newness and familiarity can be interpreted as the existence or lack of existence of certain object knowledge or methodological knowledge in the company. For example, 'a technology or service that has not formerly been embodied within products of the company' is reflected through a lack of object or methodological knowledge in the architecture. The familiarity of a technology that a company has can be reflected by the existence of object or methodological knowledge in the company that can be tapped by a new technology. From this perspective, newness and familiarity reflect the degree of connections that can be established by a technology or market towards the existing knowledge elements of the company.

Thus, the level of newness and familiarity of an innovation opportunity can be defined according to two criteria: the first is the *object knowledge integration criterion* which checks how the technologies behind an innovation project idea can be *positioned* in relation to other existing object-knowledge elements. For example, it checks how a new technology can be positioned within existing technology platforms. The second criterion is *the methodological knowledge integration criterion* that checks how the technologies behind an innovation opportunity can be *linked* with existing methodological knowledge to other existing methodological knowledge elements (see Figure 4.10). For example, it checks for a new technology, the knowledge to process it, in order to transform it into a product or a service.

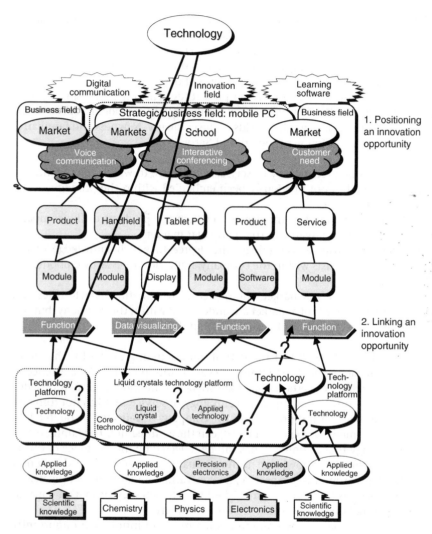

Figure 4.10 Technology positioning and linking criteria for assessing an innovation opportunity's level of newness in the innovation architecture

Best practice cases 4.12 and 4.13 show how Clariant and Topsoe take newness and risk evaluations into account when selecting and processing innovation ideas.

The newness of an innovation opportunity can be considered discontinuous if the *position* of the technology behind an innovation project idea among other elements of an IA cannot be clearly assigned and if the *links* to existing elements of the same IA are difficult to establish.

Within Clariant's business divisions there are two distinct treatments by which innovation ideas are generally managed and realized in projects. Technology and business opportunities related to the divisional core business and representing a moderate level of risk are assessed within the business divisions. The realization of such ideas in concrete projects is executed in the corresponding divisions, without any interference from the corporate level or another divisions.

Opportunities formulated by the divisions that are, however, out of the scope of existing divisional fields and implying a higher degree of risk are forwarded to an R&D Council to be discussed. This council is further provided with innovation opportunities of corporate concern gathered by the technology and innovation management entity on the corporate level.

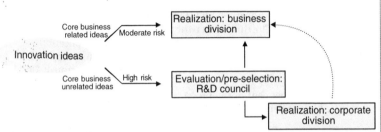

The R&D Council is composed of R&D managers of the divisions, the representatives of the different technology- and innovation management-related corporate units and leading representatives of the regional R&D centers. Its task with high risk innovation opportunities is twofold: on the one hand, it pre-selects the interesting projects to be pursued and, on the other hand, it suggests if the project realization should take place on a divisional or corporate level, possibly with the involvement of further divisions.

Upon the suggestions of the R&D Council, the final decision of major projects to realize is up to the Board of Management.

Best practice case 4.12   Clariant, risk-focused idea management and project realization
Source: Interview at Clariant, 2005, T. Jäger, M. Reisel, G. Trauffler.

Risk of an innovation opportunity

Besides checking newness of an innovation opportunity, for management purposes it is important to know what level of risk the opportunity bears for the company (see Chapter 2).

Scholars agree that one main origin of poor strategic planning of radically new technology arises from this inherent uncertainty[13] and risk[14] that is due to the described lack of knowledge and experience during the time of its emergence (Jolly, 1997: 7; Lambe and Spekman, 1997: 102; Porter, 1998: 253; Tschirky and Koruna, 1998: 292; Leifer *et al.*, 2000: 18). Thus, it is

At Topsoe the distribution of R&D activities is fixed according to the level of technology and market newness:*

Forty per cent of R&D projects are run in existing markets, on the one hand, by fostering existing technologies and, on the other hand, by researching in emerging and new technologies. Research in emerging and new technologies is very goal-oriented with specific deliverables and performances to achieve. These are set based on known weakness and problems of the existing technologies in their existing markets.

Seven per cent of the projects are conducted for existing markets. There are no reviewed deliverables or performance measurements. Thus, research in this cluster is less problem-solving focused.

Thirty per cent of the projects are done in the field of so-called focused new ventures. The business opportunities behind these projects have been identified as highly innovative and market-relevant. For most of the technologies developed in this cluster the proof of the concept is already done. They are focused towards deployment of a new market application.

Ten per cent of the projects are conducted in order to build up competencies in novel markets with novel technologies in exploratory, non-focused research.

The remaining 13 per cent of the projects support the previous ones. They are conducted in the fields of licensing, patenting, etc.

Novel technologies	7% Not reviewed deliverables, no performance measurement	10% Exploratory research
Emerging/new technologies	Reviewed deliverables and performance measurement	30% Focused new ventures
Existing technologies	40% Technology maintenance	
	Existing markets	Emerging/new markets Novel markets

* Percentages are approximate figures; they are meant to provide an impression of the project's distribution and are subject to variance.

Best practice case 4.13   Topsoe, distribution of R&D activities according to the level of newness

Source: Interview at Topsoe, 2004, G. Trauffler.

important to first understand the difference between risk and uncertainty. As Orbell (1993: 80) puts it:[15]

A decision maker confronts risk when he or she can attach probabilities to alternative states of the world with confidence; from a fair deck of cards, for example, a gambler can be confident that there is a 1 in 52 chance of drawing the ace of hearts. A decision maker confronts uncertainty, however, when there is an unknown number of cards and (or) an unknown number of aces of hearts in the deck. Under uncertainty, not only can one still lose but one does not know the odds.

The fact that uncertainty cannot be tapped with alternative states and probability makes it impossible to quantify and to measure it; in fact, 'by definition what is uncertain cannot be measured' (Gil-Aluja, 2001: 12).

As stated above, we differentiate between uncertainty and risk according to the level of knowledge available. When the implications of a technology (alternative states of outcome) are known and if their corresponding probability is known as well, management is facing risk, if both implications and/or the corresponding probability are not known, management deals with uncertainty. The interspace between both extremes of available knowledge uncertainty and risk results from partial knowledge about possible states and their corresponding probability. Ward and Chapman (2003: 100) call these interspaces the unknown-knowns and known-unknowns, while uncertainty corresponds to unknown-unknowns and risk to known-knowns. Figure 4.11 illustrates this theoretical framework, showing the knowledge areas of what is called uncertainty and risk as well as the interspace between these extremes. This view allows qualitative (knowledge about alternative states of outcome) and quantitative (knowledge about probability of the states impact) insight to be visualized when trying to assess a radically new technology. It allows uncertainty and risk to be linked by means of the degree of available knowledge.

Management should be able to decide whether to engage with a new technology or not, as soon as it has succeed in building up enough knowledge to enter in the field of risk, of known-knowns. In this area, implications and

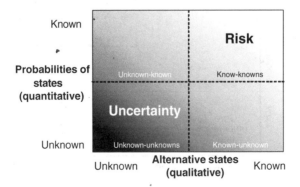

Figure 4.11   The difference between uncertainty and risk: a theoretical framework
Source: Trauffler *et al.*, 2004.

probability of a new technology are quantifiable within a certain degree of tolerance. With this knowledge it is up to the management whether it is willing to take the risk or to proceed with further investigation in order to reduce the tolerance of the information underlying the risk or to eliminate the sources of the risks.

Generally it is difficult to explore all means of eliminating uncertainty entirely in order to attain a clear level of risk. However, there are methods that help to approach this level but they should not yet be applied in this phase of the strategic planning process. In this phase of the process, the primary goal is not to assess an opportunity's risk or uncertainty level as accurately as possible; it is rather the target to roughly check all the project ideas in order to assign them to a specific and more detailed evaluation or investigation in the next phase. For this purpose, the portfolio displayed in Figure 4.12 can be used.

In this portfolio (see Figure 4.12) innovation opportunities are evaluated that are submitted in the form of roughly described R&D project ideas. The evaluation is done by market and technological risk considerations that form the two axes of the portfolio. Both risk considerations should be done within a broad risk perspective, so that assessing market risk will also include aspects such as competitive and investment risk: and technology risk should include development, manufacturing and implementation risk. Concretely speaking, such risks are, for example, the result of unforeseen problems in technical feasibility, in achieving a product-development schedule, in obtaining parts and raw materials, a change in the availability of appropriately

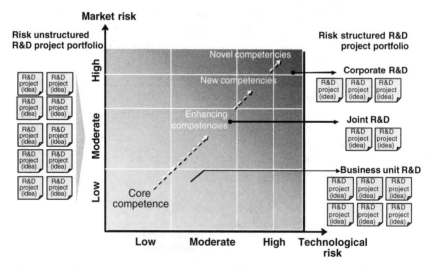

Figure 4.12 Structuring project ideas in the risk portfolio

priced and trained labor, unexpected and changing emerging standards, or product-liability problems. Market risks can arise from a change in industry growth versus assumptions, a change in competitive pricing versus assumptions, a change in market structure initiated by a new entrant or a new technology (Gupta *et al.*, 2003: 2).

The axes of the portfolio shown in Figure 4.12 are subdivided into low, moderate and high technological and market risk levels. Correspondingly the portfolio shows four areas where the same technological and market risk levels meet: the first area is spanned by low technological risk and low market risk. Project ideas that fall in this area do not represent any risk to the company; they can be considered very familiar. Usually such projects, if strategically relevant, fit with the core competencies of the company. Moderate technological and market risk span a second area. Projects that fall in this area are based on competencies existing in the company and usually extend the latter. Thus, projects in this area are called upon to enhance the company's competencies.

Clariant (see Best practice case 4.14) assigns R&D activities of projects to variable organizational entities according to their level or risk and newness.

The third and fourth areas in the portfolio are formed by the risky and highly risky project ideas. Such ideas build new competencies for the company or even novel ones. Novel competencies are not only new to the company but also to the entire marketplace. They are based on cutting-edge scientific insight.

Depending on the level of risk a project idea represents for the company, different units and processes should be assigned for the evaluation and investigation. The portfolio shown in Figure 4.12 suggests the assignment of a different unit's project according to the level of risk of a project idea. Thus, a corresponding business unit should evaluate ideas of low risk, supporting existing core competencies. For medium risk project ideas, which are expanding current core competencies, a joint team of people bringing in expertise from a business unit as well as from a corporate R&D unit should be assigned for evaluation. For risky and highly risky projects, it should be a corporate R&D team which evaluates the ideas. This way a collection of initially risky unstructured projects is structured according to their risk, and simultaneously a unit for its further assessment in the strategic planning process is suggested.

The evaluation of project ideas is best done in a workshop. Similarly to the assessment analyzing newness of innovation opportunities using the 'Innovation architecture', the risk assessment should be done with the same group of persons: business unit heads, the corresponding research heads and led by the CTO of the company. This group should have a brief look at each project idea and assess its risk from a technological and market perspective while bearing the assessment of newness in mind. This assessment should be done in a consensual way through a discussion among all the

Clariant uses three criteria to determine the structural form for the realization of new business development projects: the level of risk of the project, the remoteness from existing businesses and the potential internal divisional synergies between the company's businesses. Project risk refers to technology as well as to market aspects, the remoteness expresses the newness of the project, and potential synergies refer to the cross-section usability of the competence developed in the project for the company. Depending on these criteria new business development projects are either developed through (1) a divisionally run project, (2) a corporate new business development project or (3) an inter-divisional project with corporate commitment.

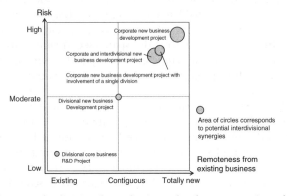

First in the case of a divisional new business development project, the division dedicates a certain amount of its laboratory and human resource capacity to pursuing the development of the new, but still adjacent business. The project is entirely financed by the division.

In the second case, a corporate unit new business development (NBD) takes the financial sponsorship as well as the strategic coordination and control of the R&D project. Operationally, however, the project is conducted within the decentralized R&D sites of the divisions. The operational project leadership is also carried out by divisional representatives.

Doing so, the required R&D facilities and human resources are functionally reallocated from their original divisional assignments to the corporate assignment, and they are grouped in a new business development project team. There is no local transfer, however; the researchers stay within their original facilities.

Once the technical feasibility as well as the producibility of a concrete product can be shown, the project is transferred into one of several suitable divisions, and the corporate financing and managerial guidance ends.

In the third case, despite the higher level of risk and newness, one or more divisions are interested in a cooperation with the corporate unit as they can anticipate concrete applications from the project. The project is then co-financed by the involved divisions as well as the corporate NBD unit.

Best practice case 4.14   Clariant, assessing risk and newness of projects

Source: Interview at Clariant, 2005, T. Jäger, M. Reisel, G. Trauffler.

members of this group. There is no list of criteria suggested in order to estimate the level of risk of a project idea, as risk really depends on the competitive situation of the individual company as well as on the internal constellation and strategic intentions of the company (Doering and Parayre, 2000: 79).

Although this check seems to be superficial as there are no fixed criteria proposed for the assessment of risk, it can be very effective when, first, experienced people, who know the company and its situation well, sit together to find a consensus and, second, if these people are aware of the danger of mixing uncertainty and risk. Experienced people that know the company and its business can intuitively distinguish very risky projects from less risky ones. If these same people are aware of the difference between risk and uncertainty, in the sense of knowing or not knowing possible alternative states and corresponding probabilities involved with a project idea, they can easily distinguish a project idea's risk levels.

Concluding the quick assessment sub-process allows two essential actions in the strategic planning process to be completed: first, differentiations between innovation project ideas according to their level of newness and risk. Furthermore, this differentiation enables specific units and experts with specific methods to be assigned for the further analysis conducted in the strategic planning process. Second, the assessment in this sub-process, especially the ones focusing on risk, reveals the level of knowledge in the company about the new project ideas. Opportunities that are uncertain and hard to assess for risk thus give clues regarding new search fields to be fixed for strategic intelligence. This way the scope of information-gathering in the strategic intelligence phase can be focused, and the overall effectiveness for the company is increased. This feedback loop relates the 'Quick assessment' step to the 'Strategic intelligence' phase and is an excellent example, which illustrates that the strategic planning process shown in Figure 4.3 is not a unidirectional process without recurrence. The process should be understood rather as a

In Hilti's innovation process the level of technological risk is one major criterion for whether to realize/continue or to reject/stop an innovation project. Furthermore, project goals and project realization forms in the innovation process differ depending on the level of risk.

When assessing risk in innovation projects Hilti applies four different risk measures with corresponding probabilities of success: very high risk, high risk, moderate risk and low risk.

Very high risk level	There are fundamental uncertainities in the physical processes on which the technology is based. It is for the moment unknown whether a solution can be found. Probability of success: about 50 per cent.
High risk level	The principal physical aspects are known, but it is not fully clear whether the mechanisms can be applied. It is open whether a solution, transferable into a commercial product, can be found. Probability of success: about 65 per cent.
Moderate risk level	The technological feasibility is verified in principle, but a limited number of problems are open and it is not fully clear whether a solution for all of them can be found . Probability of success: about 80 per cent.
Low risk level	The concept of the technology is clear. The functional prototype is available. There are some technology engineering/design questions to be solved. It is, however, quite certain that a solution can be found. Probability of success: about 90 per cent.

Best practice case 4.15   Hilti, differentiating four levels of technological risks
Source: Interview and presentation at Hilti, 2005, G. Trauffler.

self-regulating process that defines, opens and narrows its focus depending on the demand of the strategic issue that is handled.

Best practice case 4.15 illustrates how Hilti rates different levels of risk.

3.   Evaluation (concept phase 2)

Both process phases 'Investigate high risk innovation opportunities (2.1)' and 'Evaluate moderate risk innovation opportunities (2.2)' are run in parallel with the goal of analyzing innovation opportunities in detail. Phase 2.1 is focused on innovation opportunities that are risky and new for the company. Such opportunities often consist of project ideas targeting radical innovations which are based on discontinuous technologies unfamiliar to the company's existing businesses. Process phase 2.2 is concerned with more moderate and low risk innovation opportunities. The project ideas that are analyzed in this process are usually more familiar to the company's existing business. They enhance the existing businesses by generating incremental innovations, which arise from continuously evolving innovations.

The decision about which innovation opportunities to handle in which process was described in the previous phase 'Identify' (see this chapter, 'Identify all innovation opportunities').

The following two sections will be dedicated to explaining the two evaluation phases run in parallel. First, the high risk innovation opportunity's process is described, followed by the moderate risk innovation opportunity's process.

Investigate high risk innovation opportunities (process phase 2.1)

The goal of the 'Investigate high risk innovation opportunities (2.1)' process phase is to analyze innovation opportunities that have been assessed as highly risky for the company from a market and technical perspective. Often project ideas arising from such risky innovation opportunities are quite new and unfamiliar to the company. For example, they are based on emerging technologies or on the latest scientific insights that have not yet been applied in products or services. Thus, the analysis has to be designed in order to cope with a situation where there is only a limited amount of knowledge and expertise available about the project ideas – within and outside the company. It is a situation of great uncertainty under which quantitative evaluation is difficult. Therefore, the analysis in this process is focused on qualitative assessments from a company development strategic perspective. This means that it tries to recognize those innovation project ideas that, if initiated today, would allow the company to attain a targeted strategic position in the long term. These are projects that do not only affect one business in a specific field without further implications for other businesses; rather they are projects that either by themselves or together with other projects have a wide range of implications for the company, as they direct the latter, for example, in new markets or in a new competitive position.

Typically the projects they analyze in this process are not designed as new product development projects but more as competence learning and development projects that should prepare the company for the uncertain and unpredictable changes in its competitive environment. Learning can be described as 'the ways firms build, supplement, and organize knowledge around their competencies and within their cultures, and adapt and develop organizational efficiency through improving the use of these competencies' (Dodgson, 2000: 157–8).

Practice example 4.5 illustrates how Nokia built up competencies in very different fields, with a long-term perspective, that eventually let it shift its core activities form the wood business to the high-technology communication business.

An excellent example of strategic reorientation is given by the Finnish corporation Nokia. Over its history this company changed from a paper manufacturer to the world leader in mobile phones. It changed its core competencies several times in order to adapt to a changing competitive environment.

Founded in 1867, the company Nokia has its origin in paper manufacturing. In 1960 Nokia merged with two other companies, the Finnish Rubber Works and Finnish Cable Works, to become the Nokia Corporation. Although at that time Nokia was still producing products such as tires, rubber boots and cables, it was already preparing itself for a powerful strategic shift: to enter into the telecommunication business.

Thus, in the early 1960s Nokia built up new competencies in several telecommunication technologies and was able to develop, in 1963, the first radio telephones. Later, in 1965, the first data modems followed. Such devices had obviously been unfamiliar to Nokia just a few years before. They were based on cutting-edge technology of that time and were new not only for the company but also for the larger public. Throughout the 1980s Nokia continued in another new field: it produced computers, monitors and TV sets. All this knowledge, accumulated over the years in the electronics business, made the company a world leader in mobile phones by 1998.

Practice example 4.5   Nokia, a powerful strategic reorientation
Source: www.nokia.com

The need to learn is commonly explained in terms of a requirement for adaptation and improved efficiency in times of change. The greater the uncertainty in those times of change, the greater the need to learn (Dodgson, 2000: 158). The eventual goal of learning is to acquire new competencies that can be strategically used if an unexpected discontinuous change happens. In the ideal case, the company itself initiates a discontinuity by generating radical innovations based on those new competencies. Thus, these competencies learned should in the future be able to generate a wide range of new products and services to build up new businesses and markets that at the present do not yet exist and allow a strategic reorientation of the company.

The process phase 'Investigate high risk innovation opportunities' is conducted on a corporate level, and should ideally be headed by the CTO of the company. It is important to consign this phase to a corporate-level R&D unit and not to a business-level unit. Business units that are market-oriented should be focused on their existing customers, developing proven technologies and products for existing markets. Their primary goals should be to earn money for the company by delivering proven products to familiar markets in order to satisfy known customer needs. This way, they should out-perform their competitors with high-quality products, manufactured with low costs and efficient development. In order to achieve these goals, business units must work with low or moderately risky technologies with which they are familiar. Thus, a corporate unit's R&D activities should precede the business

The specialty chemical company Ciba has established a corporate-funded research fund of CHF 15 million for promoting radical innovation projects. Its goal is to finance far-sighted research projects focusing on breakthrough technologies, and products that address high-growth market opportunities within the four business segments of the company. Further, it is meant as seed money for accelerated entry into new and high risk projects. This acceleration is achieved through lean and straight decision rules around the research fund.

Projects are funded by the research fund during a maximum of three years. They are either fully corporate funded or co-funded by the segments. Over time, the corporate share of funding declines for the benefit of the funding in the segments.

Best practice case 4.16   Ciba, research fund for high risk radical innovation projects
Source: Interview and presentations at CIBA, 2005, G. Trauffler.

unit's R&D activities, handling the risky and new technologies in order to become familiar with them. Once the technologies are mastered, in that their risk can be considered moderate or even low, they can be transferred to the business units in order for product development. Incentive setting and limitation of high risk innovation project's spending can be done according to the example at the chemical company CIBA (see Best practice case 4.16).

Acknowledge (process phase 1.2.a)

The process phase 2.1 for the investigation of high risk innovation opportunities is designed in two sub-processes: 'Acknowledge' and 'Investigate'. 'Acknowledge' is a sub-process with the goal to recognize the potential of an innovation idea. It comprises two process steps: first, 'Create a frame' and, second, 'Generate issue'.

Create a frame (process phase 1.2.a)

The step 'Create a frame' is important because all the innovation ideas analyzed in this sub-process are mostly unknown or totally new to the company so that it is hard to associate the innovation project ideas with existing businesses or applications of the company and to see the benefit for the latter. Geus (1997: 31) defines this issue very sharply through two statements: first, *'We can see only what we have already experienced.'* With this statement he refers to insight from 'psychology and the study of mental maps, after which psychologists began to claim that people can only "see" what they have experienced before at least in some respect. To receive a signal from the outside world, it must match some matrix already in the mind, placed there by previous events.' Second: '*We can see only what is relevant to our view of the future.*' This statement refers to research conducted on the mechanisms of the human brain related to man's language ability and perception. 'It apparently helps men sort through the plethora of images and sensations coming into the brain, by assigning relevance to them. We perceive something as meaningful if it fits meaningfully with a memory that we have made of an anticipated future' (Geus, 1997: 35). When analyzing discontinuous technologies or potential radical innovations that nobody or only few people have experienced in similar ways, there is the danger that the opportunities behind them are not recognized as such. Thus, 'Create a frame' is the process step aiming to form *the memory of the future* of a company, enabling it to recognize innovation opportunities as such. It comprises four different analyses: (1) a company-internal analysis aiming to detect internal technological needs and vulnerabilities, (2) a future analysis aiming to explore future technology and market requirements, (3) an industry-internal analysis aiming to find potential discontinuities from the inside of industry and (4) an industry-external analysis aiming to find discontinuities from outside the industry (see Figure 4.13).

The analysis proposed to create a frame for the memory of the company's future is composed of these four analyses focusing on company-internal aspects and on company-external aspects. This composition has been chosen because of the evidence that sources of technological discontinuities can be found in a company-internal as well as in a social, political, environmental and economic company-external environment (Lehmann, 1994: 17). Thus, in the next sections, first a company-internal analysis is shown,

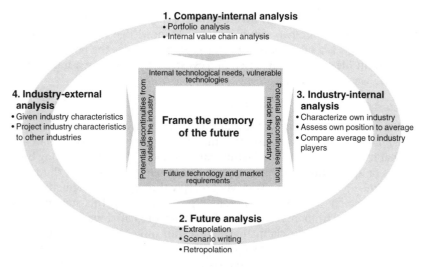

Figure 4.13   Analysis conducted in the step 'Create a frame'

followed by the future analysis that copes with internal and external company aspects. The last two analyses concentrate on company-external aspects.

Company-internal analysis

The company-internal analysis comprises, on the one hand, portfolio analysis and, on the other hand, the internal value chain analysis. First, the portfolio analysis will be described and then, in a following section, the value chain analysis.

The portfolio analysis: It is composed of three interrelated technology-focused portfolios. A first one checks internal cross-use of the technologies in the 'Platform cross-use performance portfolio'; a second one checks the technologies' external attractivity using the Boston Matrix and the third one integrates both previous considerations in the dynamic technology portfolio (see Figure 4.14).

The 'Platform cross-use performance portfolio' mirrors the technology platform's internal position. On the horizontal axis it displays the application intensity of the technologies of a platform by the number of applications it enables across the company. On the vertical axis it lists the number of applications enabled in new products. These twofold considerations reveal the internal value of a technology platform for existing and new products opposing the versatility and involvement of a platform in products (horizontal axis) to its power for innovativeness (vertical axis). This information gives a balanced image of the platform's influence for the company's creation of value. For example, the technology platform B in Figure 4.14 is a technology that is not really fostering the innovativeness of the company, as

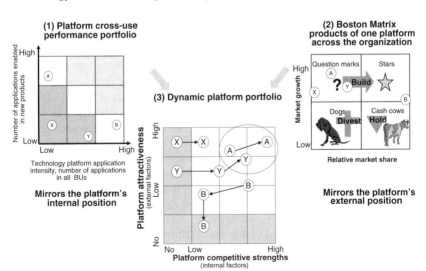

Figure 4.14   Portfolios for company-internal analysis

it only contributes to a quite limited number of new products. It is, however, still an important platform for the company as it is used in many existing products. This is an indicator of the vulnerability of this technology platform and it suggests that sooner or later a substitution platform technology should be found for it.

The Boston Matrix mirrors the technology platform's company-external position. The Boston Consulting Group Product Matrix (Henderson, 2003: 42) is an 'aid for determining the relative position of product lines based on their relative market share and the growth patterns of their markets' and, therefore, it aims 'to provide an analytical basis for strategic decisions concerning support or elimination of product lines' (Holt, 1988: 250). In this context, the Boston Matrix is used to determine growth and market share of all products across the organization in order to reach a conclusion about the external position of the technology platform enabling those products. In other words, all products enabled by one and the same platform are assessed at one time in the matrix. Doing so shows, from a market perspective, how each platform is performing.

Considering both portfolios, the 'Platform cross-use performance portfolio' and the Boston Matrix, side by side, strategic observations can be made. To pick up again the previous example of the technology platform B (see Figure 4.14) for this portfolio, it is apparent that, despite the fact that this platform is involved mostly with existing products and not with new ones in the Boston Matrix, its performance is still good. The position of a technology platform in the Boston Matrix can thus be taken as a rough indicator of the sense of urgency for substituting a technology. If the platform had been in the field 'Cash cow' migrating in the direction of the field 'Dogs', the sense of urgency to substitute platform B would be much higher.

The third portfolio is the 'Dynamic platform portfolio' derived from Tschirky's (2003a) dynamic technology portfolio. The 'Dynamic platform portfolio' is used exactly in the same way as the dynamic technology portfolio; the only difference is that the platform portfolio manages whole platforms instead of single technologies. Using the words of Tschirky (2003a: 67ff.) for the purpose of managing platforms, the portfolio can be described as follows: this portfolio rates and positions all major platforms according to their 'platforms attractiveness' with respect to their innovation and market potential, and their corresponding 'platform strength', i.e. the resources currently available within the company. Once the portfolio has been developed, its strategic evaluation can take place. This focuses on setting priorities as to the elevation or reduction of platform development resources or even the phasing-out of an aging platform. The latter decision usually follows intensive internal discussions. Besides Tschirky's criteria for assessing platform strength and platform attractiveness (see Figure 4.15), insight from both previous portfolios can be consulted in order to determine the position of a platform and its migration. The example of platform B in Figure 4.15

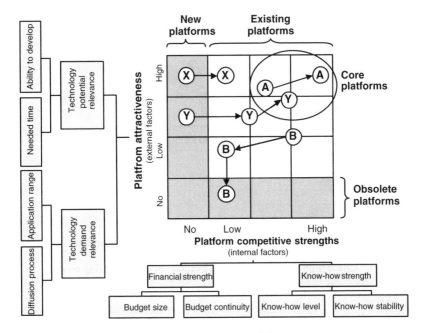

Figure 4.15   The dynamic technology platform portfolio
Source: See Tschirky, 2003a: 68.

shows that it has been recognized as a vulnerable technology: platform B will be shut down in two steps. Other new technologies platforms will be introduced, (in this example they are called platforms X and Y).

Value chain analysis: Discontinuous technologies or radical innovation often change established market patterns and disrupt existing relations between customers, customers' needs, suppliers, technological solutions and their performance. The changed framework spanned by these elements is what Christensen (1997: xv) calls a value network.[16] The value chain analysis[17] is a procedure that helps to understand the existing value network of a company in order to identify company-internal and -external technologies likely to initiate a market disruption. Knowing these technologies helps to sharpen the image of what is called the memory of the future (see section 4.3 – 'Acknowledge') of a company so that radical innovation project ideas are more easily recognized.

The value chain analysis shows the relation of suppliers and customers across multiple value-adding stages between suppliers and customers. Thus, it is especially helpful for those companies that are producing products as a supplier for other companies and not directly for the end-product market.

The 'chain' used in the value chain analysis is composed of three different elements that represent the chain's links: modules, technological solutions

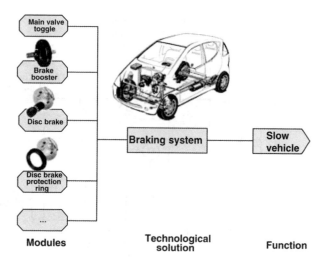

Modules   **Technological solution**   **Function**

Figure 4.16   Chain links of the value chain; example of a car's braking system

realized by these modules and functions realized by these technologies. Figure 4.16 shows an example of a car. The modules taken together form the technological solution of a braking system; the braking system fulfills the function to slow the car down.

Building up the value chain of the company is done by starting from the company's own products and services. As a premise, those products and services sold by the company are considered as modules for their customers, provided that the customers further process the bought products for manufacturing of their own products. Thus, as a first step in building up the value chain, a module is formed by integrating technological solutions, either by other complementary bought modules or others of their own modules. Second, the function that this technological solution fulfills is formulated and, third, the module formed by this technology is written down. These chain links are then further connected until the end-product market is reached. This way, the relation between supplier and customer companies can be visualized by tracking how technologies are integrated in a multitude of modules that fulfill functions (see Figure 4.17).

Figure 4.17 shows the company producing five different products: product 1 is sold to another company A; products 2 and 3 to company C; and products 4 and 5 to company D. In order to realize these products, the company uses technologies that are enabled by their own modules, modules A–F and modules bought by suppliers.

Analyzing the value chain enables the company to more easily understand and track the relationship between the causes and effects of changes in the competitive environment of the company. It allows the company a more

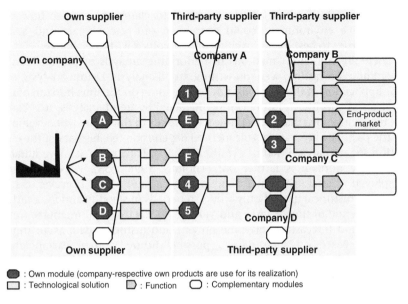

Figure 4.17 The value chain of a company

far-sighted view of the relation within its industry and with its customers. Thus, knowing how and for what the company's own products are used by the customer makes it easier to recognize those technologies that will be needed in the future as the value chain analysis allows:

- Technological changes to be anticipated, especially substitutions and their consequences for the company. Not only internally vulnerable technologies can be tracked but also those far down the value chain. This way, sources of potential substitutions and technology change can be detected and consequences for the company can be evaluated.
- Trends and future requirements to be anticipated. Instead of merely analyzing the needs of the direct customer, needs as far down as the end product can be tracked and integrated in trends and future requirement considerations. This fosters a much broader and holistic context of analysis.
- Alternative technologies and modules for existing functions to be concluded.[18] The functional concept opens up the range of possible technological solutions and modules as it expresses the purpose of the latter in an abstract and solution neutral manner.

Future analysis

Future analysis is needed for strategic planning, as the competitive environment of the company is unstable and constantly changing over the course of time. Thus, the goal of future analysis is to clarify in advance how the competitive environment could change in order to prepare and adapt the company to best meet the challenges involved with the changes.

There are numerous methods of performing analysis of possible future outcomes: forecasting, scenario writing, trend analysis, Delphi analysis, etc. The application of the methods differs depending on the time horizon of the analysis. A short-term future can be predicted by trend analysis. It is based on the central idea that the evolutionally trends in the future will develop as in the past. The accuracy of this method depends on reliable data of the evolution so far analyzed (Ramsay *et al.*, 1996: 93). Forecasting is more suitable when the horizon is farther out (Thomas, 1996: 653). It is a method employed to establish which trends will occur and when. However, if it is based on historical data, it only works in periods of stability and for a rather limited period of time (Clarke and Varma, 1999: 415). Both methods, trend analysis and forecasting, take the present and historical data as an initial position. Based on such data a possible future is then extrapolated. Following the continuous course of evolution, future analysis methods based on extrapolation are well suited to anticipating the development of incremental innovations. These innovations represent for a future analysis, events that are of *high probability and low impact*. However,

> in extrapolation, it is assumed that one or more of the components of historical data will remain constant and, in this respect at least, the future will be like the past. Inevitably, this assumption will be incorrect. Forces in the future will be different than in the past and these forces will change trends, variances, correlations, and higher frequency components. (Gordon and Stover, 1976: 191)

Thus, extrapolations do not 'tell the whole story' (Floyd, 1996: 11); they do not consider deviations from historical sequences of events and make it hard to identify events of *low probability and high impact*.

Strategic planning for discontinuous technologies and radical innovation needs, however, to cope with deviations that do not follow the usual course of the sequence in a continuous development. Their nature is by definition to not follow a continuous development, and they represent a class of events of low probability and high impact.

To anticipate future discontinuities and radical innovation it might be best to break with historical data and with present experience. Future analysis methods that do so are, for example, scenario-writing, Delphi analysis or back-casting. Scenario planning is one of the most widely used tools of foresighting (List, 2004: 24). Scenarios describe different likely futures presented in a narrative way. They describe some future state in terms of key variables and issues (Hunger and Wheelen, 2002: 187). Porter (1989: 560) describes a scenario as 'an internally consistent view of what the future might turn out to be – not a forecast, but one possible future outcome'. There are two ways of developing scenarios: one is to describe the evaluation of events from today to some point in time in the future; the second is to describe a snapshot in time from one particular instant in the future. The challenge of both methods is to sketch, in a first phase, a vision of many futures rather than to draw a detailed vision of a single future. Then probability and plausibility considerations facilitate the selection of the most likely image of the future. Such an image of the future can also be developed by a Delphi method.[19] This method is an expert survey, which leads to consensually building an image or vision of the future. This vision of the future is the initial position for the back-casting method. It is a normative approach that starts with the future and works back towards the present. This in analogy to extrapolation is called retropolation. This method was originally used in energy policy.[20] 'It is employed by starting at the particular future scenario and defining backward, step by step, which outcomes must be fulfilled or what factors must exist in order to link the future with the present' (Noori *et al.*, 1999: 549). The approach aims to find a path defined by hypothetical sequences of events connecting both end-states, the present and the future scenario.

Best practice cases 4.17 and 4.18 demonstrate how Volkswagen uses scenario techniques and trend analysis for the studying future development and probable future environments.

Following the claim for a strategic planning approach for sustained innovation management that takes into account both kinds of innovation, radical innovation followed by incremental innovation, the future analysis methods proposed in this research must be able to anticipate continuously-evolving as well as discontinuously-developing technologies. Future analysis methods fulfilling these requirements must obviously be composed of a combination of the above presented approaches. The concept of this approach is illustrated in Figure 4.18.

The future analysis concept proposed is based on a mindset that opposes technical requirement performances from the present and near future to technical requirement performances expected in the long-term future. The technical requirement performance describes the key performance of a technology required by the market at a certain point in time. The timeline is subdivided roughly in three horizons: a short-term, a mid-term and a long-term horizon. Starting from the present state, the technical requirement performances as they are required in today's industry, markets and competitive environment are extrapolated to a short- to mid-term future. Then, developing a mindset that is decoupled from today's constraints, scenarios of possible long-term futures are developed. These scenarios describe a vision of the company's future industry, its markets and corresponding technical-requirement performances. These visions of the future are the initial position for back-casting. Hypothesized sequences of events are retropolated to technical-requirement performances of a mid-term horizon. A technological

VW's Futurology core team includes fifteen to eighteen people coming from different corporate functions with interdisciplinary backgrounds. Contrary to an intuitive understanding, their primary goal is not to most accurately predict the future, but rather to try to understand the future by imagining the future, elaborated through scenarios meant as construction plans for a future reality to be created. Furthermore, the scenarios are designed to reduce the complexity of screening the present information flood by creating a perception for relevant information pieces. They help to monitor and recognize movements of reality in the direction described in the scenarios.

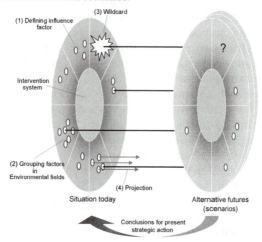

Situation today

Alternative futures
(scenarios)

Conclusions for present
strategic action

The actual scenario-building process includes four steps with distinct elements: (1) The Futurology core team first defines a great number of 'high-probability and low impact' factors influencing the intervention system, for example, a car. These factors are derived from the usual evolutionary changes in the environment. (2) Grouped according to environmental fields, each with a different topical focus, e.g. society, values, consumption, competition, politics, economy, technology, design, etc. the consequences for their present intervention system can be evaluated.

In order to also include the occurrence of disruptive events, so-called 'wild cards' are integrated into the scenario (3). Wild cards represent the positive or negative effect of highly influential events. They are 'low-probability and high- impact' events. Selectively inserted into a scenario they help to evaluate the consequences of the corresponding event, i.e. the deviation of the present scenario under the influence of an unexpected and unusual event.

Once the uncritical factors such as demographic and social actors are defined, they are projected into the future (4). This is conducted by using current forecasting methods, as well as as extrapolation and forecasting. In analogies, the critical factors for the business are projected in alternative (2–3) directions by scenarios. Based on these projections, three images of the future are elaborated. A mixture of three scenarios provide the background for strategic conclusions. The actual product strategies are then influenced on the one side by the guideline of the brand and on the other side by the strength and weakness of the product and the market.

Best practice case 4.17   Volkswagen, scenario planning and futurology

Source: Interview at Volkswagen, 2004, M. Reisel, T. Jäger, G. Trauffler.

Trend analysis and futurology at VW is attached to the Corporate Market Research unit. It covers three different areas of activity: classical market research, life-world research (Lebensweltforschung), and futurology.

Classical market research relies on statistical methods to analyze buyer patterns or customer satisfaction, etc. The main goal of these methods is to provide objectively studied, reliable, statistical data of the present and the past.

Life-world research aims to investigate everyday life patterns in society. This is achieved by face-to-face interviews during which different societal circumstances and characteristics (family life, consumer behavior, etc.) are analyzed and interrelated. The ultimate goal is the segmentation of the society into target groups, according to ways of life or societal trend profiles.

Futurology aims to identify company-external future changes in order to provide supportive guidelines for the strategy-definition process. Thinking in alternative scenarios, uncertainties and gaps in objectively analyzed data as a basis for the strategy definition process is backed up by creativity and subjective interpretation.

The methods used in classical market and life-world research are based on the evaluation of objective, precise data ('hard facts') and particular interview outcomes, whereas futurology uses hermeneutic methods. Through the combination of the three methods Volkswagen seeks to elaborate a well-balanced vision of the future.

Best practice case 4.18   Volkswagen, trend analysis and futurology
Source: Interview at Volkswagen, 2005, M. Reisel, T. Jäger, G. Trauffler.

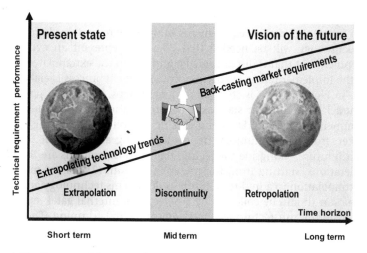

Figure 4.18   Concept of future analysis

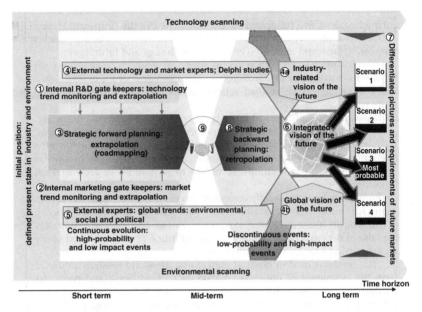

Figure 4.19   Future analysis, opposing trends to future visions

discontinuity can be expected in the case where a clear gap emerges between the extrapolated and retropolated requirement performances, or in the case where the type of requirement, the performance set apart, cannot be satisfied by any existing technology in the company. Both cases are an indicator that the steady incremental development of the existing technologies will not be able to satisfy the market requirements in the long term. In order to do so, a new technology will be needed that does not represent an evolutionary development but that is discontinued compared to the extrapolated one.

For the implementation of this concept an overall process is elaborated as shown in Figure 4.19 it is structured in nine steps. The initial position for this model is the present state as it is defined through the industrial and environmental situation. Data and experience collected from this situation are taken from (1) technology trend monitoring and extrapolated to the mid-term future. Alongside the technological considerations are the market considerations, starting from the present situation: (2) market monitoring and extrapolation to a mid-term future is done. This technology and market information should be collected by a network of internal gatekeepers aided by a constantly run technology and environmental scanning. The purpose of scanning is to identify key trends, changes and events in the organization's environment that might affect the organization's functioning (Milliken, 1990: 43). The people acting as gatekeepers should be chosen from the front-line managers of the company's business units, not from the corporate level. Research has shown that front-line managers perform best in the recognition of innovation opportunities (see Chapter 2). They should typically show a high level of communication and networking skills, have entrepreneurial ambition and should be leading small improvement teams. In order to provide these people's valuable technological and market information with the necessary attention, they should report in strategic planning meetings. Organized in a company-wide, coordinated gatekeeper's network, the persons leading this network should participate in these strategic planning meetings (3). Drafting a first forward-conducted strategic plan can consensually process the collected and analyzed information from markets and technology. This forward strategic planning can be structured through a roadmapping process.[21] The final result of the meeting is an innovation roadmap. A roadmap is a graphically based management tool that helps to structure

> the identification of the technologies underlying current and planned products and highlight the known technology developments that are anticipated, and the elements that will be needed to successfully develop the new product. These maps also identify the underlying R&D investments needed to develop the technologies and to integrate them into a new product and/or system. (Petrick and Echols, 2004: 90)

The company-internal experts' opinions are also considered; the next two steps (4 and 5) are designed to pay respect to the company's external experts who should be independent from the company. Their task is to develop a long-term image of the future. In step (4) company-external technology and market experts can either express their image of the future through a workshop or through a Delphi analysis. This image is focused on the long-term development of the company's industry and should deliver an industry-related vision of the future (4a). In this vision, markets, technologies, products, competition or scientific achievement are described that will influence the company's industry. It describes what technologies are used in which products to fulfill which functions, which new markets will emerge with what kind of new customers, which technologies will be obsolete and which kind of skills the future employee of the company will need in order to be able to deliver the expected added value. The goal of this industry-related vision of the future is to create a technology push-oriented vision showing all the possibilities of those new scientific achievements, technologies and products that could be part of life in the long-term future. Although the focus of such a vision is clearly technology-oriented, it should still be adapted to a reasonable social, political, economic and environmental context of this future, despite regarding these influences somewhat superficially (see Figure 4.20).

In step (5) a group of external experts whose expertise is in social sciences rather than in the natural sciences should also be included in a series of workshops to elaborate a more global image of the future. This global image of the future should be based on global environmental, economic and political trends in order to reflect a vision of the situation of mankind in the long-term future. It should address issues of poverty, conflicts, or terrorism as consequences of the global economy or ethnic instabilities. Other issues could be the consequences of natural resources running short: for example, oil, gas, or even water in some regions of the world, or the consequences of the aging society in western countries, the consequences of epidemic diseases in the Third World, or the consequences of the rapid and erratic growth in China and India, etc. All these consequences shape a global vision of the future that will influence the priorities and habits or even the basic needs of people. In a nutshell, the global-oriented vision of the future is rather technology pull-oriented, envisioning the needs of future societies and, as a consequence, which will be their markets (see Figure 4.21).

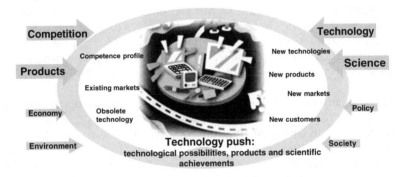

Figure 4.20   Industry-related vision of the future

Figure 4.21   Global vision of the future

A good example of such a global vision of the future is the Global Trends report of the United States National Intelligence Council (NIC).[22] This report is published every five years by the NIC, in collaboration with a great number of non-governmental institutions and experts. It aims to draw an image of the future that is fifteen years from now. It covers issues from demographics to developments in science and technology, from the global markets to implications for the United States.

Both future visions being elaborated, the technology-driven industry-related vision of the future (4a) and the market-driven global vision of future (5a), can now be opposed in order to build the integrated vision of the future (6) (see Figure 4.22). Opposing both of these visions allows technological possibilities to be considered in a global socio-political, technological and environmental context. This consideration helps to find out which technological advances imagined in the industry-related vision make more or less sense, which technologies could indeed be of a general need in the future and which not. Although it will hardly be possible to determine customer needs for future specific technological and product configurations when opposing those two visions of the future, it will, however, be possible to see whether there is a general need for the technological possibilities projected for the future. These general needs will offer clues as to how the technological performance requirements will roughly look in the long-term future.

For the elaboration of the integrated vision of the future a structured discussion in a workshop is proposed. In this workshop, the authors of the industry-related vision of the future meet with the authors of the global vision of the future for a consensus-seeking discussion. The result of this

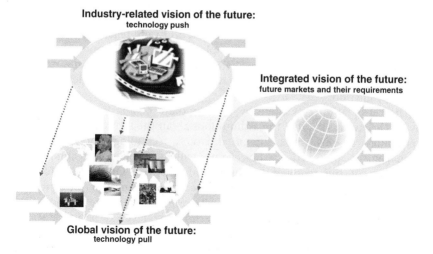

Figure 4.22   Building the integrated vision of the future

discussion will deliver the integrated vision of the future. A simple matrix that contrasts major issues of the global vision with the industry-related vision could structure the discussion. Such a discussion will enable the participants to discuss alternative perspectives of the future, but so that the delivery of one single and integrated vision including future requirements for the technologies will probably be illusory. Thus, different pictures and requirements of future markets can be developed in scenarios in order to reach consensus (see step No. 7 in Figure 4.19).

These scenarios can be developed based on the assumption that one or more of the factors influencing the integrated vision of the future, be it an environmental, political or technological factor of the global vision, will experience an unexpected deviation. Such deviations are considered discontinuous events, events of low probability but with potential high impact for the company. These events can be hypothesized from weak signals captured by the continuous technological and environmental scanning activities conducted by the company (see Figure 4.22) or by differing opinions of the experts participating in the workshop building the integrated vision of the future.

While building the different future scenarios, a number of assumptions about the future have to be taken, as a lot of constraints are not known when anticipating the long-term future. These assumptions have to be clearly formulated as they represent, together with their corresponding scenarios, the initial position for the second to last step of the proposed future analysis: backward planning and retropolation (8). Internal people who have not yet been involved in the future analysis should conduct this step. It is important not to involve the same internal people from the business units that built the integrated visions because they would tend to retropolate the scenarios and assumptions using the same mindset they already used when imagining the future. Thus, participants from the corporate level should perform the task of connecting (backwards), the long-term future perspectives with the mid-term extrapolated trends. The people seem even more appropriate when considering the fact that the deliverables of this step will be the strategic guidelines for long-term company development: the company development strategic measures.

The retroplation task done by the corporate people is to hypothesize events backwards, so that the assumptions about the future and their corresponding scenarios can be supported. From a technology and innovation-management perspective, the events will describe the technological evolution of the required technical performances. Once the mid-term horizon is reached in step (9), extrapolated technological performances of today's technologies can be compared with retropolated future technological performances. An obvious gap between those two levels of performances is an indication of an emerging technological discontinuity.

As already mentioned in the beginning of this section, the main goal of the future analysis is to anticipate changes in the competitive environment of the company. The more accurately these changes can be anticipated, the better the company can prepare for them. Thus, one goal in the above-described future analysis is to reduce the number of scenarios developed in step (7) as quickly as possible, in order to focus the following analysis on this single alternative. The method of reducing the number of scenarios consists of understanding the scenarios as receptacles for evidence supporting this scenario. The receptacle itself is spanned by the story the scenario tells, the story being founded on assumptions that are made for this scenario. Considering such a scenario as a receptacle for evidence supporting it allows it to be filled with the latter. Thus, the scenarios first have to be communicated throughout the whole company, so that every employee understands and knows about them. Once this has happened, all employees are invited to look for evidence supporting the scenarios. Every employee can collect evidence at any time at work, in daily life, or even during leisure time. The idea is not that they spend hours and hours of working time searching for information in costly databases or in specialized papers; the idea is rather that in informal exchanges, newspapers or through things they have seen on TV they come across information that can be assigned to one of the scenarios. This assignment can be realized over an information technology base platform, which can be used by everyone. With every piece of information that can be rated as evidence supporting one of the scenarios, the receptacle that this scenario represents is filled. After a certain period of time the receptacles are checked. How much supporting evidence for this scenario was collected? The scenario with the most evidence assigned can be judged as the one most likely to happen. For example, receptacle number three might be the scenario with the most assignments.

Siemens, shown in Best practice case 4.19, illustrates how it proceeds to study the future by extrapolation and retropolation.

Industry-internal analysis

The main goal of this analysis is to detect potential discontinuities that can be initiated from within the particular industry. Thus, the industry is first characterized, then the company's own position within the industry can be assessed and, lastly, companies that are susceptible to the initiation of a discontinuity are detected.

The theory backing the design of the analysis proposed in this section can be found in Christensen's (1997) book *The Innovator's Dilemma*. It describes many reasons why established companies fail to engage with disruptive technologies to generate radical innovation. One of these reasons, already described in this section, is that most established companies are part of a value network that expects those companies to produce products that correspond to a certain pattern. The application field of the product, the type of value proposition delivered by the product and the improvement trajectory of the product characterize this product pattern. The application field

The corporate technology unit at Siemens (CT) has built its own method for future analysis. The result of this analysis aims to systematize and optimize the corporation's R&D strategy and to show how the realization of this strategy can be planned. Thus a combined approach of extrapolation and retropolation is used.

Extrapolation is done by the divisions of Siemens. Based on experiences from the past and the present, projections of markets, technologies and customer needs are conducted with the goal to plan product development. This process is supported by roadmaps.

In independent projects conducted by CT in collaboration with the divisions, strategic visioning is conducted for selected Siemens' businesses. This project aims to develop a future vision of the environment of Siemens' businesses in the long-term future. The project involves an interdisciplinary team of ten to twelve experts working 50 per cent for typically six months. The experts originate from CT as well as from the corresponding Siemens businesses. Together these people elaborate the so-called 'Pictures of the Future'(PoF). The time horizon of the strategic vision, meaning how far the PoF is ahead of today, depends on the industry for which the picture is elaborated. While for the electronics industry the PoF is about four years from now, it is ten years and more for plant engineering.

The PoF support, on the one hand, the strategic planning processes in the existing businesses of Siemens and, on the other hand, they deliver evidence for emerging businesses. The PoF helps to elaborate entrance scenarios for new businesses and can also be used for deriving criteria that support go/no-go decisions in projects.

Furthermore elaborating the PoF for future competitive environments of the company supports the recognition of competencies that it is necessary to build up today in order to insure future competitive advantage. Such competencies and others are developed in the CT laboratories.

The PoF are not only useful for long-term considerations but also to derive mid-term plans. For this purpose the PoF are taken as the starting point for retropolation, pointing out the challenges that have to be tackled today in order to be successful in the mid-term future. Retropolating identifies the PoF events for the PoF to become true. Thus, the extrapolated futures can be cross-checked through the retropolations. This way discontinuities in the environment can also be detected.

Best practice case 4.19   Future analysis at Siemens
Source: Interview at Siemens CT, 2004, 2005, G. Trauffler.

describes the industries, markets and segments of the products' application in a broad sense, the value proposition defines what makes a product valuable for its customers in its defined application field and the improvement trajectory describes the main focus of innovation for defined value attributes. These three characteristics shape a certain kind of wisdom and unwritten rules of behavior in every industry. It is called the *context of the industry*. One further important aspect to fully model the industry context is a competitive marketplace. According to Burgelman and Rosenbloom (1989: 277),

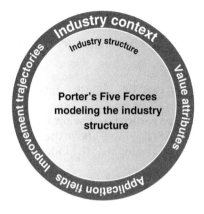

Figure 4.23   Model of the industry context and structure

the competitive marketplace within an industry context is further influenced by the five major forces structuring the industry context as described by Porter (1980): (1) rivalry among existing firms; (2) bargaining power of buyers; (3) bargaining power of suppliers; (4) threat of new entrants; and (5) threat of substitute products or services. Figure 4.23 models the industry context and its structure.

This industry context represents innovation barriers for established companies, as it hinders them from recognizing emerging discontinuities. Established companies tend to innovate in set application fields by identifying customer-oriented value propositions and by improving only along defined performance trajectories that are valued by their customers. Johnson and Hoopes (2003: 1057) explain this phenomenon from a more strategic perspective. Their explanation is based on competitive pressure and bounded rationality within the competitive environment of the industry:

> competitive pressure and bounded rationality induce agents (firms or managers) to focus their attention on nearby competitors. Thus, firms develop biased estimates of their competitive environment. These estimates correlate with the estimates of nearby firms. Thus, clusters of firms will have similar beliefs resulting in stable strategic and performance heterogeneity within an industry. (Johnson and Hoopes, 2003: 1057)

Independent from the perspective of the explanation, for established companies, the consequence is the same: a set industry context inhibits organizations from moving to uncharted territories. Routines and beliefs within this context inhibit any actions outside pre-existing patterns.

Although the vision of companies is bounded by the industry context and the competitive rules of the industry structure, companies that succeed in questioning and overcoming this bounded vision 'shatter the current advantage of their competitors and create the opportunity to build their own temporary advantage' (D'Aveni, 1994: 275). For basically questioning the rules of an industry Kim and Mauborgne (1997: 107) suggest the following four questions:

1. Which of the factors that our industry takes for granted should be eliminated?
2. Which factors should be reduced well below the industry's standard?
3. Which factors should be raised well above the industry's standard?
4. Which factors should be created that the industry has never offered?

Both authors explain their questions as follows:

> The first question forces managers to consider whether the factors that companies compete on actually deliver value to consumers. Often those factors are taken for granted, even though they have no value or even detract from value. Sometimes buyer's value changes fundamentally, but companies that are focused on benchmarking one another do not act on – or even perceive – the change. The second question forces managers to determine whether products and services have been over designed in the race to match and beat the competition. The third question pushes managers to uncover and eliminate the compromises that their industry forces customers to make. The fourth question helps managers break out of the industry's established boundaries to discover entirely new sources of value for consumers. (Kim and Mauborgne, 1997: 102)

The method proposed to assess companies susceptible to initiating a discontinuity is a qualitative analysis composed of three steps:

1. Define the context of the industry. This means that the three main patterns shaping the industry context – the value proposition, the application fields and the improvement trajectories of the industry – have to be specified (see Figure 4.23).
2. Specify the three patterns to characterize the industry context. They have to represent the norm of that industry in terms of recognized indicators of the corresponding pattern and additionally they should be quantifiable. For example, in the case of the innovation trajectory pattern of the mobile computing industry the norm innovation activity is the reduction of the size and weight of the device, the operating convenience, and versatility of the software, the battery power and the mobile connectivity features. All innovation efforts corresponding to these four activities can be considered as corresponding to the norm innovation trajectory of the mobile computing industry. A catalogue of such norm activities can be kept for every pattern.

3. Assess the position of the company as well as of competitors within the scale fixed by the norm. Additionally, assessment of the other players of the industry structures including: the suppliers, new entrants, buyers, and substitutions can be revised in order to identify whether they support or provoke deviations from the average pattern of competitors.

A visual tool, as shown in Figure 4.24, supports this three-step assessment. The three axes of the tool can be built up using the three-step procedure described above. The gray area spanned across the three axes quantifies the norm activities of each axis. Activities lying within this norm represent a 100 per cent congruency with the industry context. The companies' own assessments shown in these examples slightly over-perform the norm of the innovation trajectory in the industry; it strongly lags behind in the value proposition of its product; and it is within the norm for the application fields. The competitor's position out-performs the norm in its value propositions and in the application fields where it delivers its products. This is an indication that the activities of this competitor are deviating from the norm of the industry and that it may be planning to break with the bounded rational of the industry to introduce a discontinuity. They represent an advantageous incongruence for this competitor compared to the industry norm.

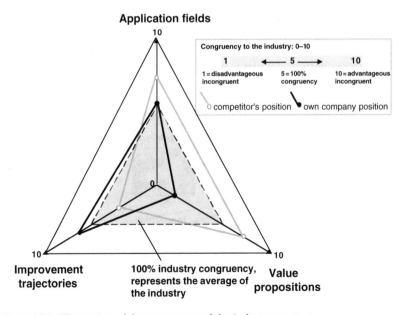

Figure 4.24 Illustration of the assessment of the industry context

Industry-external analysis

The goal of the industry-external analysis is to project the characteristics of the company's industry context on other industries in order to find alternative industries with similar application fields for their products and technologies, similar industries with similar value propositions and similar industries with similar innovation trajectories. The same analysis can be applied to the forces shaping the industry structure: find alternative industries that have similar customers, suppliers, substitutive elements emerging, or similar entrants. This is especially important as discontinuous technologies or innovations that have a radical impact on the marketplace have been shown to emerge very often from outside the industry it finally invades (see Chapter 1).

The mindset of this analysis can even be extended to analyze in which alternative industries there are companies that have similar core competencies and core technologies to the ones used in the company's own industry (see Figure 4.25).

A simple example helps to illustrate the approach of the industry-external analysis. The Swiss company Phonak produces, among other things, hearing instruments. These instruments are extremely miniaturized and require a lot of electronic and software know-how. Phonak's latest product lines of hearing devices work with digital technology. Looking for a company from a totally different industry having the same competencies in miniaturization, electronics and software engineering, a company from the electronic entertainment industry emerges: Sony. Sony produces miniaturized devices like walkmans and cameras and camcorders that use similar technologies and competencies as Phonak's. Thus, for Phonak, Sony might be a company that has the potential to initiate a discontinuity in the hearing instruments industry. The association between both companies is not obvious, but neither is it deniable.

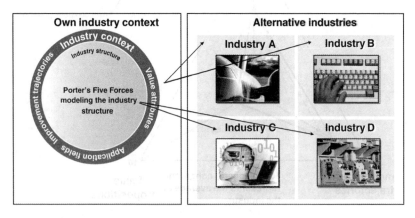

Figure 4.25 Industry-external analysis

The industry-external analysis concludes the first step of the phase 'Acknowledge' in the strategic planning process (see Figure 4.3): it was meant to build up an evaluation frame through several company-internal and -external analyses in order to facilitate the recognition of discontinuous innovation opportunities often unfamiliar to the company.

Generate issue (process phase 2.1.a)

The second step in the sub-process 'Acknowledge', called 'Generate issue' has been designed with the goal, of generating the necessary sense of urgency in order to sensitize the company to the need to further explore innovation opportunities previously detected. This step seems especially important considering that generally the sense of urgency and the priority for exploring radical innovation ideas based on discontinuous technologies is low (see Chapter 2).

The eventual goal of the sub-step 'Generate issue' is to direct the attention of the company towards a strategically important issue that is related to decisions about being explored with priority or the necessity of a great deal of resources to be allocated.

Thus, a three-step procedure is suggested (see Figure 4.26): first, to determine the scope of analysis. This step basically consists of organizing and holding a meeting where the latest version of the evaluation frame (see this chapter, 'Acknowledge') is applied in order to determine the scope of the issue that is going to be generated. Thus, in this step the goal is to pick those technologies that, according to the frame, show a potential for the long-term future of the company. The second step is to determine the nature of impact of the chosen technologies. This step is especially important when assessing discontinuous technologies, remembering that these often come from unfamiliar industries (see Chapter 2, Section 2). Thus, their impact for the company's industry is not always obvious and clear. In order to relate a technology to an industry context other than the one it originally comes from, it

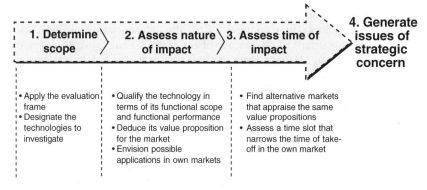

Figure 4.26 Three steps to generating issues of strategic concern

is abstracted to its functional level: the technology's functional scope and functional performances are analyzed. These functions can then be related to a changed industry context, meaning that the value proposition of the technology is assessed from a functional perspective. Possible market applications that can roughly be imagined can be a last analysis in this second step, in order to give the technology a tangible character in the changed industry context.

In a third step, after the nature of the technology's impact in the analyzing company's industry has been assessed, the moment in time when the impact will happen can be analyzed. The goal of this analysis is to determine roughly the period in time when the technology will start being attractive to a large-scale market. Among practitioners, this moment in time is called 'the time of market take-off'. It is the moment in time when the market diffusion of the technology growth behaves erratically when compared to its past. Many discontinuous technologies or radical innovations need years, even decades of basic research to become ready for commercialization. During this period of time, it is most difficult for companies to see the necessity of investing in those kinds of technologies, as the return that can be generated from them lies in a too far distant and uncertain future. For many companies the sense of urgency is not yet given in this early stage, as there is no market competitive situation in place. Most companies then decide to wait until the uncertainty inherent in the technology decreases over time. For others it is even a declared goal not to invest in basic research, but only in technologies that need three to a maximum of five years of development before commercialization is foreseeable. For all these companies, it is especially important to be able to predict the time of take-off in order to become active with the technology early enough to build up the knowledge necessary to compete.

When a company roughly knows the time of take-off, it can more accurately plan its technology and innovation strategy, especially with discontinuous technologies which are often highly resource-consuming.

Practice example 4.6 illustrates the time of take-off for an emerging technology using the case of cellular mobile phones.

As a result of these three analyses – first, the determination of the scope, second, the assessment of the nature of the impact and, third, the time of impact – finally the strategic issue of concern can be formulated. However, this formulation should not only be based on the three analyses described in this section, but should rather represent a summary of all of the strategic analyses conducted so far in the internal strategic planning process.

1. Determine scope

The determination of the scope is looking to identify those technologies that will be of strategic interest for the long-term future of the company. Thus, a meeting is suggested where the responsible persons charged with the

One example that well illustrates the time of market take-off of a former emerging technology is that used in cellular phone communication. Initial conceptual ideas and research for this wireless phone technology date back as far as 1946.

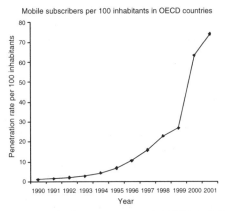

Mobile subscribers per 100 inhabitants in OECD countries

By the time the US telephone companies AT&T and Southwestern Bell introduced the first commercial mobile radio telephone service in St Louis, Missouri, the base station used for the mobile 'network' was based on six steadily assigned channels. In order to increase the performance of the network researchers had the idea to dispatch the channels dynamically on demand and to reuse the radio frequencies in the form of cell grids. Bell laboratories patented the cell principle in 1947. Today's mobile phone standards such as GSM, GPRS and UMTS are still based on this same cell principle. As this example shows, it took this technology many years of development until it was slowly introduced in 1980s and finally experienced its time of market take-off in the mid-1990s. The diagram shows the take-off of the cellular phone communication technology by mobile phone subscribers per 100 inhabitants in OECD countries from 1990 to 2001. Until the 1990s the market penetration of mobile cell phone communication had been unimportant for almost 50 years.

Practice example 4.6   Time of take-off in wireless mobile cell phone communication
Source: OECD, 1999; 2003.

creation of the evaluation frame (see this chapter, 'Acknowledge') discuss together with those responsible for strategic intelligence. All innovation opportunities that have been judged highly risky can be evaluated according to the created frame. While strategic intelligence people can explain the background of the development of the innovation idea, the front-line managers who have created the evaluation frame can judge the strategic importance of the idea. The frame promotes the recognition of technological innovation ideas, taking into account all four aspects that have been ana-lyzed when developing the evaluation frame: (1) internal technological needs and vulnerable technologies; (2) future technology and market requirements; (3) potential discontinuities from inside; and (4) those from outside the industry. Eventually this evaluation manages to relate highly innovative technology project ideas to the company, recognizing those technologies that should be further investigated. Doing so limits the scope of the innovation project ideas. Those project ideas that could not be associated with the company and its strategic future are filed in a database.

2. Assess the nature of impact

As already mentioned earlier in this publication, assessing the nature of the impact of a radical innovation idea is especially important in the frequent case where the technology underlying the innovation idea is unfamiliar to the industry that now considers using it. Thus, the goal of this assessment is to relate the technology to the context of the unfamiliar industry and to see what value proposition it brings the latter. Establishing this relation is often difficult as the technology, as it is used in its originating industry, is already used in a product. Being used in a product, an association of the technology with this specific product is already given. This makes it hard to consider merely the technology in order to analyze its benefit in a new industry. However, a separation of the technology's effects from the specific context of its product is necessary for a systematic analysis of the nature of the impact in a new industry. First, abstracting the technology to its functions and analyzing the functional scope of the product achieves this separation. The functional scope is given by the range and combination of functions of a product. Knowing the functional scope of a product, various applications across industries can be compared by comparing the functional scopes of the technologies used in different products. This comparison is the first step in assessing the impact of a discontinuous technology in an unfamiliar industrial environment. As an illustration an example applying the functional scope is described.

The example describes the emergence of a discontinuous technology in the flat panel display industry. This industry produces displays that find their use in all kinds of mobile and stationary applications, like laptops, mobile phones, computer monitors, or TV sets. For the production of such displays – for example, active matrix liquid crystal displays (LCD) – an essential process technology is a thin film coating of substrates. Substrate is the surface that is coated by a thin film of metal or an oxide, etc. Today technologies like chemical and physical vapor deposition (CVD, PVD) are used for these processes. CVD[23] is a generic name for a group of processes that involve depositing a solid material from a gaseous phase and is similar in some respects to physical vapor deposition (PVD). CVD coatings are usually only a few microns thick and are generally deposited at fairly slow rates, usually on the order of a few hundred microns per hour. PVD differs in that the precursors are solid, with the material to be deposited being vaporized from a solid target and deposited onto the substrate.

Latently the emergence of ink jet technology for the deposit of thin films has been discussed and evaluated among specialists in the display industry. This technology used today in the consumer printer industry, is most unfamiliar to the display-producing industry. The idea is to use the printer technology to dash droplets of the thin film on to the substrate instead of ink on to the paper. The nature of impact of the ink jet technology used in the display production industry being so unfamiliar to the latter makes it ideal to be assessed by functional scope analysis. In a first step the range of functions of a product where the ink jet technology is used is analyzed: a conventional ink jet printer. Figure 4.27 illustrates the result of the analysis: after listing the main modules of such an ink jet printer, every module is assigned one or more functions. First, listing the modules of the printer before assigning functions has the advantage that the level of detail of the functions will stay on the same level. In this example nine main modules have been listed for which fourteen main functions have been derived. These fourteen functions represent the functional scope of the ink jet printer. They represent the initial position to imagine new applications in the market. In this case it is the application in the display production that has been imagined.

A next step is the functional comparison of the ink jet technology and the CVD technology. Thus, from the functional scope of the ink jet technology, functions are picked that are relevant for thin film coating. The selected function's technology performance is subsequently rated according to the requirements in the thin film coating process. The rating is best done by roughly comparing the new technology's performance relative to the performance of the existing technology, the existing technology representing

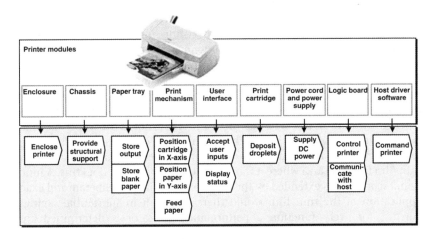

Figure 4.27   Range of an ink jet printer's functions

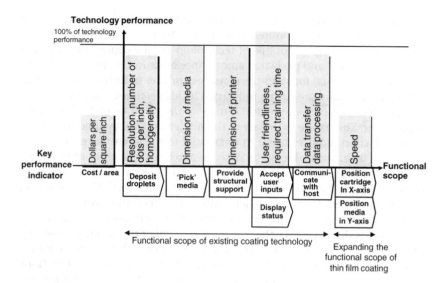

Figure 4.28   Functions of the ink jet technology relevant for thin film coating

a benchmark of 100 per cent. Those functions of the new technology that out-perform the existing technology are rated higher than 100 per cent, while those that under-perform are rated less than 100 per cent. If possible an overall performance indicator, a so-called key performance indicator that is relevant for the industry, should also be evaluated.

Figure 4.28 illustrates the second step of the functional comparison.[24] Starting from the fourteen functions forming the functional scope of the ink jet technology in the printer, eight functions were estimated to be important for the use of thin film coating in the production of flat panel displays. While six of these functions correspond to the existing functional scope of today's coating technologies like CVD, two functions extend the usual functional scope. These two functions enable specific points of the substrate to be coated instead of the whole surface all at once. As a consequence, the application of the thin film can be done only in those areas and points where it is actually necessary. With today's technologies it is not possible to control the area where the thin film should be deposited and where not as the whole substrate is coated through deposition of the chemical vapor. Thus, today's coating technologies need a second step of procedure that removes the already coated thin film from the area where it is not needed. Etching it off does this. A functional scope that is extended by the functions enabling a deliberate and exact application of the thin film would therefore result in substantial savings. Further, for every function a performance indicator is determined and assessed relative to the performance requirement in the display production. In this example, three of the performances of the ink jet technology, as it is used in the printers, obviously do not yet satisfy the requirements for the use of the same technology in thin film coating in the display production.

Analyzing the functional scope and the performances of each function of a technology facilitates the association of the benefits as well as the drawbacks of it in new application fields. In the case of the ink jet technology used in display production, a benefit could certainly be the deliberate and exact application of the thin film; however, a disadvantage is that the technology needs further development: for example, in the resolution of the droplets deposited, or on the homogeneity of the deposited film.

In conclusion it can be said that 'the technology impact analysis' sheds some light on how an emerging technology stands the test in an industry where it is totally unfamiliar. Hence the impact of the ink jet technology could roughly be predicted for the display production. Finally, this analysis could have been conducted for further alternative applications. Looking for such alternative applications means analyzing in which other markets the functional scope of the display technology applies. Doing so revealed possible applications to a production technology in the following markets: RFID, photovoltaic, tissue engineering, sensors, memory elements, toy, textiles and e-paper.

3. Assess the time of impact

This analysis tries to predict a technology's market-entry time based on its evolutionary performance development over time. The moment in time to determine is the one where the competition, based on that technology, will have a high impact; in other words it is the 'time of market take-off' (see also this chapter, 'Generate issue') that this analysis is aiming to predict. The prediction is based on the experience that the entry of different markets with similar applications of the same technology depends on the time the technology needs to reach a minimal performance which is the least required for this market.

An example is the use of image sensors, so-called CCD or CMOS chips, in many different market fields. Performance requirements for this technology are different according to the application and market field used. With the increasing performance of the technology its use was found over the years in many different applications. Early applications for image sensors included facsimile machines in the 1970s and camcorders in the 1980s. Since then, image sensors have expanded into a variety of industries, such as scientific research, computer/office applications, communications and aerospace. For instance,[25] the technology has been applied to:

- Quality control and inspection during manufacturing, since the speed and accuracy of CCD devices allow real-time inspection of manufacturing processes.
- Biological and physical sciences research, with applications ranging from fluorescence microscopy, fluorescence in situ hybridization (FISH), retinal

scanning, cancer detection and diagnosis and high-throughput drug screening to semiconductor failure analysis, laser beam profilometry, wind tunnel testing and underwater imaging.

- Aerospace and astronomy, in which CCD image sensor devices have been incorporated into instrumentation for wide field-of-view imaging, adaptive optics, satellite tracking and atmospheric monitoring.

Using the logic behind this experience, the prediction of the moment in time a technology enters a market can be assessed in four steps: (1) listing all the applications that a technology could possibly be used for (these applications can be determined by projecting the functional scope of the technology to alternative markets that show similar functional scopes); (2) estimating the minimal required performances of the technology's functions in order to be interesting for its corresponding application and market field; (3) sorting the applications in an increasing order of performance requirements; (4) determining for each of the applications a roughly estimated time of market entrance based on the technology's development speed. This way the accuracy of the predicted moment of market entrance increases, as the forecast for the market-entrance time can be done in small increments instead of in one single assessment. Each increment is provided by a market, which the technology enters by increasing its performance, so that the eventually predicted market entry is supported by a broader range of evident data rather than based on individual assumptions.

The procedure described above can be illustrated using the same example of the ink jet technology emerging in the flat panel display's production industry. The functional scope being determined, it can be used to find alternative application fields for the ink jet technology. Comparing the functional scope of the ink jet technology to the functional requirements for use in further applications, applications could be found in the following markets: RFID, photovoltaic, tissue engineering, sensors, memory elements, toy and cloth and e-paper. Once alternative applications are known, the minimal performance requirements of these alternative applications can be assessed relative to the function's performances in the display production process.

As an example, without any claim to accuracy, Figure 4.29 shows an assessment of functional requirement of the ink jet technology as it could be used in alternative markets. The assessments are done relative to the use in the display production market. All market alternatives to the display production market that show a majority of functions with performance requirements estimated to be inferior to the ones in the display market are assumed to enter the market earlier than the latter. Forecasting the time of market entrance for the alternative markets with inferior functional performance requirements narrows the time slot when the technology could be ready to enter the display market.

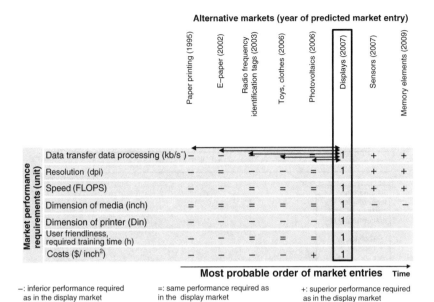

Figure 4.29 Assessment of the time of impact or 'time of market take-off'

4. Generate strategic issue of concern

Provided that the nature of impact and the time of impact are known, the generation of the strategic issue of concern can be carried out. The process step generating a strategic issue of concern has two main goals: first, to sensitize the organization to major strategic challenges assumed in the future. They are due to company-internal constellations as well as to the changes in the competitive environment of the company and likely to become the sources of discontinuities. The emphasis on this first goal is given by the explicit formulation of a list with changes that are assumed to be going to happen, including a rough indication about the moment in time they are expected. This list can further be used to deduce the expected change trends that project discontinuities in the future. Statements about projected discontinuities can be seen very roughly at this moment in time, as they are merely meant to generate an issue of strategic concern. The second goal is to present to the company a specific list of emerging technologies that might become important to keep up with the corresponding changes, in order to shape their awareness for the future importance of these technologies (see Figure 4.30).

These technologies are those coming from the high risk innovation project ideas that have been detected as relevant for the company thus far in

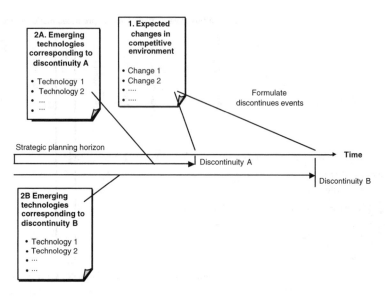

Figure 4.30   Issue generation

the course of the strategic planning process. The formulation of the list of emerging technologies also comprises a first prioritization according to strategic importance. This strategic importance can be determined through a synthesis summarizing all the analyses done so far in the strategic planning process. Thus, this synthesis comprises the original strategic search field of the intelligence from which the project idea was born, the idea's level of newness and risk, its evaluation through the evaluation frame and its nature and time of impact in the relevant industry. Such a list with emerging technologies can be structured according to the following points:

- A prioritization of technologies that represent a strategic relevance for the company. Strategic relevance is given by technologies that are important either for the present or projected future competitive situation of the company, or likely to initiate a discontinuity in the industry. This list should comprise a brief description of only that technology with the potential to contribute to the company's long-term future. Elaborating this list thus also eliminates those innovation project ideas that, according to all the strategic analyses conducted so far, obviously were not of much interest to the company. Innovation project ideas with doubtful contribution, or with a judgment that is not yet consensual, should be kept on the list. Eliminated project ideas have to be saved in a corresponding database that should be accessible company wide. The description of the selected technologies should comprise the basic functionalities and the current applications of the technology. The prioritization should show the risk and the newness of the technologies in a cross-comparison, using the risk portfolio or the integration of the innovation opportunities in the innovation architecture.

• Opportunities and threats of these technologies described in two scenarios, in the one case, when the company becomes active with the technology and, in the other case, when the company does not become active with the technology. The scenarios should not be too complex as their elaboration should be possible in a reasonable amount of time and with a reasonable amount of resources. Thus, as a basis for the scenarios, in the first place the results from the analysis conducted in order to build up the evaluation frame should be used.

Finally, 'Issue generation' is used for a company-internal communication strategy on the issues of concern. The goal of this strategy is to communicate the results of the strategic analysis done so far and later to various circles of people in different stage of the strategic planning process. It is suggested, for example, that the results of the strategic analysis so far be communicated to a circle of people composed of persons who will henceforth be increasingly involved in the strategic planning process: they are members of the top management and the board of the company. To these people, the findings are best communicated as threats rather than as opportunities. Later, after the decision is made about which innovation ideas to realize and which to drop, it is suggested to formulate the resulting strategic implementation projects be formulated as opportunities rather than as threats (see Chapter 2, 'Solutions from industry-level focused research', Cluster 1B).

Investigate (process phase 2.1.b)

The strategic analysis described in the previous sections, starting from 'strategic intelligence' to 'acknowledgment', was mainly charged with gathering information for new technologies and analyzing their resulting innovation project ideas. The examinations conducted in all those phases of the strategic planning process aimed, on the one hand, to cluster innovation project ideas, (for example, according to their level of newness or risk) and, on the other hand, to sensitize the organization to recognize those innovation ideas that could be beneficial for the company's present and projected future competitive situation, or that could trigger a discontinuity in the competitive environment of the company. As a result a list with strategic issues of concern was elaborated that comprised major and particular strategic challenges due to general technological tendencies as well as to opportunities and threats coming from concrete high risk innovation project ideas. In other words, a great number of innovation project ideas have been collected and analyzed in order to be prepared for as many possible alternative conditions or states that the company might have to adopt, in order to react to or to initiate unexpected changes in its strategic environment. Looking for so many alternatives is done with the aim of handling the origin of the inherent problem of strategic planning with discontinuous technologies and radical innovation: a situation of uncertainty (see also Chapter 1).

Being prepared for a great number of alternative company conditions increases the probability of being forearmed for unpredicted, unexpected, discontinuous technology change. The drawback of this management procedure is that the complexity of handling the problem increases with the number of alternative company conditions. Furthermore, keeping the company up for managing this complexity would be costly and inefficient in the long run.

Complexity describes the characteristic of a system to adapt to a multitude of different conditions (Malik, 2001a: 4). In this case the system is the company; it can adapt to a great number of alternative conditions according to the development of its competitive environment. This is illustrated in Figure 4.31. It shows that, although the conditions or a state a company can adopt in the past and the present can be clearly appointed, it is much more difficult or even impossible to decide on conditions to adopt in the future.

The strategic planning process described so far tried to counteract uncertainty by increasing the level of complexity. It looked at every possibility

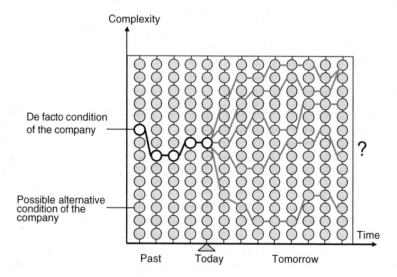

Figure 4.31   Clear conditions of the company in the past and the present – uncertain conditions in the future

Source: Tschirky and Koruna, 1998: 219.

1. Competence fit
Competence describes the *ability* to
respond to change

3. Risk response
Risk response describes tactics to
minimize risk

2. Strategic flexibility
Flexibility describes the *agility* to
respond to change

Figure 4.32   Three criteria in 'Investigate' to reduce complexity

that supports the company in order to be able to adopt a multitude of alternative conditions. A second management procedure counteracting uncertainty is to reduce complexity by limiting the number of possible conditions to create transparency (Tschirky and Koruna, 1998: 219).

Reducing complexity is the main goal of the step 'Investigate'. In order to reduce the number of innovation project ideas that shape the condition of the company, 'Investigate' uses a number of criteria. There are three different criteria, (1) one for competence fit, (2) one for strategic flexibility and (3) one for risk response. The criteria are designed to select a minimum of innovation project ideas out of the prioritized list elaborated in the previous process step, so that the company still maintains the best possible initial position to adapt to or to initiate discontinuous technology changes in its competitive environment. Thus, the *competence fit criteria* aims to select all those innovation project ideas that create within the company the ability to react to strategic changes. These abilities should be built up through various technological competencies. The *strategic flexibility criterion* aims to select all those innovation project ideas that create within the company the agility to react to strategic changes. The agility to react to changes qualifies the multitude of alternatives to do so in terms of timing. The *risk response criterion* aims to select those innovation project ideas with a manageable overall risk (see Figure 4.32). All three analyses are conducted just as the previous analysis on high risk innovation project ideas; they are performed and coordinated by a corporate unit.

Competence fit (process phase 2.1.b)
As already mentioned above, the competence fit criterion aims to select all those innovation project ideas that create within the company the ability to react to unexpected environmental changes. Thus, an ability to react to unexpected changes has to be built up by learning those technological competencies in advance that are fundamental to the change.

Competence is the ability of an organization to sustain coordinated deployment of assets and capabilities in ways that help the organization achieve its goals. Note that this concept of competence has three essential elements: (1) coordination of assets and capabilities; (2) intention in deploying assets and capabilities to specific purposes; and (3) goal-seeking as the driver of organizational action. (Sanchez, 2001: 7)[26]

According to this definition, the competence fit analysis has to select and manipulate assets and capabilities in such a way as to achieve the goal of reducing the company's vulnerability to failing in the face of discontinuities. In the context of strategic technology planning, these assets and capabilities are based on a number of technology innovation project ideas that are analyzed in the strategic planning process. Competence fit aims to learn in advance about technological assets and capabilities so that the uncertainty inherent to discontinuities can be relieved, then deployed if necessary, to master the initiated discontinuous changes.

As it is difficult to know which competencies to select, the 'competence fit' step is designed to choose more than just one technological competence to learn. It rather suggests choosing a full range of competencies covering the whole variety of uncertainty in the competitive environment of the company. Due to generally limited resources, it is, however, not always possible for a company to learn a multitude of competencies at the same time in order to only use a handful of them in the case where a discontinuous change happens. Thus, a balanced portfolio of competencies to learn has to be elaborated. This portfolio should be managed in a profitable way in order to stay independent from third party budgeting decisions within the company. In order to compose the right portfolio, the 'competence fit' process step is composed of three analyses: (1) elaborate which competencies are hidden behind a selected combination of technology project ideas; (2) analyse how learning these competencies covers uncertain changes that are hard to predict in the competitive environment and create a strategic option for the future; (3) analyze how learning these competencies supports existing competencies and expected changes in the competitive environment. The last analysis is done in order to attain the previously mentioned balance of the portfolio. It aims to also include project ideas that are not exclusively designated to uncertainties by building up competencies that will probably only be needed with a low degree of probability, but also to have projects that will be needed and out of which a return can be generated.

1. Elaborating the competencies behind technologies

The elaboration of which competencies are hidden behind a selected combination of technology project ideas is essential in order to formulate which general benefit is apparent from the selection and learning that those competencies can bring. The benefit should be held neutral and not specifically related to the company, formulated in a general way, held qualitative and free from a strong goal or application orientation. This way the whole competence potential of a set of innovation project ideas can be assessed, rather than when it is assessed right from the beginning within a specific company focus. This assessment can be done in a workshop regrouping R&D specialists from the corporate level together with external technology consultants or venture capital specialists. This assessment seems most effective if the people involved are not too business-oriented or market-focused.

This publication promotes the development of long-term new competencies by a corporate R&D unit instead of a business unit. However, corporate R&D units have become unpopular in certain industries (see Practice example 4.7) as it was difficult to directly measure their return on investment; Practice example 4.8 shows a number of arguments supporting such organizations.

Corporate units in research and technology began to become popular during the economic boom of the 1960s. Major companies created such units in order to promote research in novel and high risk fields with the hope of generating radical innovation. During these times of economic wealth effectiveness of research activities and market relevance in research was secondary. In big companies these units were basically allowed to do blue sky research representing a grassy play area for outstanding researchers.

With the increasing competition and changing economic pressure in the 1970s and 1980s many of these corporate units were shut down and the remaining ones had to justify their existence by beginning to generate return. Today, more than ever, corporate research units have to prove that the research they do is relevant to the market and contributing to future return. Thus, corporate units face a fundamental dilemma: on the one hand, the research they do should be relevant for the market; on the other hand, falling back on mere incremental innovation is fatal as their existence is justified by the mission to generate radical innovation.

In order to overcome this dilemma this thesis presents the options approach described in the 'competence fit' phase with the matrix matching innovation project ideas as strategic options with key uncertainties encountered in the company units. As soon as an innovation project idea can be placed as an option to cover an uncertainty in the strategic plan of a unit, the relevance for the market is given as a business unit's plan is market focused. Thus, the market relevance of a corporate unit high risk innovation project idea is more market relevant and of higher strategic importance the more business units see its relevance demonstrated in the matrix. Project ideas that cannot be placed as options thus do not show market relevance and can be eliminated.

The key to this inquiry for market relevance of corporate unit research project ideas is the approach to project the high risk innovation ideas on the long-term future of a business unit perspective.

Practice example 4.7   The market use of high risk competence learning projects

ABB's decision in favor of a corporate research unit is based on the following seven points:

1. *Risk pooling*: High risk (technology risk) projects are pooled in corporate research for an upfront technology evaluation. This way those projects do not interfere or break with ABB's business areas' R&D plans and budgets.
2. *Competence/resource pooling*: The number of people including lab infrastructure critical for high risk technology projects is not justified for an individual business area (BA) or business area unit (BA-U). Pooled at Corporate Research it is, however, accessible as competence for the whole ABB group. Thus, competent people can be deployed more flexibly in various businesses across organizational and country boundaries.
3. *Internal technology transfer and synergies*: When Corporate Research acts as a central information hub, newly developed technologies can be multiplied for various BAs and BA-Us. A silo view towards specific technology solutions can be avoided.
4. *Neutral technology partner*: Corporate Research represents an independent and impartial body inside the company providing technology advice to BA/BA-U.
5. *Technology scouting*: Corporate Research can explore emerging technologies or new areas, e.g. in collaboration with universities in very early stages where BA/BA-U relevance and assignments are not yet clear.
6. *Protection from short-termism*: Not being fully absorbed by short-term daily business, Corporate Research creates an innovative climate that allows medium and long-term views.
7. *Technology showcasing*: Corporate Research represents a central place for demonstrating the company's latest technology findings to customers, analysts, journalists, universities, etc.

Practice example 4.8 ABB, seven reasons in favor of a corporate research unit
Source: Interview at ABB, 2005, M. Reisel, T. Jäger, G. Trauffler.

2. Covering uncertainties with competencies: create a strategic option for the future

After this first general non-company-related assessment about what competencies the technology innovation projects could bring, the second analysis in 'competence fit' is company-specific. Its task is to determine what benefit the formulated competencies bring to the company in order to counteract an unpredictable development of the environment.

Concretely speaking, the project idea's competencies formulated in the previous analysis are opposed to uncertainties that business and corporate units encounter when dealing with long-term strategic planning in order to detect those ideas that most absorb and counteract uncertainty. Those uncertainties should be key uncertainties, depending on which whole alternatives elaborated strategically would become entirely obsolete. These uncertainties in a way represent major turning points in the future that can only be predicted with very low accuracy, but depend on which totally different strategic measures have to be taken.

Best practice case 4.20 shows how Philips tries to focus the R&D activities of its corporate units on the market.

Miller and Waller (2003: 100) suggest structuring uncertainties according to three main categories: general environmental uncertainties, industry uncertainties and company uncertainties. Table 4.2 clusters the three main categories in subcategories and provides some specific examples of uncertainty. The typology of the uncertainties listed in Table 4.2 provides a framework for managers to identify relevant uncertainties. Once managers identify the relevant uncertainties, they can think about how the uncertainties interrelate and the nature of their effects on the company's competitive environment and their consequences for the business's performance. Scenario planning helps to identify those uncertainties that could have the most significant effect on changes in the company's competitive environment. These uncertainties can be considered as key uncertainties.

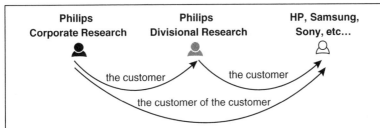

In order to secure the market relevance of corporate research, Philips introduced the customer of the customer policy. One measure within this policy is that Philips Corporate Research organizes fairs for the customers of its customers. The customers of Philips Corporate Research being the company internal divisions, their customers of the customers are, for example, the big electronic companies buying at Philips, such as Sony, HP, Samsung, etc. Invited are the top management of these companies as well as researchers and marketing people. The goal is to show the customers of the customers what long-term research is being conducted at the Philips corporate labs. Feedback from the attendees is a good indicator for the market relevance of the research done. Additionally 'research can become a commercial tool' as the marketing effect of such fairs is not to be underestimated.

If the fair succeeds in getting its attendees enthusiastic about its research, the divisions will be delighted too as the knowledge developed in corporate research will eventually come up to the divisions.

Best practice case 4.20   Ensuring market relevance at Philips Corporate Research
Source: Interview at Philips, 2004, G. Trauffler.

Table 4.2   Three main categories of uncertainty

General environmental uncertainties	
Political:	Terrorism, war, changes in government
Government policy:	Fiscal and monetary policies, trade restrictions, regulations affecting the business sector, tax policy
Macroeconomic:	Exchange rates, interest rates, inflation, terms of trade
Social:	Social unrest, shift in social concerns
Natural:	Variations in weather, natural disasters
Industry uncertainties	
Input market:	Quality of inputs, supply relative to industry demand
Product market:	Consumer tastes, market demand, availability of substitutes
Competition:	Pricing and other forms of rivalries, new entrants, product and process
Company uncertainty	
Operations:	Labor relations, availability of inputs, production variability and downtime
Liability:	Product liability, emission of pollutants
R&D:	R&D activities, regulatory approval of new products
Credit:	Problems with collectibles
Behavior:	Opportunistic behaviors by managers or employees

Source: Miller and Waller, 2003: 100.

Following Miller and Waller (2003: 100ff.) it is suggested that this analysis should begin on the business unit level, as different businesses face different uncertainties. As an initial position for this analysis, scenario planning is recommended. For this purpose, either new scenarios can be developed or the images of the future developed in the 'Acknowledge' phase (see this chapter, 'Acknowledge') can be used. In the most probable image of the future that was going to be used for the elaboration of the long-term strategy, key uncertainties have to be identified. These uncertainties are so essential that so far they represent the weak points of the scenarios hindering the formulation of a clear strategy. The key uncertainties can be structured according to the framework given in Table 4.2.

After determining the key uncertainties for each business, findings should be checked across the units to see how or whether uncertainties affect other units:

Certain contingencies may be relevant to only one business. Others may have broader effects across businesses. These effects across businesses could be similar (i.e., the businesses benefit together) or in opposing directions (i.e., some businesses benefit and others are harmed). By identifying the relevant contingencies across a firm's portfolio of businesses, managers gain an understanding of the aggregate corporate-level exposure profile. This information is essential for formulating hedging strategies. Managing overall corporate risk is a higher priority than managing the risks of individual business units. An understanding of how environmental uncertainties affect the company as a whole guides corporate-level hedging strategies. (Miller and Waller, 2003: 101)

Such a cross-check can be easily performed using a matrix, placing the key uncertainties on the vertical axis and the units on the horizontal axis. In this matrix, every uncertainty can be checked to determine whether it affects units other than the one it initially issued from.

Eventually those innovation project ideas within the company that create the ability to react to unexpected environmental changes are selected according to the degree to which the competencies that they bring to the company help to cover the uncertainties detected previously in the scenarios. The logic behind this is that the innovation projects that best counteract unexpected changes in the competitive environment are those that best counteract the uncertainties that might be the cause of the change's unpredictability. Additionally, the innovation project ideas to select from have already been identified as the innovation ideas with the greatest potential for initiating a discontinuity or a radical innovation. Thus, matching the uncertainties from the most probable scenarios with the competencies provided by the innovation project ideas, which are most likely to initiate a discontinuity, seems to be a favorable procedure.

For those innovation project ideas with the power to counteract or to weaken an uncertainty, an initial investment might be considered in order to build up first competence probes. Doing so enables the company not only to better know the potential of the technology and its competence, but it also creates a possibility for the company to further invest in the technology in order to further develop the first probe of it made so far. This approach follows 'the probe and learn' procedure described in Chapter 2, 'Solutions from the company-level focused research', Cluster 2B. From a strategic point of view it is similar to the rationale of the real options approach.

The real options approach was derived from finance research, where options analysis was created to quantitatively value investments under uncertainty. 'An option is the right, but not the obligation, to take an action in the future' (Amram and Kulatilaka, 1999: 5).

Real options have only recently begun to influence management practice (Miller and Waller, 2003: 94). The real option approach described in this publication is qualitative rather than quantitative. It follows the approach described by Miller and Waller (2003), who give a brief and very clear description of the history and rationale of real options in the following quotation.

Real options at a glance

In 1977, Stewart Myers published an influential article in the *Journal of Financial Economics* in which he noted that company value results from both (1) assets in place and (2) opportunities to purchase real assets at potentially favorable prices in the future. He termed the latter asset category 'real options', drawing attention to the similarities to financial call options. Broadly categorized, real options confer possibilities either to acquire assets (call options) or divest assets (put options) in the future at prices that may be attractive relative to those faced by parties not holding options. Whereas financial options confer rights to buy or sell financial assets, real options have physical and, knowledge-based resources as their underlying assets. Financial options have precise exercise prices and fixed expiration dates. By contrast, real options generally are not specified contractually, so their exercise prices and expiration dates are functions of the resources involved and the competitive context. The threat of preemption by competitors is a key determinant of when real options expire (i.e., their durations).

At the heart of the real option perspective is the notion that the values of real resources vary over time in ways that cannot be fully predicted. By holding a call option on a strategic resource, the firm stands to capture any value above the exercise price. The exercise price is the additional investment required to deploy the resource (e.g., the cost of expanding production capacity to bring a new product to market). Alternatively, by holding a put option, the firm can avoid any loss of resource value below the exercise price. For a put option, the exercise price is the net value realized when exiting a business. In short, by holding an option, the company can take advantage of resource price moves, but avoids exercising the option if losses would result. In this way, option holders limit adverse outcomes (i.e. downside risk).

There are many examples of real options. Companies purchase real call options by making foothold investments in new markets. Investments in R&D activities and equity positions in other companies are common examples of real call options. The flexibility to scale back (or exit entirely) is the essential characteristic of put options. Examples of real put options include the use of temporary workers, rented plants and equipment, and exit provisions in joint venture contracts. Options to switch between modes of production, products, or distribution channels involve both a put (i.e., abandoning one mode) and a call (i.e., adopting another mode). In each case, by making an initial investment in flexibility, the company reduces its subsequent cost of altering its strategy.

Under uncertainty, real options are valuable because they give management the flexibility to acquire, divest, and switch resources when such moves prove advantageous. Waiting for the resolution of uncertain contingencies can greatly enhance the value of investments relative to go/no go commitments that do not allow for flexibility and discretionary timing. Additionally, managers are not relegated to passively holding real options, allowing forces outside their control to determine their values. Instead, managers seek to enhance the values of their real options by positively affecting the values of the underlying real resources. (Miller and Waller, 2003: 97)

Projecting the real options theory described above to the present analysis, when trying to match uncertainties and technology competencies that absorb these uncertainties, the competencies represent the real options. They create a strategic option (call option) for the future by an initial investment to build up first competencies in the chosen technology. Doing so opens the possibility for the company to later further invest in this technology once the initial uncertainty this option was covering turns out to be the initiator of a discontinuous change in the company's competitive environment. In this case, initial competencies already existing, deepening the latter can be done much faster than competitors. This is equivalent to exercising the technology option and capturing the value above the exercising price. This is possible due to the first-mover advantage of a more rapid market entry which enables the acquisition of rapid market share combined with the creation of entry barriers for competitors.

A match between uncertainties detected, on a corporate and/or on a business unit level, with a counteracting competency, results in positioning a strategic option. In such a mindset, a bundle of technology project ideas represent a competence within the context of competition. A competence then represents an option in the context of uncertainty. For positioning options the strategic options can be found using a simple matrix similar to that shown in Figure 4.33.

	BU 1	BU 2	BU 3	BU 4	Corporate
Solidity of the supply chain (imaging chips)	Option A	X	Option A	–	X
Internet hype (connectivity, networking)	X	Option B	Option F	X	Option D
Technology standards (CMOS/CCD)	Option D	–	–	–	–
Accepted quality ('good enough' picture)	–	Option D	Option C	Option B	X
Key uncertainty 5	Option C	–	X	X	Option E
Key uncertainty 6	...	...	...	...	...

–: not matching   x: matching   Options A–E: matching and covered by an option

Figure 4.33 Matrix matching strategic options with key uncertainties encountered in several business units: example of the uncertainties involved with the emergence of the digital imaging technologies in the traditional photography industry

The matrix in Figure 4.33 opposes key uncertainties to business units and the corporate level. As an example Figure 4.33 lists some of the uncertainties traditional photo camera manufacturers faced at the beginning of the last decade, the period when digital imaging technologies emerged.

If a key uncertainty concerns a business unit, the matching field is filled by an 'X' indicating its affiliation, or by an option that can counteract this uncertainty in its corresponding business unit. A dash symbolizes that the uncertainty does not affect the corresponding business unit. An option placed in a field of the matrix counteracts one or more key uncertainties in one or various business units. Such an option is composed of one single technology innovation project idea or of a combination of project ideas providing the competencies to absorb the matching uncertainty.

Technology project ideas and their corresponding competencies, which could be positioned in this matrix in the form of a strategic option, should be included in a special portfolio. This portfolio represents a first choice of high risk technology innovation project ideas that have been collected and examined all along the strategic planning process so far. Elaborated with the goal of building up new competencies, it is called a 'competence-building portfolio'. It includes a handful of project ideas, which have shown a 'competence fit' with the strategic needs of the company, providing it with strategic options for the long-term future. These project ideas have the power either to initiate themselves a discontinuity in the competitive environment of the company or to counteract and absorb the consequences of an unexpected discontinuous change in the latter. The axes of the portfolio measure, on the one hand, the number of uncertainties covered by the project and, on the other hand, the risk of the project (see Figure 4.34). *Those innovation project ideas that are the basis for most options are the ones with the highest strategic importance.*

3. Support of existing competencies and/or expected changes in the competitive environment

The concluding analysis in the 'competence fit' step examines how learning from the competencies initially formulated supports existing assets and capabilities of expected changes in the competitive environment of the company. As mentioned above, this analysis is done in order to balance the competence-building portfolio of technology innovation projects that so far only contains high risk project ideas for the use of uncertain happenings. For the project ideas that are new and highly risky for the company it is not even certain if the competencies built up by their realization is needed, as the event that they are realized for is uncertain. Thus, these projects risk generating a lot of expense without yielding any certain return. Keeping this in mind, the present analysis aims to find additional, more reliable uses for the competencies built up by these same high risk projects. To do so, the competencies the project ideas provide are assessed for their use in existing or

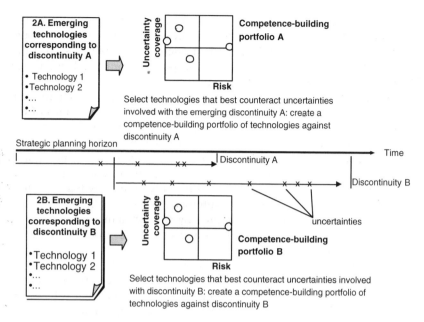

Figure 4.34 Creating the competence-building portfolio

planned company applications in order to prepare expected changes in the competitive environment. This analysis is relatively easy to perform in a workshop held on the business unit level with managers that are involved with the formulation of business unit strategy formulation.

Strategic flexibility (process phase 2.1.b)

In the previous analysis 'competence fit' provided the ability to react strategically to major changes such as discontinuities in competition by selecting a first set of high risk innovation project ideas in order to learn new competencies. The actual analysis aims to examine the strategic flexibility of those selected project ideas. Strategic flexibility describes the agility of the company to adapt to unexpected strategic changes. Agility takes a general and time-valuing perspective of those projects enabling strategic changes in periods of uncertainty (Hitt and Freeman, 2001: 97). When valuating flexibility, Ansoff (1984: 76ff.) differentiates between external and internal strategic flexibility.

External strategic flexibility addresses issues of risk diversification; competencies should not be selected so that the company becomes overly dependent on one business unit to the extent to which an unexpected or discontinuous change in its strategic environment can 'cripple it'. Furthermore, cross-vulnerabilities among business units should be limited while still respecting the synergic effect between them. A single discontinuity should not impact the firm simultaneously in several business areas. Thus, business units should be aligned in order to depend on different assets and capabilities such as different technologies, economic, cultural and political climates. Thus, a high degree of external flexibility is reached by technological and market diversity.

Internal strategic flexibility influences the speed with which internal changes can be performed. It depends on how easily configurations of the company's resources, capabilities and skills can be shifted for use in other additional purposes, and how rapidly they can be shifted from one unit to another. This is, however, a difficult goal to achieve, as the ultimate flexibility would be 'total financial liquidity' – having the firm's assets quickly convertible into money. But this path is possible only in the very few firms that are neither capital nor technology intensive. For most, the potential for enhancing internal flexibility is limited by the inherent convertibility of technology skills, equipment, facilities and inventories from one business unit to another (Ansoff, 1984: 78).

Internal and external flexibility are in conflict. A high level of external flexibility based on highly diversified positions in markets through a wide range of assets is counter-productive to internal flexibility that is based on convertibility of assets allowing the alternative and rapid reuse of existing assets for different purposes. For competencies to be highly convertible, a focused rather than a diversified portfolio of assets is advantageous. Thus, a high level of external flexibility decreases internal flexibility and vice versa.

The formulation of strategic flexibility as a criterion for determining whether to include a specific technology innovation project idea or not into the portfolio of competence building can be based on the conflict described above between external and internal strategic flexibility. In the case of the high degree of external flexibility, the diversity of competencies to include in the portfolio of innovation project ideas is eminently important. This means that the company can react to a variety of unpredictable changes that might happen in the competitive environment. Thus, external flexibility is important as long as the range of possible alternatives of changes is great. This is usually the case the more uncertain and unforeseeable and the more distant in the future the moment of change is supposed to be.

However, with decreasing uncertainty in the course of time, the range of change alternatives consolidate, and external flexibility becomes less important. The more accurately the alternatives of change can be narrowed, the more focused the management of the portfolio of competence building. With the moment of change approaching, it then becomes more and more important to be able to rapidly and smoothly perform the change. To do so, internal flexibility is most important as it enables resources to be converted rapidly, so that they can be used in alternative ways. Thus, the use of the criterion of strategic flexibility for selecting innovation project ideas to include in the portfolio of competence building depends on the type of flexibility needed.

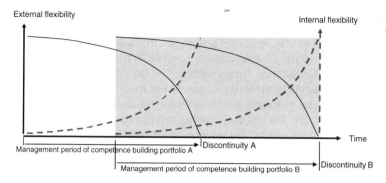

Figure 4.35 Balance between internal and external flexibility in the course of time

External flexibility provided by the competencies of a specific innovation project idea is the selection criterion as long as there is a great deal of uncertainty around the alternatives of changes. This is usually the case the further in the future a discontinuity is assumed to be.

Internal flexibility provided by the competencies of a specific innovation project idea is the selection criterion as soon as the alternatives of changes decrease and the sooner the discontinuity is expected. The balance between internal and external strategic flexibility that should be followed in the course of time is illustrated in Figure 4.35.

Risk response (process phase 2.1.b)

This third analysis of the 'Investigate' process phase is applied after the two previous criteria, 'competence fit' and 'strategic flexibility', have already reduced the initially great number of high risk innovation project ideas to a handful of selected projects. The projects that are going to be considered in this analysis obviously are or might become of great strategic importance for the company. Along the whole strategic planning process they have managed to attract enough attention so that they have been forwarded for further strategic analysis. Despite their actual or potential importance, one has to bear in mind that all these project ideas have been rated as high risk right from the beginning by a rough risk assessment (see this chapter, 'Quick assessment').

It is the aim of the actual 'risk response' step, now that the number of project ideas is manageable, to examine more in detail and to explicitly formulate the initially detected risk and to elaborate alternatives for risk response. The logic behind this step is a risk-focused input–output consideration. The desired output is that the company can estimate the benefit it may receive from the realization of a specific innovation project idea. It can be confirmed by all the analysis conducted so far. Knowing the desired output 'risk response' checks what input is necessary for the realization of a project idea.

An obvious disproportion between input and output, detected by 'risk response' represents the last selection criteria for the innovation project ideas.

A further goal of 'risk response' is to summarize and simultaneously review the consistency of the analysis conducted so far in the 'Decide and formulate' phase in a condensed way. This is achieved by the design of the process used to systematically elaborate a risk response. For most of the data processed in this process, access to former analysis conducted along the strategic planning process is necessary. The process is presented in Figure 4.36.

The risk response process is based on the understanding of risk described in this chapter, 'Quick assessment'. Following this understanding, risk consideration should always include previous uncertainty considerations as well. Thus, systematically reaching a level of risk that is acceptable for management decisions to be taken, the process starts from a state of uncertainty. For this purpose, a double iterative process approach is suggested. In a first process loop, the management of uncertainty through an iterative process is suggested. The goal is to find out what alternative stages of outcome a technology innovation project could provoke in the industry it affects. In a second loop, building on the insight from the first one, the technology is related to the company context. Through the management of risk, the company should strive to formulate the influence of a technology by determining risk as precisely as possible and avoiding it if this risk is not acceptable.

As an initial step in the first loop, different scenarios have to be built. The scenarios describe how the technology will evolve in performance and price, and how it will affect the industrial context and its competitive environment. To build the scenarios, data from the 'Acknowledge' process phase

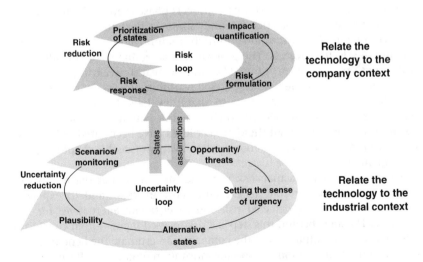

Figure 4.36   Process for systematic elaboration of risk response

may be accessed. This previous phase of the strategic planning process has elaborated a number of scenarios and images of the long-term future (see this chapter, 'Acknowledge'). From the most likely scenarios, the effect of the technology will be qualified in terms of opportunities and threats that will impact the company. These opportunities and threats can be taken to reformulate and detail the initial sense of urgency formulated also in the 'Acknowledge' phase. This step in the uncertainty-reducing process is an opportunity to recall the sense of urgency originating from the competitive environment or from a specific technology. Recalling the sense of urgency seems to be even more important here, as the 'Decide and formulate' phase is approaching.

As opportunities and threats are interdependent (Ward and Chapman, 2003: 98), a set of specific opportunities and threats together form a stage or a possible outcome. By combining interdependent opportunities and threats, a number of stages may be formed. Further, the plausibility and, for a later point in time, the probability as to whether these stages will happen or not, is assessed. Estimating exact probabilities right from the very first attempt of evaluating a stage is difficult; it is only through the course of time that knowledge can be built up in order to substitute plausibility considerations with probabilities.

Thus, at first this step in the process is the transition from the initial position of uncertainty; the unknown-unknown to the known-unknowns and unknown-knowns. It is what Gil-Aluja (2001: 26) calls the attempt to jump from uncertainty to randomness. This step is an essential one when trying to set a basis for decision-making as it represents the transition from subjectivity to objectivity. According to Gil-Alunja (2001: 26):

uncertainty is insufficiently structured and when explaining it, this is done subjectively. Randomness, on the other hand, is tied to the concept of probability, which in itself is a measurement of observations repeated over time and/or in space; randomness is a measurement of observed facts, as it constitutes an evaluation which should be as objective as possible.

As already mentioned in this chapter, 'Process and methods overview', given that objectivity is not possible in an uncertain phase and that subjectivity alone is not sufficient for effective decision-making, the next best choice is what Tschirky (2003b: 28) calls 'inter-subjectivity'.

Inter-subjectivity is consensus-oriented decision-making among people with different backgrounds from inside and outside the company. A possibility to promote inter-subjectivity in a company may be reached, for example, through the gatekeepers system (see this chapter, 'Structures overview'). Inter-subjectivity might be one solution to the problem of assessing qualitatively (and especially quantitatively) the implications, impact and probability of new technologies. Beside inter-subjectivity, decision-making in the uncertainty process loop needs the support of monitoring activities conducted with every completed iteration. Its task is to provide the latest information required to build up further knowledge and to eliminate uncertainty. Once probabilities have been attached to possible alternative states, one can proceed to the second loop, as the states together with probability represent risks.

The conclusion of the uncertainty management cycle delivers alternative states composed of the combination of opportunities and threats. These states represent the input for the risk management cycle indirectly relating the technology innovation project idea to the company context. The analysis done in the risk management cycle consists of exploring the consequences of different states for the company after having prioritized the latter according to their level of plausibility or probability. This prioritization can be checked for consistency with the prioritization done earlier in the 'Acknowledge' phase – setting the sense of urgency (see this chapter, 'Acknowledge'). Further, the quantitative impact is estimated in the case of the occurrence of a specific stage and the consequences for the company are described. Eventually the consequences are formulated as risks. In order to formulate risks it is necessary to project impact and probability of a state to the company. When trying to assess the impact of specific opportunities and threats, management has to make certain assumptions as not all the facts are known. It is very important to be aware of the assumptions made at this point in time, as the validity of impacts depends greatly on them. In order to guarantee the validity of projected impacts, management has to make sure that assumptions will be able to be proven in the future. Proving these assumptions is the task of the uncertainty management cycle, as assumptions have to be made out of lacking knowledge, meaning out of uncertainty. Trying to do so, the uncertainty-reducing process loop occupies a major information coordination role in the whole strategic planning process. On the one hand, it has to cooperate tightly with strategic intelligence in order to receive that information needed to support the assumptions and, on the other hand, a close cooperation with the risk-reducing process loop is needed to refine the assumptions that are the basis for the risk-impact estimations.

Applying the risk-management process simultaneously to the uncertainty process that checks and revises the assumptions made permits risk to be detailed and eliminated in each iteration.

Best practice case 4.21 illustrates how intensively Intel uses risk management over all its innovation activities in order to prevent and reduce the risk of innovation endeavors.

Evaluate moderate risk innovation opportunities (process phase 2.2)

The process phase 'Evaluate moderate risk innovation opportunities (2.2)' is the counterpart of the phase (3a). Both process phases are run in parallel but

Intel intensively uses risk management to handle financial, technical and social risk in order to insure the quality of innovation projects. Risk management at Intel is meant not only to minimize the probability and impact of adverse events *but also* to maximize probability and impact of positive events to project objectives. Thus the company has developed its own risk-management process which is designed as an iterative process circle with six steps (see diagram to the right): (1) risk management planning is the first step of the process deciding how to approach and plan risk;

management activities for the innovation; (2) risk identification, identifies which risks might affect the innovation; (3) risk prioritization assesses the impact and probability of identified risks and prioritizes them according to their potential effect on planned innovation project objectives; (4) quantitative risk analysis applies numerical analysis on probability of each risk, on the impact on project objectives and on the extent of overall risk; (5) risk response planning determines actions to explore opportunities and to reduce threats to objectives; and (6) risk tracking and control keeps track of identified risks, monitors residual risks, identifies new risks, ensures execution of risk plans and evaluates their effectiveness in reducing risk. This last sixth step is considered especially important at Intel, as tracking risks helps to understand the origin of risks so that they can be avoided in the future. The arrows cross connecting the steps (6) and (2), and (3) and (5), indicate that after the process has been run for a first time not all the steps have to be used in every iteration.

Intel uses the risk-management cycle, as described above, over all phases of an innovation project: from the emergence of the innovation idea in the exploration phase to the commercialization of the final product. In every phase, different risk issues have to be managed. This understanding is illustrated in the diagram below with an exemplary innovation process. People involved in the risk considerations along such a process include innovators, change agents, decision-makers and innovation champions.

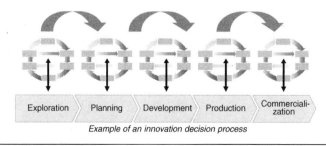

Example of an innovation decision process

Best practice case 4.21   Risk management at Intel

Source: Interview and presentation at Intel, 2003, G. Trauffler.

with a different focus. The focus of the present phase is to evaluate moderate risk innovation opportunities delivered in the form of technology-innovation project ideas. Usually these innovation opportunities are of a moderate level of newness to the company and enhance the existing businesses of the company. Thus, this process phase is run within each of the business units.

As displayed in the overall process, in Figure 4.3, this phase comprises three different analyses that are to be processed in every business unit and in collaboration with the operational product and business intelligence processes: (1) a strategic fit evaluation; (2) a quantitative and qualitative evaluation; and (3) a make or buy–keep or sell evaluation. This analysis is well described in the work of Sauber (2004: 128ff.). Thus, explaining these different evaluations, the following paragraphs will focus on a brief overview of Sauber's descriptions.

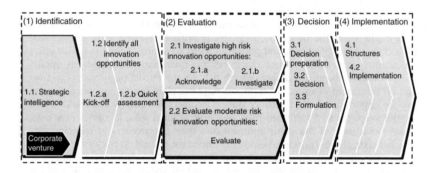

Strategic fit (process phase 2.2)

Strategic fit evaluation aims to check the consistency of the innovation opportunities. Consistency is itself evaluated among the innovation opportunities and with its company-internal and -external environment. The evaluation of consistency follows the three different types of strategic fits according to Porter (1996: 70ff.):

1. First-order fit is simple consistency between each activity.
2. Second-order fit occurs when activities are reinforcing.
3. Third-order fit goes beyond activity reinforcement to optimization of effort.

Sauber (2004: 135f.) suggests a set of tools to check the strategic fit of innovation opportunities. These tools answer the key questions of this first evaluation:

- Is the consistency between each innovation opportunity and the overall consistency insured, especially the fit between market pull and technology push?

- Do the innovation opportunities reinforce each other and the company activities in terms of its competencies, and especially its core competencies?
- Do the innovation opportunities optimize the efforts for the future, in terms of scenarios?
- Do the innovation opportunities conform to the corporate/business unit strategy?

The more positively these questions can be answered, the higher the level of the strategic fit of the innovation project idea.

Quantitative and qualitative (process phase 2.2)

Quantitative and qualitative evaluation aims to find out if innovation opportunities are feasible in terms of knowledge, in terms of time and if they are profitable. For this analysis Sauber (2004: 136) suggests, first evaluating feasibility and calculating the degree profitability. The degree of feasibility qualitatively checks what knowledge is missing in the company and how much time will be needed for the realization of an innovation project idea; the evaluation of profitability includes qualitative resource allocations and profitability calculations. At last, aided by the dynamic technology portfolio (see also this chapter, 'Acknowledge', Company internal analysis) the decision about which moderate risk innovation project idea to chose might be prepared. This choice is paraphrased by Brodbeck (1999: 2) with the question: 'which way to go?'

The key questions to be answered, according to Sauber (2004: 141), after the quantitative and qualitative evaluation are:

- Is the knowledge gap and this gap's strategic importance for each innovation opportunity known?
- Is the planning time necessary to develop an innovation opportunity known in detail?
- Are the financial key figures, required in the context of the company, for the innovation opportunities known?
- Is the dynamic technology portfolio meaningful?
- Can a decision be taken in terms of which way to go?

Make or buy/keep or sell (process phase 2.2)

Make or buy/keep or sell evaluation functions to prepare the decision about whether a part or a whole innovation opportunity is to be developed internally or externally, and if existing company assets should be kept or sold. For this analysis Sauber (2004: 141) reverts to Brodbeck's research (1999) and suggests the use of the innovation architecture.

Make or buy decisions consider the following aspects, according to Brodbeck (1999: 99):[27] the limited resources, development time, fixed costs, coordination, sourcing alternatives and cultural fit to the cooperation partners, etc.

Keep or sell decisions consider aspects, according to Brodbeck (1999: 114),[28] such as the internal return on investment, the possibility of selling as a basis for a higher market development, possible utilization alternatives, joint use of R&D learning curve, etc.

At the end of this analysis, Sauber (2004: 143) suggests the following key questions to be answered in a bundle:

- Has each innovation opportunity of the innovation architecture been analyzed in detail regarding how to develop it? Make it internally or buy externally?
- Is each bundle of object, methodological and meta-knowledge analyzed to determine if it is still needed? Should it be kept internally or should it be sold?
- Is the strategic path for each innovation opportunity known?

4   Decision (concept phase 3)

The strategic concept phase 'Decision (3)' uses all of the decision-preparing analysis done in phases (2.1) and (2.2) concerned with high and moderate risk innovation opportunities coming from both types of strategic units: from the corporate unit and from the different business units of the company. The goal of the phase 'Decision (3)' is to come to a decision about which innovation project ideas should be realized and how they should be realized. Finally, based upon these decisions, this phase is also where the formulation of an innovation strategy for the company's strategic units as part of, and aligned with, the corporate strategy takes place.

The tasks in the concept phase 'Decision (3)' may be structured in three parts in the process. These are: (1) decision preparation, (2) the decision itself and (3) the formulation of the decision and its consequences for the realization.

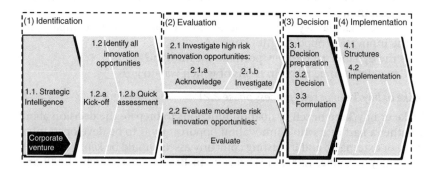

Decision preparation (process phase 3.1)

The input for the 'Decide and formulate' phase is given by those innovation project ideas that have been found strategically relevant after the analysis done in the processes (3a) and (3b). With this input, the 'Decide and formulate' phase is started by the elaboration of two different types of strategic documents. These documents are called strategic decision agendas. They are meant to prepare the decisions that form the strategic unit's innovation strategy by structuring the discussions along the 'Decide and formulate (4)' phase. The first type of strategic agenda is elaborated for discussions around high risk innovation opportunities supporting the decision of development strategic measures. This document is elaborated with the insight the people from the corporate unit gained during the process phase (2.1) analyzing the high risk innovation project ideas. The second type of strategic agenda is elaborated for discussions around medium risk innovation opportunity supporting the decision for competitive strategic measures. It is elaborated with the insight from people of different business units gained during the process phase (2.2) analyzing the medium risk innovation project ideas. The content of both strategic agendas[29] is structured in five discussion points (see Figure 4.37). There is one single strategic agenda for the corporate unit handling the discussions of high risk innovation opportunities and one strategic agenda for every business unit managing the discussions of medium risk innovation opportunities.

The strategic agenda's goal is to ultimately encompass the strategic decisions about which high and which medium risk innovation opportunities should be realized and how best to realize them. This decision is taken after point number five of each agenda has been reviewed. All previous points,

Strategic agenda for HIGH risk innovation opportunities (development strategic measures)	Phase	Strategic agenda for MEDIUM risk innovation opportunities (competitive strategic measures)	Phase
1. Trends and scenarios		**1. Initial position**	
• Vulnerability/requirements	3a	• Strength/weakness and core competences of the past	2a
• Potential disruptions	3a	• Short- and middle-term environmental, social, technology trends	3a
2. Uncertainties		**2. Innovation opportunities**	
• BU level uncertainties	3a	• Specific and potential fields of innovation opportunities	2a
• Corporate-level uncertainties	3a	• Demonstrate and retain potential varieties of future activities	2a
3. Technological opportunities			
• Newness	2b	**3. Strategy and gaps**	
• Risks	2b	• Identify gaps with the strategic fit	3b
• Risk response and uncertainty	3a	• Identify gaps for technological realization	3b
• Assumptions			
• Value proposition	3a		
• Flexibility and business relatedness	3a		
• Timing	3a		
4. Strategic options and competence building		**4. Innovation objective**	
• Competence fit and strategic importance	3a	• Decide which innovation objective to follow	3b
• Evaluate and place strategic options	3a	• Detail decision	3b
5. Organizational learning plan		**5. Business unit business plans**	
• Innovation project proposals			
• Innovation program proposals			
• Implementation procedures			

Figure 4.37   Strategic agenda for high and medium risk innovation opportunities as preparation for decisions about the innovation strategy

one to four in both agendas, are treated as information that is meant to justify and explain this last point. This information reviews the essentials of all the analysis conducted so far along the strategic planning process. The fifth and final point contains the learning plan for the high risk strategic agenda and the business plan for the medium risk strategic agenda. Both plans are the explicit formulations of high and medium risk project proposals that are used for the decision.

The content of a typical business plan following Hofmeister (1999: 190ff.) and a suggestion of a learning plan is shown in Figure 4.38. The learning and business plans are derived from the strategic agendas. There is one single learning plan for the corporate unit and one business plan for each business unit.

Details about the elements of a business plan can be found in literature: for example, in Ludolph and Lichtenberg (2001), Hofmeister (1999) or Bischof (2000). Generally speaking, a typical business plan is focused on short-term goals and describes, for example, the business, the marketing and operational procedures, or financial data. Thus, the project ideas that are submitted as proposals in the form of a business plan are projects that in the first place are product development projects based on mastered technologies with moderate risk and a moderate degree of newness. These mastered technologies are exactly the technologies that the company previously had to learn as part of competence-building goals. In order to learn about such technologies and to get to know their level of risk and newness to finally master it, the technologies have been submitted and accepted as proposals for competence learning in a learning plan. These activities show that the technologies submitted in a learning plan are of a much longer-term horizon than the ones in the business plan.

For every major competence the worth of which a company should judge, a separate learning plan may be submitted. One competence being based on at least one technology project idea, the company can thus decide upon the realization of many project ideas by looking at a few formulated learning plans.

The learning plan is designed to indicate opportunities to learn new competencies and acquire expertise in the long term by the realization of risky and radically new innovation project ideas.

The position 'I. The competence' in the learning plan as suggested in Figure 4.38 describes (A) the competence desired to build up, (B) the R&D activities that are necessary in order to do so, (C) the competitive advantage that the learning of these competences promise in the long-term future and (D) the development procedure. The development procedure roughly formulates the projects necessary to develop the competence in the form of a proposal. Realizing the definite formulation of the projects is done only after the decision about which competences to build up has been taken.

The position 'II. The expertise' in the learning plan describes in more detail some learning-related premises, such as the (A) patents and licenses

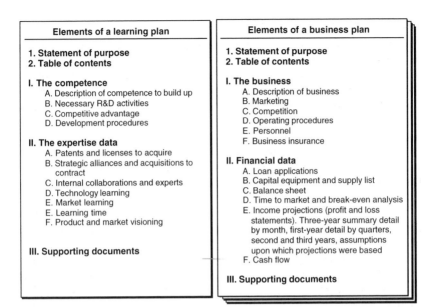

Elements of a learning plan	Elements of a business plan

1. Statement of purpose
2. Table of contents
 	
I. The competence
  A. Description of competence to build up
  B. Necessary R&D activities
  C. Competitive advantage
  D. Development procedures
 	
II. The expertise data
  A. Patents and licenses to acquire
  B. Strategic alliances and acquisitions to
    contract
  C. Internal collaborations and experts
  D. Technology learning
  E. Market learning
  E. Learning time
  F. Product and market visioning
 	
III. Supporting documents
	1. Statement of purpose
	2. Table of contents
	
	I. The business
	  A. Description of business
	  B. Marketing
	  C. Competition
	  D. Operating procedures
	  E. Personnel
	  F. Business insurance
	
	II. Financial data
	  A. Loan applications
	  B. Capital equipment and supply list
	  C. Balance sheet
	  D. Time to market and break-even analysis
	  E. Income projections (profit and loss
	    statements). Three-year summary detail
	    by month, first-year detail by quarters,
	    second and third years, assumptions
	    upon which projections were based
	  F. Cash flow
	
	III. Supporting documents

Figure 4.38 Content of a typical business plan, and suggested content for a learning plan.

needed in order to build up the targeted competences, (B) the partners for strategic alliances and company acquisitions, (C) the internal collaboration within the company and with experts outside it, (D) the learning goals about the technologies and (E) the markets involved. Competence learning here is described according to the 'probe and learn' approach (see Chapter 2, 'Solutions from the company-level focused research', Cluster 2B). This position concludes with (F) the first draft on the vision for the products and the markets emerging from the new competences are to be developed.

Both the two main positions, the competences and the expertise that can be acquired should be stated in a short description at the beginning of the learning plan as a statement of purpose (position 1 in the learning plan of Figure 4.38). This short description can be understood as a summary of the most essential goals that should be realized by the competences to build up.

The preparation of the decision through elaborating the agendas and the business and learning plan is the task of those people that have been involved with the processes 'investigate (3a)' and 'evaluate (3b)'.

Decision preparation is considered to be concluded as soon as the strategic agendas are elaborated and the business and learning plans are ready to be presented for decision.

The decision (process phase 3.2)

The actual decision about innovation-strategic goals and paths is taken based on proposals in the form of business and learning plans. They deliver, within the set strategic boundaries that are given by normative-level company policy, the content for possible configurations of innovation strategic goals and paths.

A tool supporting the systematic elaboration of goals and path configurations supporting the composition of the innovation strategy is the strategy morphology (Figure 4.39).

The morphology is structured with strategic goals and paths as the main strategic elements with corresponding specifications. The content of both the main elements and the specifications are derived from the business and learning plans.

The morphology is elaborated in a workshop involving the CEO and CTO of the company together with those people who have been in charge of leading phases (2.1) and (2.2): the heads of the business units and their corresponding R&D heads. For each strategic unit, a morphology is elaborated for the composition of this same unit's innovation strategy. In this workshop, structured according to the strategic agendas, the submitted business and learning plans are reviewed one by one. Doing so in a consensual discussion, the morphology is elaborated: first the strategic goals and their specifications are fixed, then the strategic path and their specifications are set. It is not mandatory to fill in all the boxes for specification; on the contrary, those boxes left empty also

	Strategy element	Specifications			
Strategy goals	Strategic purpose	O internal growth	O external growth	O internal and external growth	O
	Return in equity (ROE)	O 8%	O 10%	O 12%	O
	Return on investment (ROI)	O 10%	O 12%	O 14%	O
	Annual sales in three years (million yen)	O +5000	O +7000	O +10000	O
	Long-term sales growth-	O 5%	O 10%	O 15%	O
	Innovation rate	O 10%	O 15%	O 20%	O
		O	O	O	O
Strategy path	Innovation field: polymers	O	O polymer belts	O polymer cables	O medical polymers
	Innovation field: optical fibers	O	O optical switches	O optical data transfer	O
	Innovation field: smart materials	O	O acoustic attenuation	O smart belts	O
	Innovation field xy:	O	O	O	O
	Business field: polymers	O	O belting market	O electronics market	O health care market
	Business field: optical fibers	O	O electronics market	O automotive market	O
	Business field: smart materials	O	O automotive market	O entertainment market	O
	Business field xy:	O	O	O	O
	Overall market strategy	O leader strategy	O follower strategy	O	O
	Regional market strategy	O Japan	O Japan + US	O Japan + US + Europe	O
	Market collaboration strategy	O no collaboration	O majority partnership	O minority partnership	O
	Market collaboration partners	O no partner	O company A	O company B	O company x
	Technology strategy	O no collaboration	O inner innovation	O JV competence	O new strategy competence
	Make or buy strategy	O in-house R&D	O contract research	O joint R&D	O
	Technology collaboration partners	O no partner	O university X	O company Y	O company Z
	Acquisition candidates	O no candidate	O company C	O company A	O company B
	Innovation strategy options	O Option 1	O Option 2	O Option 3	O Option 4

Figure 4.39 The strategy morphology: the elaboration of innovation strategy options

represent a choice, that of ignoring a strategic element. Setting the strategic goals and path for the technology and innovation strategy has to be done as part of, and in alignment with, the corporate strategy.

Once all of the innovation-strategic goals and paths, including their specifications, are filled in in the morphology, the combination of these elements results in the formation of alternative strategy options. These options are the ultimate innovation strategic choices that the members of the workshop have to decide about. In fact, one option represents one possible innovation strategy comprising a specific combination of strategic goals and the strategic path.

The further functional strategies, such as the technology, product and business strategies, are deduced from the innovation strategy (Tschirky and Koruna, 1998: 294) (see Figure 4.40). There is one innovation strategy

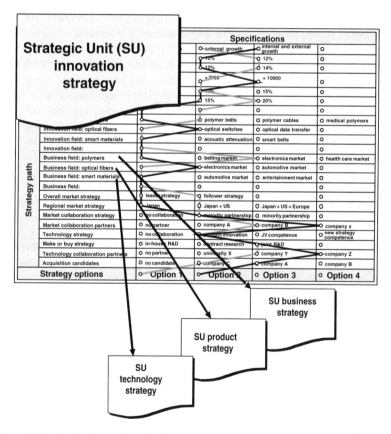

Figure 4.40 Deduction of technology, product and business strategy from the innovation strategy

per strategic unit with its corresponding technology, product and business unit strategy: one for the corporate unit and one for every business unit.

Formulation (process phase 3.3)

The formulation of strategic decisions comprises three issues that prepare the strategic level for the operational implementation of the strategy. These issues are the compilation of strategic projects, the form of their structural realization and their scheduling.

Compilation of strategic projects

The input for the compilation of strategic projects is given by the technology and innovation strategy and by its deduced product and business strategies. As these strategies are, in general, highly interdependent across units and across their corresponding functional emphasis, the implementation requires a lot of coordination. This coordination can be optimized by the formulation of appropriate strategic projects. As already mentioned in Chapter 2, strategic projects as described by Tschirky (2003b: 73) are a management instrument for the coordination of strategy implementation. Tschirky's instrument is adapted for the purpose of this research. One strategic project regroups a number of R&D projects that are all directed towards a common strategic goal. Thus, strategic projects regroup R&D projects with different foci – such as technology development and research, product development or business development – and different ownerships, across the strategic units of the company. One strategic project can comprise at the same time technology strategy R&D projects, product strategy or business development R&D projects.

The R&D projects that are part of one strategic project can be owned by different business units or by the corporate unit as part of their business, product, or technology strategy. The ownership of one whole strategic project is best assigned to one single member of the board. As a rule of thumb established in practice, one member should not manage more than two strategic projects at the same time.

The coordination of strategic projects with corresponding R&D projects can be organized as shown in Figure 4.41 in the 'strategic project compiler': every strategic project is coordinated and owned either by a business unit or by the corporate unit. One strategic project regroups a number of R&D projects that are backed, on the one hand, by existing technologies and, on the other hand, include new technologies as proposed by the business plans and learning plans. The three types of technologies are intertwined in different R&D projects that are managed according to their corresponding strategies: technology strategy, product strategy or business strategy.

The compilation of strategic projects follows the rationale of a differentiated management of high risk innovation projects and moderately risky innovation

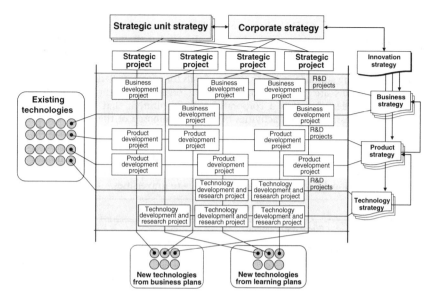

Figure 4.41   Network of existing and new technologies and projects in the strategic project compiler

Source: Adapted from Tschirky and Koruna, 1998: 348.

projects. Thus, strategic projects (including new technologies from the learning plan that are considered high risk), always include at least one competence-building technology development and research project before being related to a product or business development R&D project. Doing so first builds up the competence behind the technology so that it is mastered before it is used for the development of products and businesses. Such strategic projects should be headed and coordinated from the corporate unit.

New technologies that are proposed as a part of a business plan are mastered technologies or technologies of moderate risk. These technologies can directly be used in product and business development projects within one strategic project. A business unit that already knows in which market the product can be placed best manages this strategic project itself.

Best practice case 4.22 illustrates how DSM proceeds to formulate and decide about major R&D programs and projects.

Form of structural realization of strategic projects

The elaboration of a strategic project's form of structural realization evaluates how the sum of its R&D projects is best positioned organizationally in the company for its implementation. The form of structural realization determines, for example, whether an R&D project should be realized in

Every business unit at DSM writes an annual 'strategy dialog paper'related to the strategy update. This paper is the basis for the annual strategy dialog meeting that targets synchronizing strategies across the company and using synergies. Beside the strategic alignment, this meeting is also the platform for discussing and formulating strategic projects and proposals for corporate R&D programs.

The proposals are projected into a virtual organization, the Global R&D Network, for decision. It is a corporate-level organization that steers, with a long-sightedness, the R&D activities of DSM. Composed of the business unit R&D heads, it is led by the CTO. The CTO directly reports to the board of directors.

The Global R&D Network manages 20 percent of the corporate R&D money and decides about the realization of corporate R&D programs and strategic projects; additionally it can allocate R&D money to universities.

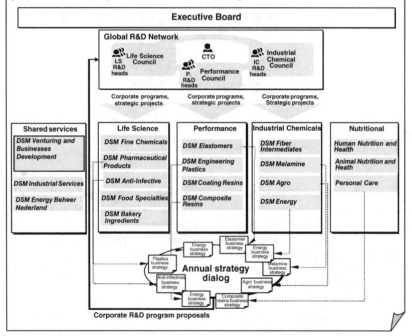

Best practice case 4.22 Formulation and decision about corporate R&D programs and strategic projects at DSM

Source: Interview at DSM, 2004, G. Trauffler.

a separate research team inside or outside the company, in the corporate unit of the company or in a specific business unit in the company, and which constellation of company-internal and external parties the realization entails.

The various forms of organizational embedding of a R&D project as shown in Figure 4.42 can be designed according to two characteristics: on the one

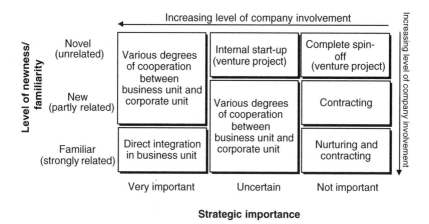

Figure 4.42 Forms of structural realization of R&D projects in a strategic project depending on operational relatedness and strategic importance
Source: Adapted from Burgelman, 1984.

hand, according to the project's strategic importance (see also this chapter, 'Competence fit') and, on the other hand, according to the project's level of newness or familiarity (see also this chapter, 'Quick assessment') to the company and its units. Both characteristics influence the level of company involvement in a project calling for different forms of structural realizations.

As described in this chapter, 'Competence fit', the strategic importance of a technology development and research project is determined according to the number of uncertainties it covers in the long-term strategic plan of the unit. Besides the number of uncertainties covered in a unit, the level of completeness of coverage is relevant too. To bring it all together, the more strategically important a technology development project is considered to be for a unit, the more uncertainties it will cover and the more completely it will cover these same uncertainties. Thus, a strategic unit that rates a project strategically as highly important, as it increases the accuracy of its long-term strategic planning, is automatically more motivated to be more directly involved with a project. Similarly projects that are rated as not strategically important will be less interesting.

For the assessment of the level of newness/familiarity of an innovation project idea, the newness is performed in phase 1.2 (see this chapter, 'Identify all innovation opportunities') using the IA (see this chapter, 'Kick-off'). Within a project, the more difficult it is to *position and link* a technology to existing knowledge in the company, the more new and the more unrelated it is to the company. Thus, the newer or more novel the technologies are to develop in an R&D project for a strategic unit of the company, the less existing knowledge can be associated with it. Similarly, the easier it is to position and link the technologies of an R&D project to existing knowledge in the company, the less new or the more familiar and related they are. Thus, the more familiar the technologies behind an R&D project are for a strategic unit of the company, the more existing knowledge can be associated with it.

Best practice cases 4.23 and 4.24 show how Philips and Bayer assign different types of innovation projects to different organizations within their company for realization.

A strategic unit, especially a business-oriented unit that rates an innovation project familiar and strongly related to it, will be motivated to get involved with it as it can use and exploit its existing knowledge. For the strategic unit, participating in (or independently running) such projects means that it can reap benefits for its own business at a very low level of risk. Vice versa, a strategic unit, especially a business-oriented unit that rates an innovation project novel and unrelated, will be averse to getting involved with it as, at first, there is no great contribution it can bring in and, second, a possible benefit is uncertain and risky.

By understanding how the strategic importance and the level of newness/familiarity influences the motivation of strategic units to become involved

Philips differentiates the organizational realization of R&D projects according to a market criterion and a research-type criterion. The market criterion distinguishes between existing markets and new markets. The research types are differentiated according the their application focus in products. There are three types: an early stage applied research, advanced stage applied research and product-oriented research and development. The matrix below visualizes the choice of the organizational realization depending on the combination of both criteria.

	Existing markets	New markets
Early stage applied research	Corporate research project	Corporate research project
Advanced stage applied research	Joint project: corporate research and product division	Create a start-up company
Product-oriented research and development	Product-division project	–

Best practice case 4.23   Philips, differentiating organizational realization forms of R&D
Source: Interview at Philips, 2004, G. Trauffler.

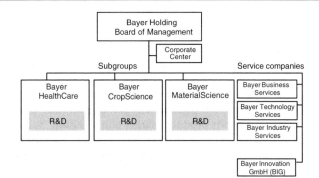

Since the latest corporate reorganization in 2002, Bayer has been structured as a holding organization hosting three market-oriented subgroups: Bayer HealthCare AG, Bayer CropScience AG and Bayer MaterialScience AG. All three subgroups are fully owned by the holding organization. Beside the subgroups, there are three service companies, also entirely owned by Bayer. They provide different kinds of functional services to the subgroups and to strategically relevant external customers. Bayer Business Services, Bayer Technology Services and Bayer Industry Services are legally incorporated with their headquarters in Leverkusen. Furthermore, Bayer Innovation GmbH is a subsidiary with headquarters in Dusseldorf, Germany. Its aim is to market concepts and innovative products to supplement Bayer's business portfolio, and to access new markets with strong growth potential, such as medical and security technology.

Directly subordinate to Bayer's Board of Management, the so-called Corporate Center comprises a number of staff functions. Among the staff functions within the Corporate Center, Corporate Development deals with the management of the current business portfolio elements and the planing of strategic innovation.

As R&D is performed in a decentralized way, all three subgroups of Bayer, HealthCare, CropScience and MaterialScience, follow their own R&D activities. These are, in the first place, focused on applied research and (product) development, fostering the existing core businesses, but also have new business areas like 'New Business Ventures' in BioScience or the 'New Business' center for MaterialScience. R&D efforts regarding the development and implementation of technology platforms spanning several subgroups that support the advancement of the company's core technologies and processes are taken care of by Bayer Technology Services.

Bayer Innovation GmbH develops business ideas that cannot be related to existing businesses. The underlying technology of those businesses should, however, correlate with Bayer's existing competencies. Bayer Innovation GmbH's mission is to develop new business opportunities by evaluating the degree of fit possible for new portfolio elements with the corporate vision. The declared objective is to enrich and complete the holding's business portfolio and to penetrate into potential growth market.

Best practice case 4.24   Bayer, R&D structures adapted to types of innovation

Source: Interview at Bayer, 2005, T. Jäger, M. Reisel, G. Trauffler.

with R&D projects, the explanations of the different structural forms of project realization shown in Figure 4.42 become obvious:

- *Direct integration in a business unit*: A direct integration of an R&D project makes sense if this project is familiar and strategically quite important for that unit. Usually, such project ideas have already been analyzed in the 'Evaluate (2.2)' phase along the strategic planning process in this same business unit, and have been presented as part of a business plan targeting a specific and well-known product market constellation. Such technologies should already be mastered and of medium risk, and they should be used in new product and business development projects following set product and business strategies (see Figure 4.41).
- *Various degrees of cooperation between business units and the corporate unit*: Such cooperation applies whenever a strategically very important project is new or novel to the company's business unit, or when a strategically uncertain project is new or unfamiliar to the whole company. This constellation of strategic importance and level of newness/familiarity results from R&D projects that are of high risk for the business units. Usually the projects that fall into this constellation are projects that have been suggested as part of a learning plan in order to build up new strategically relevant competencies for the future.

  In cooperation projects between various business units aiming to acquire new competencies, the corporate unit should organize and lead the project team. The composition of such projects varies from case to case. Almost exclusively members of the corporate unit might do some projects with advisory support from business unit members, and other projects may be realized in a balanced assignment of business and corporate unit members. This assignment depends on the risk/reward calculations of the business units according to the strategic importance and the level of newness/familiarity.

  In order to keep the risk of such cooperation projects limited, the project team should not exceed more than 25–30 people from the various business units, and its duration should be strictly limited to two to three years. Furthermore, it is widely acknowledged that the more unrelated and uncertain such a project is, the more urgently it is recommended not to realize it within an existing business unit. The realization of the project should be done in a new location outside the usual environment of the units, and all the people involved with the project should be relieved of their obligations and duties in the units for the duration of the project.

  The resources are brought in by the participating business units as well as by the corporate unit.

Best practice cases 4.25 and 4.26 illustrate how corporate unit and business unit can collaborate together on a flexible base.

- *Internal start-up*: An internal start-up[30] is a new company that is created within the parent company especially for the realization of an R&D

At Syngenta, many management activities and, among others, R&D activities, are run in interdisciplinary project teams that are composed of people from the corporate level and people from the business-unit level.

The project team is typically created on the business-unit level run by the business-unit people.

These people form the core project team, they have the responsibility of the project.

The core project team has the opportunity to access specific expertise from the corporate level. This expertise is organized in knowledge silos that comprise six global function pooling experts of specific knowledge backgrounds, such as research, regulatory, marketing, intellectual property, traits and genetics, and health assessment and environment safety.

People from these global functions can be assigned to temporarily support a core project team according to the required expertise.

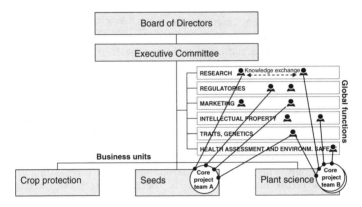

Pooling the experts at the corporate level in global functions has two significant advantages: first, various degrees of intensity in cooperation between the business-unit level and the corporate level is facilitated as corporate experts can be deployed flexibly across the whole organization in one or more projects, allowing a rapid compilation of project structures. Second, there is a great deal of knowledge exchange on the corporate level that the whole company can benefit from.

Best practice case 4.25   Syngenta, flexible cooperation between corporate units and business units

Source: Interview at Syngenta, 2005, M. Reisel, T. Jäger, G. Trauffler.

project. The start-up company is financed by corporate money and managed following the rules of venture capitalism. The management of such ventures is to be secured by the venture unit that should be part of the corporate unit (see also this chapter, 'Back-end intelligence aided by corporate venturing'). Thus, an internal start-up as a realization form is also called a venture project.

At Degussa the collaboration between business units and the corporate unit for high risk innovation projects exploring new technologies is processed through an organizational structure called the 'project house'. Project houses are a joint effort of business units together with Creavis, the operational arm of the corporate unit responsible for high risk innovation projects. It is a physical group composed of 20-30 company internal specialists collaborating with academia and external research institutions. Team members are delegated from their business units into a central location away from their organizational home unit. Their participation as a team member is promoted by incentive plans.

Project house

20–30 specialist
physical group
Own budget/Incentive plan
3-year limited period

External cooperations

The project is managed and coordinated by Creavis. It has its own budget funded 50 per cent by the participating business units and 50 per cent by the corporate unit.

The primary goal of a project house is to develop new knowledge as a basis for new competencies in emerging technology areas that are of long-term benefit for all participating business units. The newly developed knowledge as well as the infrastructure used in the project house is accessible company wide. One condition for starting a project house is the participation and commitment of a significant number of Degussa's business units. This condition not only splits the financial commitment of the participating units, but also secures the market relevance of the endeavor as the interest of business units is a clear indicator of market relevance.

Project houses are run for no longer than three years. After this period, the team members, including the corresponding infrastructure, are reintegrated into their operational home ensuring the transfer of the newly elaborated knowledge. For newly developed knowledge with high market potential that does not fit into the existing businesses of the parent organization, there is the possibility of a new business.

Best practice case 4.26   Collaboration of business units and corporate units in project houses at Degussa

Source: Interview and presentations at Degussa, 2003, G. Trauffler.

This form of structural realization for an R&D project applies in the case where it is of an uncertain strategic importance coupled with a high level of newness or novelty. This constellation of strategic importance and newness of R&D projects may issue from former competence-building projects, yielding additional competencies to those targeted but, however, may not be directly related to the existing business activities of the company. If such additional competencies are based on mastered technologies, which represent a business opportunity, the creation of an internal start-up is the most suitable form of realization. The argument not to sell the technology, as it is not relevant to the parent company's existing business, is the uncertain strategic importance. In the case where the competence and technology developed in the internal start-up eventually turns out to become relevant for the business of the parent company, the latter still the possibility of accessing the generated knowledge or integrating the start-up company into the parent company as part of an existing business unit, or even as a whole new business unit.

- *Complete spin-off, contracting and nurturing and contracting*: A spin-off is a particular type of start-up; it can be understood as any process that leads to a new firm out of the existing-parent organization. The spin-off is managed similarly to the internal start-up by the internal venture unit as a venture project.

Contracting means contracting with a third company or an external research laboratory as a partner. Nurturing and contracting represent a higher level of involvement of the contracting company with its partner. These three forms of realization for an R&D project apply in the case where the latter is not strategically important for the company. A complete spin-off is recommended when the project is also not related or particularly new to the company. Contracting with a third company or an external research laboratory and nurturing and contracting is suggested in the case of a low strategic importance coupled with a lesser degree of newness or a degree of familiarity of the project to the existing business of the company. Both procedures allow the company to observe how the project and the competencies generated evolve without being too intensively involved.

In this case, usually neither the business units nor the corporate unit are interested in directly participating, as the risk of this project is too high and the benefit is questionable. Usually the projects that are realized as internal start-ups are driven by the will of the corporate unit to build up a totally new competence with a long-term goal of diversification.

The issue of securing the transfer of knowledge is not to be underestimated when R&D projects are shifted from one organizational unit to another in the course of their development. Practice example 4.9 shows how ABB deals with this challenge.

Scheduling of strategic projects

As the readily compiled R&D projects of strategic projects are not all realized at the same time, a scheduling of the latter is inevitable. One example was indicated in the previous section; some strategic projects that include competence-building R&D first need to be completed before their related product and business development projects can be started.

Besides informal knowledge transfer between the corporate R&D unit and the divisions, ABB has incorporated processes for this specific purpose.

Corporate Research focuses on exploring new technologies for their deployment in second next and further-generation products, while the divisions conduct product-focused R&D for actual and next-generation products. Both development processes on the corporate level and on the division level follow an ABB-specific stage gate process model with seven gates.

According to this model, the research process on the corporate level starts with the kick-off of a technology development project (1). When the project reaches the execution phase (Gate G3), concerned product developers from the divisions join the gate assessment teams in order to gain insight into the development of the new technology (2).

At the moment in time where the technology reaches Gate G5, the end of its actual development, a product development project is kicked off in a corresponding division (3).

At the technology development project closure (Gate G7), Corporate Research personnel might be transferred into the product development team in the division (4). This transfer concludes the knowledge transfer from corporate to divisional research.

One condition for this method of knowledge transfer to be applicable is the proximity of Corporate Research centers to their corresponding product development units in the divisions, the business area unit R&D.

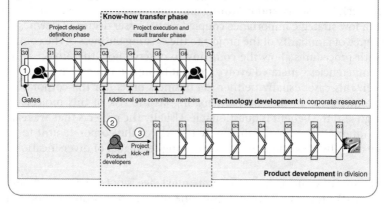

Practice example 4.9   ABB, insuring knowledge transfer from corporate R&D to division
Source: Interview at ABB, 2005, M. Reisel, T. Jäger, G. Trauffler.

A strategic instrument that has gained more and more popularity since the 1990s is the strategic product-technology roadmap. It comprehensively visualizes how the strategic projects and their corresponding technology strategy, product strategy and business strategy projects are related along a planning timeline in order to meet goals in timing. For incremental innovation projects such goals in timing are, for example, the moment of market entry of new products by a business strategy project. For radical innovation projects, a goal in timing can be the development of a specific competence within a certain time through the realization of a strategic project. Furthermore, the resources to allocate to strategic projects can be planned.

Figure 4.43 shows in six layers an example of a product technology roadmap scheduling competencies, resources, strategic projects and their corresponding R&D projects in technology, products and business issues.

All the information from the roadmap can eventually be compiled to elaborate an innovation strategy. An example of how an innovation strategy can look is shown in Figure 4.44.

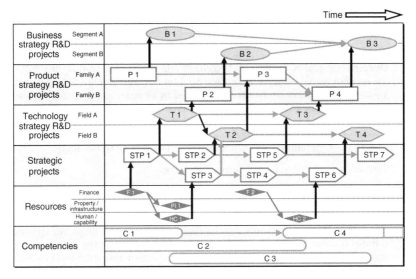

Figure 4.43   Product-technology roadmap for scheduling strategic projects and their corresponding R&D projects

Source: Bucher, 2003: 246.

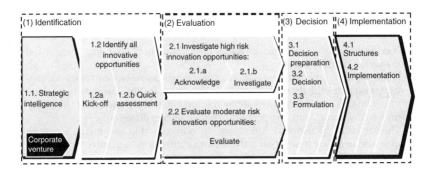

Pixel Inc.'s Strategy Paper

Revenue in 2003:	2 bn. EUR; EBIT: 1.8 mn EUR; # employees: 10,500;
Headquarters:	Zurich, Switzerland, Zürichbergstr. 18
Businesses:	Digital cameras
Vision:	CAPTURE, ENJOY AND SHARE YOUR UNIQUE MOMENTS IN LIFE
Mission statement:	Based on our current core competencies in the fields of digital photography we are becoming a full solution provider to our current and potential customers. Thus, in line with our vision, we aim to offer the full range of functions to enable our customers to save, visualize and distribute their precious moments.

Corporate strategy
Our strategic goal is, by 2007, to become number two in the worldwide market for amateur digital cameras. Revenues of 2.5 bn EUR and an EBIT of 10 per cent are targeted. These objectives will be realized by improving our profitable core in chip design, by extending our current activities and embracing technology-push innovation fostering inorganic growth opportunities. Besides insuring business continuity through incremental innovation, it is our aim to generate growth through radical innovation using even disruptive technologies.

Innovation strategy as part of corporate strategy

I. Prologue
In the past, the main performance driver for our products was the density of pixels per chip and the overall quality of the picture itself. However, since our competitors have successfully developed the 12 mio. pixel chip, our current number three position in the market is under threat. Thus, in the future besides insuring the present market position, the main performance driver will change in order to provide increased convenience in managing and sharing visual images. This change will be realized by a dual strategy approach. On the one hand a short- and mid-term competitive development strategy will secure today's competitiveness through continuity and incremental changes and, on the other hand, a long-term company development strategy will set the company up for fundamental and radical changes in the environment.

II. Our strategic objective
In response to the challenges in our competitive environment:

It is our objective to become the leader in the domain of enabling, sharing and managing digital images.
A full solution range of products and services will allow our customers to capture, visualize and share their precious moments in life. The aim is to share visual images with increasing ease by minimizing the complexity of the procedure while maximizing the possibilities of wide data diffusion.
The focus on incremental innovation in our core chip technologies will be extended to radical innovation activities with cutting-edge disruptive technologies

from the field of info-imaging. A special emphasis will be on biometric pattern recognition.

This strategic objective will change our understanding in developing new products.

III. Our strategic path
The understanding has an impact on our innovation activities:

An important investment in improving our core domain of chip design will insure the competitiveness of our basic technology. The aim is no longer to be the first in the high-end digital imaging market but to secure a position in the consumer market.

In the middle of 2006 we will offer full solution products and services. These solutions should contain a wireless data transfer system connected to an online data management and sharing system aided by biometric pattern recognition software permitting pictures to be classified and administrated directly from the camera.

Competencies in wireless data communication technologies will be built up in-house extending our core domains.

Technological knowledge for the competence of developing management and sharing software will be acquired by the acquisition of the start-up company called 'I-Manager'.

The acquisition of competencies in the field of biometric image pattern recognition will be built up internally through a strategic alliance with the ETH Zurich artificial intelligence lab.

A new competence-building research program on 'image management and sharing' will be founded. The program will establish the basis for a broad range of innovations affecting all kinds of digital imaging applications.

In the long run this strategic path will enable the company, on the one hand, to rapidly enter into many different new market fields that today still seem uncertain and, on the other hand, it will continue to enhance the company's presence in existing markets of digital photography.

Figure 4.44   Example of the innovation strategy of a fictional company: Pixel Inc.

Best practice case 4.27 shows how Infineon works with roadmaps for the planning of their technology projects.

5   Implementation (concept phase 4)

The concept phase 4, 'Implementation', concludes the strategic planning process. Its goal is, on the one hand, to deduce in a systematical way the corporate organizational structures (see next section) and, on the other hand, to prepare an effective and rapid implementation (see this chapter, 'Optimizing the implementation').

In the three business groups of Infineon a technology innovation officer (TIO) runs a roadmap for strategic planning of the corresponding group. Within a business group the TIO is responsible for the coordination of all R&D activities. Concretely speaking he initiates R&D projects, manages the project review process and elaborates the group roadmap. These group roadmaps are collected at the corporate level in order to synchronize the company-wide activities. The result is a combined corporate roadmap that is used for detecting potential synergies of product line technologies and product development projects between the business groups. This synergy potential, together with additional information collected by corporate technology intelligence, is communicated as a proposal back to business groups.

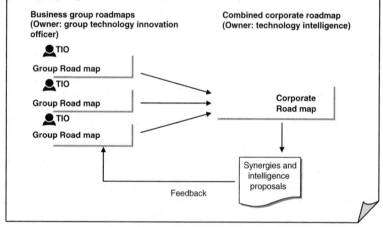

Best practice case 4.27   Infineon, synchronizing roadmaps company wide

Source: Interview at Infineon, 2005, M. Reisel, T. Jäger, G. Trauffler.

Deduction of corporate organizational structures (process phase 4.1)

According to Chandler's principle that 'structure follows strategy' (1962), the roll-out phase describes how the organizational structure already shown in Figure 4.5 can be updated once the strategy has been formulated.

As an initial position for this update the latest 'Innovation architecture' elaborated by the company is taken. It visualizes, on the corporate level, the main technologies of the company, and also the main markets where it competes. Technology and market information are the inputs for the 'Strategic impact analysis' (see Figure 4.45).

It is the goal of the 'Strategic impact analysis' (see Figure 4.46) to reduce the overall complexity of a company's technology and business interrelations by breaking down its interaction in three steps. First, the so-called strategic

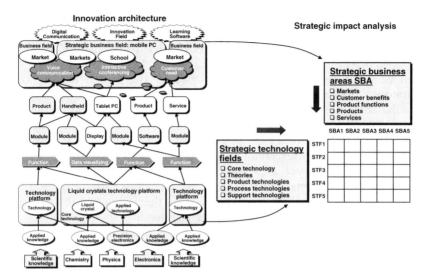

Figure 4.45   The innovation architecture as an initial position for the impact analysis

business areas (SBAs) are reflected. SBAs are dedicated sectors of the overall marketplace in which the company intends to position itself. The selection of SBAs includes strategic considerations of which markets and customer benefits to address, which product functions to fulfill and which concrete products and services to offer. The creation of SBAs follows the theory of the market-based view which suggests that companies build up competitive advantage by positioning themselves in markets with the highest business potential (see Porter, 1985). Once a company has selected its SBA, it should try to align its internal business structures according to the chosen sectors of the marketplace. Usually creating business divisions and/or business units achieves this alignment. Second, from the large number of technologies available in a company, strategic technology fields (STFs) are created. They represent a specific competence of the company materialized through a set of identified core technologies of the company, including their corresponding basic theories, product technologies, process technologies and support technologies. The creation of STFs follows the theories of the knowledge-based view that encourages companies to create competitive advantage through building up company-internal core competencies that are evaluated in the market (see Prahalad and Hamel, 1990). In a third step, the STFs are opposed to the business structure of the company, so that so-called technology platforms can be created. Technology platforms emerge when a certain constellation of one or more core technologies with corresponding product, process and support technologies can be used as a basis to create value in many business divisions or units of a company. As mentioned in this chapter, 'Structures overview', platforms represent a collection of competencies serving one common purpose. From a technology-management view these competencies are enabled by technological knowledge; the technology fields can be partitioned into technology platforms. The second task for the 'Strategic impact analysis' is to optimally align this internal technology-market combination in order to use the given technological resources as efficiently as possible. This alignment consists of placing the platforms within the divisions so that the knowledge can be used in as many as divisions as possible. This is the impact of the technology towards the divisions.

The 'Strategic impact analysis' being completed, the update of the corporate organizational structure as shown in Figure 4.5 can be done. This updated organization is the initial position for the 'roll-out' of the strategy through its implementation of the strategic projects.

Optimizing the implementation (process phase 4.2)

The optimization of the implementation of the strategic planning concept includes its *customization* to a specific company situation that can be *systematized* and *accelerated* by explicitly proposing an implementation plan. This plan describes which activity of the process has to be executed when and by whom. In other words, laying down the process in an organization means agreeing on a number of management meetings to be held throughout

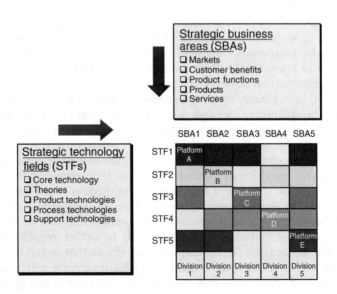

Figure 4.46   Strategic impact analysis

CIBA specialty chemical company has elaborated a system for measuring the company's innovation performance. Coupled to an existing database system every market item has been equipped with three additional main innovation indicators.

The indicators are (1) the time of market launch, (2) the patent situation, and (3) overall innovativeness. The indicator for overall innovativeness asks, for example, if the newly launched product has been developed from their own R&D efforts or if its underlying technology has been bought or licensed; if the developed product, in the case of a molecule, is a newly developed molecule, or if it is a composition of existing molecules, etc. The data base is fed and maintained by product managers and the sales force.

Using the data base, innovation performance is measured on a business line level. There are six quantified items on this level: (1) sales and net margin of new products (≤five years old), (2) sales and net margin with patented products, (3) number of innovative products launched, (4) patents: number of priority filing cases, (5) patents, total valid intellectual property rights, and (6) patent expenses.

Best practice case 4.28   Ciba, measuring innovation performance
Source: Interview at CIBA, 2005, G. Trauffler.

the year. In each of these meetings specific activities described in the generic process of Figure 4.3 have to be discussed and decided. Figure 4.47 shows how mapping it in an implementation plan with fixed-date management meetings can customize the generic process.

The implementation plan precisely describes which meetings are necessary and when they have to take place. It also fixes responsibilities, the decisions to be taken, the participating employees, the information needed in order to take decisions as well how to document the information elaborated during the meetings and, finally, it fixes the frequency of the meetings. The customization of the generic strategic process can be done by running through the implementation plan in a scheduled calendar year, and by adapting and changing activities, tasks, responsibilities and agendas of meetings in order to best fit the needs of the individual company. At the end of the strategic planning process, strategic project descriptions are formulated and ready to be started. They will finally yield innovation performance.

Best practice case 4.28 illustrates how CIBA measures the yield of its company's innovation performance.

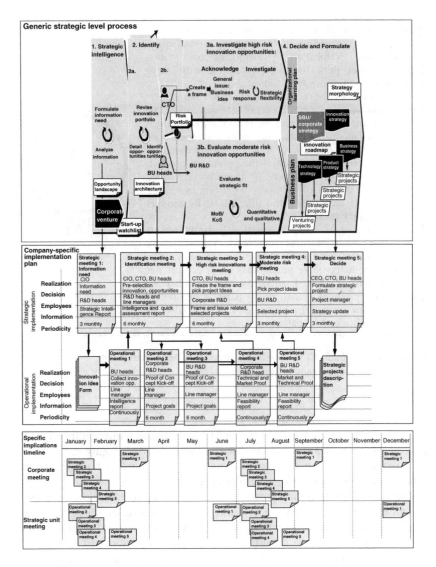

Figure 4.47 Mapping an implementation plan on the strategic-level process

6 Summary and conclusion

Within this chapter a strategic planning concept for the management of sustained innovation was developed. The concept comprises an integrated strategic management process including structures and methods with the goal of systematically guiding the manager while elaborating an innovation strategy for a technology-driven company.

The foundation for the concept is based, on the one hand, on research from current management literature (Chapter 2) and, on the other hand, on research in state-of-the-art management practice conducted in three in-depth company cases (Chapter 3). The quintessence of this research has been synthesized in nine propositions that formulate the requirement for a strategic concept for sustained innovation management.

As a conclusion it can be said that the concept designed to fulfill all of the nine propositions is one possible solution for the strategic management of sustained innovation. It thus represents one potential contribution to the lack of concepts for successfully mastering sustained innovation. It should not be regarded as the *only effective way* to achieve sustained innovation. Further, the concept is focused exclusively on the procedure of strategic innovation planning. There may be other factors that also play an important role besides choosing the right procedure for planning.

In order to assess the effectiveness of this concept a validation case study was conducted. The case study analyzed the relationship between the success of a company and the number of key elements taken from the presented concept that it had implemented in its strategic and operational management. Success of the company was measured by net margin and EBIT margin of the latter. The case study encouraged the assumption that the more elements of the concept for sustained innovation a company had implemented, the more successful it was. Furthermore, the case study could support the assumption that this concept best applies to large-sized and R&D-intensive companies.

5
Management Principles

The goal of this chapter is to make a major contribution towards fulfilling the need in practice (see Chapter 1). This need represents a call from reality for management guidelines that support the practitioner in designing and implementing a strategic planning procedure for sustained innovation management in innovation-driven enterprises. Therefore, this chapter is the practical answer to the questions about how to design, direct and develop strategic planning processes, structures and methods involved in discontinuous technologies and radical innovation, in order to achieve the implementation of sustained technological innovation.

The nature of this chapter is different from that of the other chapters. While the latter follow scientifically sound argumentation, the thinking in this chapter is more normative and hands-on. Therefore, proposals in this chapter are not thoroughly argued, but quite straightforward. Based on theory and, most of all, the practical experience gained during this research, they should be taken as general management principles for technology-driven companies in the field of strategic planning. This also implies that the principles do not strictly follow the elaborated solutions offered during the course of this research.

The principles are structured following the two strongest beliefs gained during this research in the field of strategic planning with discontinuous technology and radial innovation, calling for: *(1) the minimization of risk and (2) the maximization of strategic flexibility.*

1 Minimization of risk

One of managers' greatest concerns when deciding about whether or not to enter into a new and uncertain field related to the development of a discontinuous technology is the possibility of losing an investment in an uncertain technology development effort. It represents the financial risk associated with the decision to be taken. The following management principles represent guidelines to minimize this risk.

Principle 1: fund R&D projects like in the venture business

In most decisions about new technology development endeavors, the risk associated with it is acknowledged; however, it is not explicitly quantified. This is due to the way resources are allocated to projects in many companies: through the establishment of budgets. Allocating resources in the form of budgets means that fixed sums of money are given to specific projects for a specific period of time. After this period of time has passed, a new budget is allocated; this way the money is allocated to the projects, period after period. This manner of resource allocation blurs the perception of the possibility of loss – of risk – as a budget is handled as money that has been granted and, therefore, is meant to be spent, at best entirely. This way, projects risk costing a lot more than they, in fact, need to cost. Thus, instead of the money coming to the projects, make the projects come to the money. Just as in the venture business, projects should have to show what their anticipated outcome would be, they should apply for money and they should be funded in stages with reviews of previously fixed goals. This way money will not be perceived as a granted sum to spend but as a means necessary to achieve set goals. It is believed that this simple differentiated matter of perception helps to minimize the risk of spending more money on research projects than is really necessary.

Principle 2: frame clear manageable risk entities

The decision to strategically plan in favor of an uncertain research project is often difficult, as it seems that the inherent risk cannot be kept within reasonable limits. Indeed, if a risk associated with a project is not clearly defined and limited, projects can become very costly. As a matter of fact, in most large companies, researchers can describe projects that are run over years and years, swallowing enormous sums of money, while those responsible for the project keep on claiming to be just at this moment within easy reach of the breakthrough discovery or achievement. In order to avoid these uncomfortable situations, risks inherent in such projects should be clearly framed in limited and quantifiable time and resource entities. Having these entities defined, it is much easier for the manager, on the one hand, to compare risks among multiple projects and, on the other hand, to balance risk against the expected reward of a single project. For example, the time allowed for a risky technology development project should be limited to three years with a maximum sum to be allocated in several rounds within that period of time. This way the risk of the project is perfectly calculable, regardless of the uncertainty of the technology.

Principle 3: shift development risks on to innovative start-ups

It is common knowledge that established, large companies have difficulties realizing breakthrough ideas that eventually lead to radical innovations.

Those more successful in doing so are generally dynamically run, young start-up companies. Thus, for big companies, access to the start-up scene represents at present a secondary source of radical innovations in addition to their often sluggish internal development efforts. Thus, instead of internally running the risks inherent with the development of radically new technologies, this development risk can be shifted to innovative start-up companies. However, before an established company can become involved in the knowledge developed in a start-up company, for example, by financing its research, by offering synergies, or by simply acquiring the start-up itself, it has to first be detected as interesting. Therefore, established companies should create technology intelligence assignments that identify and set up contact with the right start-up companies.

Principle 4: differentiate according to risk and newness

Strategic analysis is the part in planning sustained innovations that most essentially prepares and influences the decision to realize or eliminate an innovation opportunity. Within this part of the process, it is critical for an appropriate strategic assessment to differentiate in the analysis, according to the risk and newness these opportunities represent for the company. Innovation opportunities with a moderate level of risk and newness have to be assessed with different measurements and for different strategic purposes, then, from those with a high level of risk and newness. While the first should be analyzed with the prospect of their contribution to attain short- and mid-term competitive strategic goals, the latter should be analyzed with the prospect of their contribution to long-term development strategic goals. Such a mindset minimizes the risk of a distorted strategic analysis and increases the accuracy of strategic decisions.

Principle 5: differentiate technology development from product development

Minimizing the risk in developing radical technological innovations while following the concept of sustained strategic innovation planning means developing the innovations in two stages: in the first stage the technology underlying the product is developed for purposes of familiarity. The primary goal should be to eliminate uncertainties and risks so that the technology can be considered as mastered. In the case where the technology is new to the company this first stage of technology development generally takes at least three years and often more. In a second stage, this mastered technology can be deployed in the development of new products. The primary goal in product development is to adapt the technology to the customers' needs. The time horizon in this second stage is much more compressed, as it is in technology development. It is determined by the competition and the industry. Generally, this 'time to market' should not exceed three years; however, there are cases such as in the pharmaceutical industry where this development takes much longer. To bring it all together, technology development and product development should not be mixed as they follow different rules that are determined by their distinctive goals and time horizons.

Principle 6: develop a risk-taking and a failure-accepting culture

Risk minimizing in strategic planning presumes risk-taking as a company culture. Generally speaking, in Europe risk-taking still needs to be promoted as a key element of company culture. This is certainly also related to the low tolerance of accepting failure. Too often failure is considered as a sign of incompetence and ignorance instead of an opportunity to learn. Thus, looming failure in projects tends to be hushed up or ignored until the struggle against an unfortunate situation is definitely hopeless. Such struggles often swallow resources that could be used more effectively elsewhere. Such cases can be avoided in a failure-accepting culture that promotes 'fast failure' and learning rather than stalling and punishing mistakes.

2 Maximization of strategic flexibility

An implicit insight from the experience gained in the course of this research is that, despite all efforts, anticipation of and preparation for a discontinuity will remain a challenge in strategic planning. Thus, companies that operate in dynamic, rapidly changing competitive environments should maximize their strategic flexibility. As mentioned in Chapter 4, strategic flexibility is the agility with which one can adapt to unexpected changes in the environment, where this has not been anticipated.

Principle 7: establish competence learning as a strategic goal

Agility when adapting to discontinuous changes in the competitive environment implies the ability to do so with a short reaction time. Reacting rapidly to changes in the competitive environment usually means that a company must be in a position to adapt, change, or exchange its products according to unexpectedly changing competitive rules. The reaction time thus depends on the time needed to develop and commercialize the adapted products; it is the 'time to market' that represents the most critical factor. However, an efficient time to market can only be guaranteed in the case where the technology behind the product is already mastered. In order to be able to instantly deploy a technology for product development in the case of a discontinuity, the company already needs to be familiar with the technology, to a certain degree.

However, the chance of accurately anticipating the technology that will initiate the discontinuity is limited. Thus, the approach promoted here is one of continuous competence learning as a strategic goal. Competence learning comprises the learning of a set of technologies that are considered most likely to be present at the initial stages of a discontinuity. It should be established as a development strategic goal of a company that allows the realization of high risk technology learning projects. In these projects the question about the yield of products should be subordinated to the question of which competencies to acquire. The question about which products to develop can be raised after the technology is mastered (see also Principle 5).

Principle 8: set up differentiating project realization structures

It has been shown in this research that R&D projects with varying strategic importance and levels of newness are best realized in different realization structures. Within this mindset, maximal flexibility in changing the realization structure promotes knowledge transfer in the company and accelerates the development time. The changes in the structures of realization should be performed according to evolving strategic importance and evolving levels of newness in the course of the realization. For example, if a technology that has been developed by an internal start-up company, separated from the parent company, becomes strategically important for a specific existing business of the company, it is best to reintegrate the start-up and to change the organizational structure of realization.

Principle 9: create knowledge networks

Strong knowledge networks throughout the company increase the flexibility of deploying competencies rapidly as the knowledge is not concentrated in local units or teams. It is especially important to promote the exchange and synchronization of knowledge when there are many different units and R&D project-realization forms generating this new knowledge. Redundant development effort can be avoided and the transfer of knowledge across the various units and R&D project realization forms is accelerated when the knowledge needs to be shifted.

Principle 10: use uncertainties to place strategic options

In order to maximize flexibility when discontinuous changes develop in the competitive environment, technology competences (Principle 7) should be placed as strategic options to cover uncertainties in the strategic planning of long-term business units' planning. Thus, these uncertainties represent useful backgrounds for the development of flexibility; they represent those events in planning in which a company needs to show flexibility – the ability to adapt to unexpected changes. Technology competences can be systematically built up to counteract these uncertainties, creating a strategic option for further research and market entry in the case where the uncertainty turns out be susceptible to the competence.

6
Outlook and Management Summary

1 Outlook

This research studied how innovation-driven companies can strategically plan to successfully cope with discontinuous technologies and radical innovation while simultaneously fostering incremental innovation. This approach, which pays attention to both radical and incremental innovations in strategic planning, is called sustained innovation management. The corresponding question of the publication was: 'How processes, structures and methods of strategic planning with discontinuous technologies and radical innovation should be designed, directed and developed in order to achieve the implementation of sustained technological innovation.' The analysis in theory and in practice of state-of-the-art management in strategic technology management, as well as in strategic innovation management, revealed the absence of a satisfactory answer to this question. This absence represented the twofold gap in theory and in practice.

Based on the twofold gap, nine propositions were formulated representing the requirements for the design of a strategic planning concept for sustained innovation management. Action research and best practice in technology-driven companies provided implementation and validation elements of the generated solution concept. The findings from action research and the best practice cases were used to discuss the solution concept and eventually a new set of management principles could be deduced as a contribution towards closing the twofold gaps in theory and practice.

The suggested solution in this book represents one possible solution for strategic planning of sustained innovation management. It should not be regarded as a prescription for success for all kinds of strategic innovation management challenges and certainly needs to be adapted to company and industry specifications. However, through consideration of the presented management principles, the accuracy of strategic planning and the sustainability of the innovations can very likely be increased.

Some general research challenges and issues in the field of strategic planning for sustained innovation management emerged during this research work:

- *Broader empirical basis for the generated solution*: The generated solution, in particular the strategic planning process, methods and structures, are based on case study research in three technology-driven enterprises. Therefore, the empirical basis is, due to the nature of case study research, narrow. Further case studies would provide a broader basis and would provide deeper insight into today's state-of-the-art management.

- *Complete validation of the generated solution*: In the action research cases, as well as through the best practice case, only elements of the strategic planning process could be implemented. To completely validate the solution of this work, an entire concept of the process, including structures and methods, should be implemented.

- *Broader validation of management principles*: In addition to the generated solution of strategic planning for sustained innovation management, further validation of the management principles would be of scientific and practical interest. Hence, each management principle could be a hypothesis. While this publication's research design did not include the testing of such hypotheses, further research could envisage empirically testing these hypotheses derived from the management principles.

- *Broader insight into the interaction between the strategic planning process and other management processes*: It is practically impossible to set clear limits between different management issues (e.g. innovation management and technology management) and different management processes (e.g. innovation strategy formulation process and business unit strategy formulation process); they are nested and interrelated. A detailed examination of the interaction with, and the impact on, most current management processes of strategic planning process would upgrade the holistic understanding of an integrated strategic management approach.

Furthermore, some particular solution elements addressed during the elaboration of the concept revealed interesting research topics that could benefit from further research:

- *A practitioner-oriented quantitative strategic-options approach for competence learning*: The strategic options approach introduced in this research (see Chapter 4) is of a qualitative nature based on the basic concept of real options. In order to increase the accuracy of the options approach in strategic planning, a practitioner-oriented qualitative approach would be interesting. However, the real-options approach is of a qualitative nature; its use in the context of strategic planning within this concept seems to be difficult as such quantitative analysis is not very straightforward.

- *Strategic risk management approach*: In the presented strategic planning concept, risk considerations have been addressed in several phases of its planning process. During the search of existing strategic risk management approaches it became obvious that this field of research still represents a large potential for management research. Most risk management approaches address project management risks focusing exclusively on the operational level.

These issues and topics represent challenges to both management practitioners and management scientists. They close this research work; however, they might represent a trigger for further research efforts in the field of strategic management.

2 Management summary

'Limiting damage and catching up' is still the motto by which many companies strategically manage discontinuous technology changes in their environment and radical innovations in their marketplace. Considering the increasing frequency of discontinuous technologies and radical innovations disrupting established industries, this cannot be considered an appropriate motto. Rare are those companies that actively seize the challenge of designing their management approaches and organizational structures in a way that takes competitive advantage of discontinuous technologies or that actively and consciously generates radical innovations. The poor performance of companies meeting this challenge is rooted in two main gaps. On the one hand, the understanding of implications of today's management approaches for this management challenge is missing. On the other hand, there is a lack of applicable concepts for the strategic management of discontinuous technologies and radical innovation.

This publication investigates the understanding of the implications of today's management approaches by analyzing state-of-the-art theory and practice through literature and case study research. From this understanding nine propositions for processes, methods and structures were derived. Formulated as requirements for a concept of strategic management, these propositions set the guidelines for the design of a strategic management concept which actively handles the challenges of discontinuous technology and radical innovation. The propositions generally involve processes, methods and structures of a strategic management concept that support differentiated but simultaneous considerations of strategic issues according to their level of risk and newness for the company. Furthermore, a systematic and coordinated dispatching of strategic activities directing operational activities over the entire strategy development process is demanded.

The strategic management concept designed according to the propositions acts at the core as a process with a twofold evaluation and investigation process limb working in parallel. Both process limbs are connected to an input and output phase. At the input end it is connected with a strategic idea gathering and pre-selection process, and at the output end it is connected to a decision and strategy formulation process. The process includes methods and supportive structures and is designed as a concept that enhances the strategic management of technology and innovation as part of general management.

The applicability of the concept is discussed based on the action research findings after their implementation in practice, and on a validation case study. The publication ends with management principles, which will be used as guidelines for practice. Thus, this book contributes to theory and practice by explaining how to master the strategic management of discontinuous technologies and radical innovation.

Appendix: List of Interviews

List of companies interviewed that are mentioned in this book

Company	Industry	Date of interview/ interview review	Location of the interview	Interview partner
ABB AG	Power and automation	02.12.2004	Dättwil, Switzerland	Head ABB Corporate Research Center Switzerland
BASF AG	Chemicals and specialty chemicals	10.12.2004	Ludwigshafen, Germany	Senior Manager University Relations and Research Planning Project Manager BASF Future Business GmbH
Bayer AG	Health care, crop protection, materials	07.12.2004	Leverkusen, Germany	Corporate Development Innovation, R&D Planning Tools
Beiersdorf AG	Branded consumer goods	03.12.2004	Hamburg, Germany	Corporate Vice President Research and Development
Ciba Specialty Chemicals Holding Inc.	Chemicals and specialty chemicals	25.02.2005	Basel, Switzerland	Head Corporate Technology Office
Clariant AG	Specialty chemicals	27.01.2005	Frankfurt, Germany	Research and Development Knowledge Management
Degussa/Creavis AG	Chemicals and specialty chemicals	27.11.2003	Marl, Germany	Project Manager Corporate Venture
DSM Inc.	Chemicals and specialty chemicals	07.04.2004	Heerlen, Netherlands	Director Business Creation
Givaudan SA	Flavors and fragrances	01.04.2004	Dübendorf, Switzerland	Vice President Delivery Systems

Haldor Topsoe Inc.	Catalysis and specialty chemicals	30.04.2004	Copenhagen, Denmark	Director, R&D Division
Heidelberger Druckmaschinen AG	Printing equipment	23.12.2004	Heidelberg, Germany	Senior Vice President Research and Development
Hilti GmbH	Construction tools	25.06.2004	Schaan, FL	Corporate Innovation Manager
IBM Corp.	Data processing equipment	17.01.2005	Philadelphia, United States	Program Manager, Business Transformation Architect
Infineon Technologies AG	Semiconductors	28.01.2005	Munich, Germany	Director Technology Strategy, Senior Director Strategy Development
Intel Corp.	Semiconductors	17.01.2005	Philadelphia, United States	Quality Technology Research
Logitech GmbH	Personal interface products	25.11.2004	Romanelle-sur-Moge, Switzerland	Director Research and Development, Vice President Control Devices Engineering
Maxon Motor GmbH	Electronic drives	19.01.2005	Sachseln, Switzerland	Technical Support Sales/Marketing Strategic Marketing
Novartis AG	Pharmaceuticals	14.01.2005	Basel, Switzerland	Head of Corporate Research
Philips Corp.	Semiconductors and others	13.05.2004	Eindhoven, Netherlands	Director Research Strategy and Business Development
Phonak AG	Digital hearing instruments	11.01.2005	Zurich, Switzerland	Vice President Research and Development
Siemens AG	Semiconductors and others	10.03.2005	Munich, Germany	Vice President Corporate Technology

Continued

Company	Industry	Date of interview/ interview review	Location of the interview	Interview partner
Sulzer AG	Mechanical engineering	12.01.2005	Winterthur, Switzerland	President Sulzer Innotec
Swisscom AG	Telecommunication	13.12.2004	Zurich, Switzerland	Swisscom Innovations
Syngenta AG	Crop protection, seeds	16.11.2004	Basel, Switzerland	Head Plant Science Development
Volkswagen AG	Automotive	26.09.2004	by phone, Wolfsburg, Germany	Corporate Market Research, Futurology
Weidmann Plastics Technology AG	Injection molding	01.03.2004	Jona, Switzerland	Director, Sales & Marketing

Notes

1 Introduction

1. An index consisting of 500 stocks chosen for market size, liquidity and industry group representation. It is a market-value weighted index, with each stock's weight in the index proportionate to its market value (www.investopedia.com).
2. Within this publication the term discontinuity always refers to a discontinuity triggered by an unexpected technology change.
3. Analysis of economic data has led to the conclusion that there is among others, a 50-year cyclical trend in the economic performance of OECD countries. This phenomenon, called the Kondratiev cycle, is named after its initial explorer (Rothwell and Wissema, 1991: 11).
4. Compare Duijn (1983).
5. In this publication industry is defined as 'a group of firms procuring a similar product or service' (Hunger and Wheelen, 2002: 35).
6. 'Radical innovation' will be used throughout this work to represent all these different terms.
7. Besides the chip technology, other complementary technologies such as memory, battery or data processing technologies have become necessary for digital photography to enter the consumer market. However, the chip technology can probably still be regarded as the main trigger.
8. 'Older technological orders seldom vanish quietly; competition between old and new technologies is fierce. New technologies are disparaged when they are introduced because they frequently do not work well and are based on unproven assumptions and on competence that is inconsistent with the established technological order. The response of the existing community of practitioners is often to increase the innovativeness and efficiency of the existing technological order. For example, mechanical typewriters, piston airplanes, telegraphy, gas lighting, mechanical watches, and *sailing vessels* all experienced sharp changes' (Anderson and Tushman, 1990: 611).
9. Improvements of established product cannot be considered as real innovations; however, they use a big part of research and development budgets.
10. Uncertainty can be defined as 'an inability to predict future outcomes' (Burkhardt and Brass, 1990: 106).

11. 'Established firms are those that have been in the industry prior to the advent of the technology in question, practicing the prior technology' (Christensen, 1997: 9).
12. The term 'sustained innovation' is not to be confused with the term sustainable development that was originally used by the United Nations in the 1987 publication 'Our Common Future' (World Commission on Environment and Development, 1987). It has nothing in common with the corporate perspective of sustainable development referring to companies that are committed to minimizing the environmental footprint of their operations, while simultaneously contributing to the economic and social advancement of communities in which they operate (Schofield and Feltmate, 2003).
13. There is evidence from research that most companies do not have or do not utilize a systematic and structured process for managing discontinuous technologies (Veryzer, 1998a: 305).
14. 'A competence is the ability of an organization to sustain coordinated deployments of assets and capabilities in ways that help the organization achieve its goals. . . . Capabilities are repeatable patterns of action that an organization can use to get things done. Capabilities reside in groups of people in an organization who can work together to do things. Capabilities are thus a special kind of asset, because capabilities use or operate on other kinds of assets (like machines and the skills of individuals) in the process of getting things done' (Sanchez, 2001: 7).
15. 'Exploitation is the use and development of things already known' (Kraatz and Zajac, 2001: 634). 'Exploitation has to do with refinement, choice, efficiency and implementation' (Leifer, 1998: 130).
16. The strategic perspective of the terms exploration and exploitation will be explained in further detail in Chapter 4, 'Front-end intelligence aided by the opportunity landscape'.
17. The claim for a sustained innovation management approach is elaborated in further detail in Chapter 2, 'Management implications'.
18. Exploration is the pursuit of new knowledge (Kraatz and Zajac, 2001: 634). 'Exploration is defined by terms such as search, risk taking, experimentation, discovery and innovation. This idea suggests something totally new including new product, processes combinations of the two, raw materials and technologies' (Leifer, 1998: 130).

2   State of the Art in Management Theory

1. Compare also Teece (1990: 40), Welge and Al-Laham (1992: 2356), Hauschildt (1997: 25), Maurer (2002: 17), and Hunger and Wheelen (2002: 2).
2. 'Innovativeness paraphrases the ability of individuals and organizations to perform changes' (Tschirky and Koruna, 1998: 9).
3. For further reading see: Hitt and Ireland (1985), Amit and Schoemaker (1993), Barney and Zajac (1994).
4. In alignment with the concept of Chandler (1962: 14), 'structure follows strategy'.
5. See this chapter, 'Basic functions of management in an integrated company context'.
6. See this chapter, 'Basic functions of management in an integrated company context'.
7. Theories are universal statements, which lead unknown phenomena back to known phenomena. Furthermore, theories explain the causes and effects of retrospective and prospective views.
8. See Tschirky (Tschirky and Koruna, 1998: 194) for a detailed discussion of various approaches.

9. For a discussion of company potentials, see Tschirky (Tschirky and Koruna, 1998: 215, 245, 246).
10. Technology-based firms are 'firms that rely on technology for their ability to compete' (Dodgson, 2000: 134).
11. Wolfrum (1991: 72) defines the purpose of technology strategies as follows: 'Which technology from which source should be used when and on which performance level and for what purpose?'
12. For more detail on the strategic goal and path see this chapter, 'Strategy'.
13. Compare Martino (1993).
14. See Lichtenthaler (2000).
15. In this publication storage is considered part of technology acquisition. For more explicit approaches to storage of technology refer to the literature on knowledge management: Leonard-Barton (1995), Thierauf (1999), Ruggles (1997), Cross and Israelit (2000).
16. For a list of definitions and an evolution of the term innovation, refer to Schaad (2001: 13f.).
17. 'Architectural innovation is the reconfiguration of an established system to link together existing components in a new way' (Henderson and Clark, 1990: 12).
18. See Seibert (1998: 107); Hauschildt (1993a: 15); Herzhoff (1991: 11); Trommsdorff and Schneider (1990: 3); Kaplaner (1986: 15).
19. For further readings in innovation strategy formulation refer to Sauber (2004).
20. A technological paradigm is a model and solution approach of specific technological problems. It is based on determined principles of scientific disciplines and specific material technologies (Dosi, 1982: 152).
21. A technological trajectory represents the 'usual' regime to solve a problem given within the guidelines of a technological paradigm (Dosi, 1982: 152).
22. Recently authors have suggested differentiating further the competence-destroying and competence-enhancing concept stating that they are composed of two distinct constructs that, although correlating, separately characterize an innovation: new competence acquisition and competence enhancing/destroying (Gatignon *et al.*, 2002: 1103).
23. Projects with a five to ten times improvement in performance, 30–50 per cent reduction in cost and/or new-to-the-world performance (Rice *et al.*, 1998: 52).
24. A product's technology base includes all the technologies – specific areas of technical competence – which are needed to design and produce the product (Ehrnberg and Jacobsson, 1993: 28).
25. Exception to this market perspective is the description from Green *et al.* (1995: 203ff.).
26. Macroeconomics deals with economic behavior of entire industries.
27. Not all the findings point in the same direction; for example, Herstatt and Lettl (2004) descibe a case where customers were successfully involved in the development of radical innovation products; see also von Hippel (1988).
28. Most statements of causes and effects are given by the industry-level focused research. However, these would need higher specification in order to be used as an initial position for the redesign of management concepts.

3 Managing Radical Innovation – Corporate Case Studies

1. Savioz (2002: 17) has made an attempt to distinguish between high technology or technology-based industries and low-technology industries. He discusses several input and output based measures such as R&D expenditures (e.g. OECD has set the limit at 3.5 per cent) or innovation rates and came to the conclusion that

neither methodology fully captures the essence of the industry dynamics. Thus, the definition in this book focuses on the external demand for innovativeness and does not consider the company-specific reaction to it in terms of R&D investments. This definition of innovation-driven industries could eventually be further detailed by characterizing them as industries where the participants' p/e (price/ earnings) ratio correlates with their innovativeness. A similar study was conducted by ADL (1986–96), which showed the correlation between the average annual shareholder return and the innovativeness of a sample of 600 US companies between 1986 and 1996.

2. Nanotechnology is 'the ability to do things – measure, see, predict and make – on the scale of atoms and molecules and exploit the novel properties found at that scale. Traditionally, the Nanotechnology realm is defined as being between 0.1 and 100 nanometres, a nanometre being one thousandth of a micron (micrometer), which is, in turn, one thousandth of a millimetre' (Holister, 2002: 4). In the nanometre range properties of substances differ substantially from the properties of macroscopic solids. Not only the chemical composition but also the size and shape of particles determine their properties.

3. Goals following the CTI Webpage (October 2004): http://www.temas.ch/nano/ nano_homepage.nsf/vwAllByKey/homelen

4. The three companies that collaborated in the first set of the case studies requested anonymity. Thus, those three names Injec-Tech, Quali-Chem-Tech and Pro-Chem-Tech do not correspond to any company existing in reality.

5. See Chapter 1.

4 Sustained Innovation Management

1. Visions usually cover 'long-term objectives, main areas of activities, geographical dimensions of businesses, major resources and competencies, innovative ambitions, the desired relationship with customers, attitude towards societal and ecological expectations, the role and development of human capital and the values which determine communication and collaboration' (Tschirky, 2003b: 33).

2. According to Hunger (Hunger and Wheelen, 2002: 9) a policy 'is a broad guideline for decision making that links the formulation of strategy with its implementation. Companies use policies to make sure that employees throughout the firm make decisions and take actions that support the corporation's mission, its objectives, and its strategies.'

3. For further readings on definitions of intelligence, refer to Savioz (2004).

4. For further readings on the strategy implementation phase refer for example to Sauber (2004: 151).

5. For companies operating in industries with highly variable types and frequencies of orders, a flexible project structure is recommended rather than a business unit structure that pools resources.

6. For detailed descriptions on the tasks of strategic intelligence, especially in the context of technology, refer to Savioz (2002: 54ff.) and Lichtenthaler (2000: 330ff.).

7. ' "[F]uzzy front end" of product development, [is] also known as the "pre-development" phase, "pre-project activities" or "pre-phase 0". . . . the front end ranges from the generation of an idea to either its approval for development or its termination' (Herstatt, Verworn and Nagahira, 2004: 43.)

8. For further literature on Communities of Practice refer, for example, to Wenger *et al.* (2000) and Wenger (1998).

9. This process phase will be described as a summary based on the research conducted by Sauber (2004). For more detail refer to his work.
10. For the theoretical background of the innovation architecture and details on how to develop, refer to Sauber (2004: 98).
11. Sauber (2004: 100) defines three different dimensions of knowledge in the innovation architecture: '(1) object knowledge is the knowledge about objects and information in our environment. In innovation, the object knowledge is the knowledge about customer needs, products and services, modules, technologies and scientific insights applied. In contrast, (2) methodological knowledge is the knowledge to act and to comply actions. Thus, it is the knowledge about how to proceed and behave, what specific steps and tasks to initiate, and with which procedure to complete the tasks. Especially, the methodological knowledge enables the creation, processing and transfer of object knowledge. (3) Meta-knowledge encompasses knowledge about the source, reliability, importance, and transferability of the knowledge as well as the cognitive capabilities available to the knowledge development.'
12. For the theoretical background of the functions and details on how to develop a functions for a specific management, refer to Sauber (2004: 79).
13. Uncertainty in industrial engineering means: 'Unknown future events which cannot be predicted quantitatively with useful limits' (Williams and Chair, 1989: 2–23).
14. Yates and Stone (1992: 4) say risk is 'the possibility of loss'.
15. There is a recent tendency to break with this strict separation of risk and uncertainty and advocate its convergence (Ward and Chapman, 2003).
16. Value network: 'A value network is the context within which a firm establishes a cost structure and operating processes and works with suppliers and channel partners in order to respond profitably to the common needs of a class of customers. Within a value network, each firm's competitive strategy, and particularly its cost structure and its choices of markets and customers to serve, determines its perceptions of the economic value of an innovation. These perceptions, in turn, shape the rewards and threats that firms expect to experience through disruptive versus sustaining innovations' (Christensen and Raynor, 2003: 14).
17. The concept of the value chain analysis has been elaborated based on the idea of Andreas Biedermann's diploma thesis at ETH Center for Enterprise Science in 2004.
18. For further detail about functions refer to this chapter, 'Kick-off'.
19. For further literature of Delphi methods refer to: Linestone (1975), Brockhaus and Mickelson (1976; 1977).
20. For further detail refer also to Robinson (1982), and Lovins (1976).
21. 'Technology road-mapping is a needs-driven technology planning process to help identify, select, and develop technology alternatives to satisfy a set of product needs. It brings together a team of experts to develop a framework for organizing and presenting the critical technology-planning information to make the appropriate technology investment decisions and to leverage those investments. Given a set of needs, the technology road-mapping process provides a way to develop, organize, and present information about the critical system requirements and performance targets that must be satisfied by certain time frames. It also identifies technologies that need to be developed to meet those targets. Finally, it provides the information needed to make trade-offs among different technology alternatives' (Walsh, 2004: 166). For further readings on roadmapping refer to Bucher (2003) and also to this chapter, 'Formulation'.

22. The National Intelligence Council's Global Trend report is available on the Web: http://www.cia.gov/nic/NIC_home.html
23. Source: www.azom.com
24. The assessment of this figure does not claim any accuracy. In the first place they are meant to simply illustrate the method of assessing the impact of an industry-unfamiliar technology.
25. http://www.pro.on.ca/about_us/newsletters/newsletter_may_98.htm
26. Assets are anything tangible or intangible that an organization could use in the pursuit of its goals. Capabilities are repeatable patterns of action that an organization can use to get things done. Capabilities reside in groups of people in an organization who can work together to do things. Capabilities are, thus, a special kind of asset, because capabilities use or operate on other kinds of assets (like machines and the skills of individuals) in the process of getting things done (Sanchez, 2001: 7).
27. Brodbeck (1999: 99) discusses the make or buy decision in the context of technology. Nevertheless these findings may also be taken in the context of innovation.
28. Brodbeck (1999: 14) discusses the keep or sell decision in the context of technology. Nevertheless these findings may also be taken in the context of innovation.
29. The strategic agenda for medium risk innovation opportunities has been developed following Sauber (2004: 147ff.).
30. 'A broad definition of start-ups encompasses all firms in an early life-cycle phase. Sometimes start-up refers also to recently incorporated enterprises, which are characterized by a high level of dynamics and future orientation' (Luggen, 2004: 13).

Bibliography

Abell, D. F. (1999). 'Competing Today While Preparing for Tomorrow'. *Sloan Management Review* (Spring): 73–81.

Abernathy, W. J., and Clark, K. B. (1985). 'Innovation: Mapping the Winds of Creative Destruction'. *Research Policy* 14: 3–22.

Abernathy, W. J., and Glark, K. B. (1991). 'Innovation: Mapping the Winds of Creative Destruction'. In M. L. Tushman and W. L. Moore (Eds), *Readings in the Management of Innovation*, Vol. 2, New York: Auflage: 55–78.

Abernathy, W. J., and Utterback, J. M. (1978). 'Patterns of Industrial Innovation'. *Technology Review* 6/7: 41–7.

Afuah, A. (1998). *Innovation Management: Strategies, Implementation and Profits*. Oxford: Oxford University Press.

Allen, T. J. (1986). *Managing the Flow of Technology*. Boston: Massachusetts Institute of Technology.

Amit, R., and Schoemaker., P. J. (1993). 'Strategic Assets and Organizational Rent'. *Strategic Management Journal* 14 (January): 33–46.

Amram, M., and Kulatilaka, N. (1999). *Real Options*. Boston, MA: Harvard Business School Press.

Anderson, P., and Tushman, M. L. (1990). 'Technological Discontinuities and Dominant Design: A Cyclical Model of Technological Change'. *Administrative Science Quarterly* 35: 604–33.

Andrews, K. R. (1987). *The Concept of Corporate Strategy* (3rd edn). Homewood, Illinois: Irwin.

Ansoff, H. I. (1981). 'Die Bewältigung von Überraschungen und Diskontinuitäten durch die Unternehmensführung – Strategische Reaktionen auf schwache Signale'. In H. Steinmann (Ed.), *Planung und Kontrolle*. Munich, Vahlen.

Ansoff, H. I. (1984). *Implementing Strategic Management*. London: Prentice-Hall International.

Ashton, W. B., Kinzey, B. R., and Gunn, M. E. (1991). 'A Structured Approach for Monitoring Science and Technology Developments'. *International Journal of Technology Management* 6(1/2): 91–111.

Ashton, W. B., and Stacy, G. S. (1995). 'An Introduction in Business: Understanding Technology Threats and Opportunities'. *International Journal of Technology Management* 10(1): 79–104.

Barney, J. B., and Zajac, E. J. (1994). 'Competitive Organizational Behavior: Toward an organizationally-based theory of competitive advantage'. *Strategic Management Journal* 15: 5–9.

Basalla, G. (1988). *The Evolution of Technology*. Cambridge: Cambridge: University Press.

Berth, R. (2003). 'Auf Nummer sicher'. *Harvard Business Manager* (June): 16–19.

Biedermann, M. (2002). Course: 'Value Engineering Management'.

Birkenmeier, B. (2003). *Externe Technologie Verwertung*. ETH, Zurich.

Bischof, F.-G. (2000). *Der professionelle Business Plan: Geschäftsideen erfolgreich umsetzen*. Munich: Humboldt.

Black, J. (2002). *A Dictionary of Economics*. USA, Oxford University Press.

Bleicher, K. (1991). *Das Konzept Integriertes Management*. Frankfurt: Campus.

Bleicher, K. (1992). *Das Konzept Integriertes Management* (2nd edn). Frankfurt: Campus.

Booz-Allen, H. (1982). *New Product Management for the 1980s*. New York: Booz, Allen and Hamilton.

Bower, J. L., and Christensen, C. R. (1995). Disruptive Technologies: Catching the Wave. *Harvard Business Review* 1995 (January–February): 43–53.

Brockhaus, W. L., and Mickelsen, J. F. (1976). *The Delphi Method and its Applications*. Washington: A Bibliography.

Brockhaus, W. L., and Mickelson, J. F. (1977). 'An Analysis of Prior Delphi Applications and Some Observations on its Future Applicability'. *Technological Forecasting and Social Change* 10: 103–10, Elsevier.

Brockhoff, K. (1997). *Forschung und Entwicklung. Planung und Kontrolle*. Munich: Oldenbourg.

Brodbeck, H. (1999). *Strategische Entscheidungen im Technologie-Management*. Zurich: Industrielle Organisation.

Brodbeck, H., Birkenmeier, B., and Tschirky, H. (1995). 'Neue Entscheidungsstrukturen des Technologie-Managements'. *Die Unternehmung* 2: 107–23.

Brodbeck, H., Bucher, P., Birkenmeier, B., and Escher, J.-P. (2003). 'Evaluating and Introducing Disruptive Technologies'. In H. Tschirky, H.-H. Jung and P. Savioz (Eds), *Technology and Innovation Management on the Move*. Industrielle Organisation: 137–51.

Bucher, P. (2003). *Integrated Technology Roadmapping: Design and implementation for technology-based multinational enterprises*. Zurich: Swiss Federal Institute of Technology.

Burgelman, R. A. (1984). 'Managing the Internal Corporate Venturing Process'. *Sloan Management Review* (Winter): 33–48.

Burgelman, R. A., and Rosenbloom, R. S. (1989). 'Technology Strategy: An Evolutionary Process Perspective'. *Research on Technological Innovation, Management and Policy* 4: 1–23.

Burkhardt, M. E., and Brass, D. J. (1990). 'Changing Patterns or Patterns of Change: The Effects of a Change in Technology on Social Network Structure and Power'. *Administrative Science Quarterly* 35(1) (Technology, Organizations, and Innovation): 104–27.

Carroad, P., and Carroad, C. (1982). 'Strategic Interfacing of R&D and Marketing'. *Research Technology Management* 25(1): 28–33.

Chamberlin, E. H. (1933). *The Theory of Monopolistic Competition*. Cambridge, MA: Harvard University Press.

Chambers, F. A., and Taylor, M. A. P. (1999). *Strategic Planning: Processes, Tools and Outcomes*. Ashgate: Athenaeum Press.

Chandler, A. D. (1962). *Strategy and Structure. Chapters in the History of Industrial Enterprise*. Cambridge, MA/London: MIT Press.

Christensen, C. M. (1997). *The Innovator's Dilemma, When New Technologies Cause Great Firms to Fail*. Boston: Harvard Business School Press.

Christensen, C. M., and Raynor, M. E. (2003). *The Innovator's Solution.* Boston: Harvard Business School.

Clark, G. (2002). The Disruption Opportunity. *MIT Sloan Management Review* summer: 27–32.

Clark, G., and Bower, J. L. (2002). 'Disruptive Change'. *Harvard Business Review* (May): 3–8.

Clarke, C. J., and Varma, S. (1999). 'Strategic Risk Management: the New Competitive Edge'. *Long Range Planning* 32(4): 414–24.

Cooper, A., Gadson, J., Nielsen, K., and Philips, C. (2001). 'Corporate Venturing, Gold Mining or Fool's Gold'. *Kellogg TechVenture 2001 Anthology.* Evanston, IL: 1–28.

Council, R. T. E. (2001). 'Idea-Sensing Efficiency – Practices for Broadening Access to External Technology Innovations'. *Research and Technology Executive Council* 10: 5ff.

Cross, R. L., and Israelit, S. B. (Eds) (2000). *Economy: Individual, Collective and Organizational Learning Process.* Wobum, MA: Butterworth-Heinemann.

Damanpour, F. (1988). 'Innovation Type, Radicalness, and the Adoption Process'. *Communication Research* 15(5): 545–67.

D'Aveni, R. A. (1994). *Hypercompetition: Managing the Dynamics of Strategic Maneuvering.* New York: Free Press.

D'Aveni, R. A. (1995). *Hyperwettbewerb Strategien für die neue Dynamik der Märkte* (trans. P. Künzel). Frankfurt/New York: Campus.

Day, J. D., Mang, P. Y., Richter, A., and Roberts, J. (2001). 'The Innovative Organization: Why New Ventures Need More than a Room of Their Own'. *The McKinsey Quarterly* 2: 21–31.

Dodgson, M. (2000). *Management of Technological Innovation: An International and Strategic Approach.* New York/Oxford: Oxford University Press.

Doering, D. S., and Parayre, R. (2000). 'Identification and Assessment of Emerging Technologies'. In G. S. S. Day, J. H. Paul and Robert E. Gunther (Eds), *Wharton on Emerging Technologies.* New York: John Wiley & Sons: 75–98.

Dosi, G. (1982). 'Technological Paradigms and Technological Trajectories'. *Research Policy* 11: 147–62.

Drucker, P. (1969). *The Age of Discontinuity.* New York: Harper & Row.

Duijn, J. J. v. (1983). *The Long Waves in Economic Life.* London: George Allen & Unwin.

Ehrnberg, E. (1995). 'On the Definition and Measure of Technological Discontinuities'. *Technovation* 15(7): 437–52.

Ehrnberg, E., and Jacobsson, S. (1993). 'Technological Discontinuity and Competitive Strategy – Revival through FMS for the European Machine Tool Industry?' *Technological Forecasting and Social Change* 44: 27–48.

Floyd, C. (1996). 'Managing Technology Discontinuities for Competitive Advantage'. *Prism* (Second Quarter): 5–21.

Foster, R. N. (1986). *Die technologische Offensive.* Wiesbaden: Gabler.

Foster, R. N., and Kaplan, S. (2002). *Schöpfen und Zerstören.* Vienna/Frankfurt: Redline Wirtschaft bei Ueberreuter.

Frauenfelder, P. (2000). *Strategisches Management von Technologie und Innovation. Tools and Principles.* Zurich: Industrielle Organisation.

Gälweiler, A. (1990). *Strategische Unternehmensführung* (2nd edn). Frankfurt: Campus.

Garcia, R., and Roger, J. C. (2002). 'A Critical Look at Technological Innovation Typology and Innovativeness Terminology: A Literature Review'. *Journal of Product Innovation Management* 19: 110–32.

Gatignon, H., Tushman, M. L., Smith, W., and Anderson, P. (2002). 'A Structural Approach to Assessing Innovation: Construct Development of Innovation Locus, Type and Characteristics'. *Management Science* 48(9): 1103–22.

Gertsen, F. (2003). 'Editorial: Continuous Innovation'. *International Journal Technology Management* 26(8): 801–4.

Geus, A. P. d. (1997). *The Living Company*. Boston: Harvard Business School Press.

Ghoshal, S., and Moran, P. (1996). 'Bad Practice: A Critic of Transaction Cost Theory'. *Academy of Management Review* 21: 13–47.

Gil-Aluja, J. (2001). 'Management Problems in Uncertainty'. In J. Gil-Aluja (Ed.), *Handbook of Management under Uncertainty*. Dordecht: Kluwer Academic Publishers: 11–32.

Gilbert, C. (2003). 'The Disruption Opportunity'. *MIT Sloan Management Review* (Summer): 27–32.

Gordon, T. J., and Stover, J. (1976). 'Using Perceptions and Data about the Future to Improve the Simulation of Complex Systems'. *Technological Forecasting and Social Change* 9: 191–211.

Grant, R. (1996). 'Towards a Knowledge-based Theory of the Firm'. *Strategic Management Journal* 17(Winter Special Issue): 109–22.

Green, S. G., Gavin, M. B., and Aiman-Smith, L. (1995). 'Assessing a Multidimensional Measure of Radical Technological Innovation'. *IEEE Transactions on Engineering Management* 42(3): 203–14.

Gupta, J. P., Chevalier, A., and Dutta, S. (2003). 'Multicriteria Model for Risk Evaluation for Venture Capital Firms in an Emerging Market Context (article in press). *European Journal of Operational Research 2003*. Corrected proof available online 10 April 2003.

Hamel, G., and Prahalad, C. K. (1994). *Competing for the Future*. Boston: Harvard Business School Press.

Hammer, R. M. (1998). *Strategisch Planung und Frühaufklährung*. Munich/Vienna Oldenburg.

Harmann, B.-G. (2003). Patente als strategisches Instrument zum Management technologischer Diskontinuitäten (Dissertation). Bamberg: Difo-Druck GmbH, Bamberg.

Hauschildt, J. (1993a). 'Innovationsmanagement'. In E. Frese (Ed.), *Handwörterbuch der Organisation*, Vol. 3. Stuttgart: Poeschel: 1029–41.

Hauschildt, J. (1993b). *Innovationsmanagement*. Munich: Franz Vahlen.

Hauschildt, J. (1997). *Innovationsmanagement*. Munich: Franz Vahlen.

Henderson, B. D. (2003). 'Das Konzept der Strategie' (1980). In B. v. Oetinger (Ed.), *Das Boston Consulting Group Strategie-Buch*. Munich: Econ: 26–55.

Henderson, R. M., and Clark, K. B. (1990). 'Architectural Innovation: The Reconfiguration of Existing Product Technologies and the Failure of Established Firms'. *Administrative Science Quarterly* 35: 9–30.

Herstatt, C., and Lettl, C. (2004). 'Management of "Technology Push" Development Projects'. *International Journal of Technology Management* 27(2/3): 155–75.

Herstatt, C., Verworn, B., and Nagahira, A. (2004). 'Reducing Project Related Uncertainty in the "Fuzzy Front End" of Innovation: A Comparison of German and Japanese Product Innovation Projects'. *International Journal of Project Development* 1(1): 43–65.

Herzhoff, S. (1991). *Innovation-Management, Gestaltung und Prozessen und Systemen zur Entwicklung und Verbesserung der Innovationsfähigkeit von Unternehmungen*. Bergisch Gladbach: Josef Eul.

Hippel, E. von (1988). *The Source of Innovation*. New York: Oxford University Press.

Hitt, M. A., and Freeman, R. E. (2001). *Hand book of Strategic Management*. Oxford, Blackwell.

Hitt, M. A., and Ireland, R. D. (1985). 'Corporate Distinctive Competence, Strategy, Industry and Performance'. *Strategic Management Journal* 6: 273–93.

Hofmeister, R. (1999). *Der Business Plan: Geschäftsidee prüfen Firmengründung planen – Finanzierung sichern.* Vienna: Wirtschaftsverlag Ueberreuter.

Holister, P. (2002). *Nanotech: The Tiny Revolution.* CMP Scientifica. July 2002: 1–34.

Holt, K. (1988). *Product Innovation Management* (3rd edn). London: Butterworth.

Hunger, J. D., and Wheelen, T. L. (2002). *Essentials of Strategic Management* (3rd edn). New Jersey: Prentice Hall.

Johnson, D. R., and Hoopes, D. G. (2003). 'Managerial Cognition, Sunk Costs, and the Evolution of Industry Structure'. *Strategic Management Journal* 24: 1057–68.

Jolly, V. K. (1997). *Commercializing New Technologies.* Boston: Harvard Business School Press.

Jung, H.-H. (2003). *Technology Management Control Systems in Technology-based Enterprises.* Zurich: Industrielle Organisation.

Kantrow, A. M. (1980). 'Keeping Informed'. *Harvard Business Review*: 9–12; 17–18; 21.

Kaplaner, K. (1986). *Betriebliche Voraussetzung erfolgreicher Produktinnovationen.* Munich: GBI.

Kassicieh, S. K., Walsh, S. T., Cummings, J. C., McWhorter, P. J., Romig, A. D., and Williams, W. D. (2002). 'Factors Differentiating the Commercialization of Disruptive and Sustaining Technologies'. *IEEE Transactions on Engineering Management* 49 (4, November): 375–87.

Kessler, E. H., and Chakrabarti, A. K. (1999). 'Speeding Up the Pace of New Product Development'. *Journal of Product Innovation Management* 16: 231–47.

Kim, W. C., and Mauborgne, R. (1997). 'Value Innovation – The Strategic Logic of High Growth'. *Harvard Business Review* (January-February): 103–12.

Knight, K. E. (1967). 'A Descriptive Model of the Intra-Firm Innovation-Process'. *The Journal of Business* 40: 478–96.

Koruna, S. (2001). 'External Technology Commercialization: Policy Guidelines'. Washington: Academy of Management Conference.

Kostoff, R. N., Boylan, R., and Simons, G. R. (2004). 'Disruptive Technology Roadmaps'. *Technological Forecasting and Social Change* 71: 141–59.

Kraatz, M. S., and Zajac, E. J. (2001). 'How Organizational Resources Affect Strategic Change and Performance in Turbulent Environments: Theory and Evidence'. *Organization Science* 12(5): 632–57.

Kunz, P. (2002). 'Strategieentwicklung bei Diskontinuitäten', dissertation. Universität St Gallen, Hochschule für Wirtschafts-, Rechts- und Sozialwissenschaften (HSG), St Gallen.

Kusunoki, K. (1997). 'Incapability of Technological Capability: A Case Study on Product Innovation in the Japanese Facsimile Machine Industry'. *Journal of Product Innovation Management* 14: 368–82.

Lambe, C. J., and Spekman, R. E. (1997). 'Alliances, External Technology Acquisition, and Discontinuous Technological Change'. *Journal of Production and Innovation Management* 14: 102–16.

Lehmann, A. (1994). *Wissensbasierte Analyse technologischer Diskontinuitäten.* Wiesbaden: Deutscher Universitätsverlag.

Leifer, R. (1998). 'An Information Processing Approach for Facilitating the Fuzzy Front End of Breakthrough Innovations', Conference Proceedings IEMC: 130–5.

Leifer, R. (2000). *Radical Innovation.* Boston: Harvard Business School Press.

Leifer, R., McDermott, C. M., O'Connor, G. C., Peters, L. S., Rice, M. P., and Veryzer, R. W. (2000). *Radical Innovation.* Boston: Harvard Business School Press.

Leonard-Barton, D. (1992). 'Core Capabilities and Core Rigidities: A Paradox in Managing New Product Development'. *Strategic Management Journal* 13: 111–25.

Leonard-Barton, D. (1995). *Wellsprings of Knowledge*. Boston: Harvard Business School Press.

Lichtenthaler, E. (2000). 'Organisation der Technology Intelligence: eine empirische Untersuchung in technologieintensiven, international tätigen Grossunternehmen'. Zurich: Dissertation ETH Zurich Nr. 13787.

Linstone, H. A. (1975). *The Dephi Methods*. Reading, Mass.: Addison-Wesley.

List, D. (2004). 'Multiple Pasts, Converging Presents, and Alternative Futures'. *Futures* 36: 23–43.

Lovins, A. (1976). 'Energy Strategy: The Road Not Taken?'. *Foreign Affairs* (October).

Ludolph, F., and Lichtenberg, S. (2001). *Der Businessplan: professioneller Aufbau und überzeugende Präsentation*. Munich: Econ.

Luggen, M. (2004). *Technology and Innovation Management in New Technology-Based Firms*. Zurich: ETH-Zurich.

Lynn, G. S., Morone, J. G., and Paulson, A. S. (1996). 'Marketing and Discontinuous Innovation'. *California Management Review* 38(3): 8–37.

Macharzina, K. (1984). 'Bedeutung und Notwendigkeit des Diskontinuitätenmanagements bei internationaler Unternehmenstätigkeit'. In K. Macharzina (Ed.), *Diskontinuitäten Management, Strategische Bewältigung von Strukturbrüchen bei internationaler Unternehmenstätigkeit*. Berlin: Erich Schmidt: 1–19.

Malik, F. (2001a). 'Strategische Unternehmungsführung als Steuerung eines komplexen Systems', *MZSG Seminardokumentation*: St Gallen.

Malik, F. (2001b). *Management-Perspektiven – Wirtschaft und Gesellschaft, Strategie, Management und Ausbildung* (3rd edn). Bern/Stuttgart: Haupt.

Marchetti, C. (1980). 'Society as a Learning System: Discovery Invention and Innovation Cycles Revisited'. *Technological Forecasting and Social Change* 18: 267–82.

Martino, J. P. (1993). *Technological Forecasting for Decision Making* (3rd edn): New York, McGraw-Hill.

Mascitelli, R. (2000). 'From Experience: Harnessing Tacit Knowledge to Achieve Breakthrough Innovation'. *Journal of Product Innovation Management* 17: 179–93.

Maurer, P. J. (2002). *Das Informationsmanagement der Innovatik*. Diss., Technische Wissenschaften ETH Zürich, Zurich.

McDermott, C. M., and O'Connor, G. C. (2002). 'Managing Radical Innovation: An Overview of Emergent Strategy Issues'. *Product Innovation Management* 19: 424–38.

McKee, D. (1992). 'An Organizational Learning Approach to Product Innovation'. *Journal of Product Innovation Management* 9(3): 232–45.

McKelvey, M. D. (1996). 'Discontinuities in Generic Engineering for Pharmaceuticals? Firm Jumps and Lock-in in Systems of Innovation'. *Technology Analysis and Strategic Management* 8(2): 107–16.

Meier, M. (2002)'Produktfunktion festlegen'. http://e-collection.ethbib.ethz.ch/cgi-bin/show.pl?type=lehr&nr=40; accessed 9.07. 2003.

Mensch, G. (1975). *Das technologische Patt – Innovation überwindet die Depression*. Frankfurt: Umschau.

Mensch, G. (1979). *Stalemate in Technology: Innovations Overcome the Depression*. Cambridge, MA: Ballinger.

Meslem, A. (2003). 'Image numérique. Les capteurs photosensibles'. *SVM* (March): 158–61.

Meyers, C., and Tucker, F. (1989). 'Defining Roles for Logistics During Routine and Radical Technological Innovation'. *Journal of Academic Management Science* 17(1): 73–82.

Miller, K. D., and Waller, G. H. (2003). 'Scenarios, Real Options and Integrated Risk Management'. *Long Range Planning* 36: 93–107.

Miller, W. L., and Langdon, M. (1999). *4th Generation R&D, Managing Knowledge, Technology and Innovation*. New York: John Wiley & Sons.

Milliken, F. J. (1990). 'Perceiving and Interpreting Environmental Change: An Examination of College Administrators' Interpretation of Changing Demographics'. *The Academy of Management Journal* 33(1): 42–63.

Mintzberg, H. (1994). *The Rise and Fall of Strategic Planning*. Hertfordshire: Prentice Hall International (UK).

Mintzberg, H., and Lampel, J. (1999). 'Reflecting on the Strategy Process'. *Sloan Management Review* (Spring): 21–30.

Mintzberg, H., and Waters, J. A. (1985). 'Of Strategies, Deliberate and Emergent'. *Strategic Management Journal* 6: 257–72.

Moore, G. A. (1999). *Crossing the Chasm*. New York: HarperCollins Publishers.

Müller-Stewens, G., and Lechner, C. (2001). *Strategisches Management*. Stuttgart: Schäffer-Poeschel.

Myers, S. C. (1977). Determinants of Corporate Borrowing, *Journal of Financial Economics* 5 (2), November: 147–75.

Nahm, F. C. (1986). 'There is a Method to Do This Management: How to Set Up Strategic Planning – and Keep it Going'. *Currents* 12(10): 44–8.

Nault, B. R., and Vandenbosch, M. B. (1998). 'Eating your own Lunch: Protection through Preemption'. In A. Y. Ilinitsch, A. Y. Lewin and R. A. D'Aveni (Eds), *Managing in Times of Disorder: Hypercompetitive Organizational Responses*. Sage Publications, Thousand Oaks: 171–206.

Nayak, P. R., and Ketteringham, J. M. (1986). *Breakthroughs!*. New York: Rawson Associates.

Noori, H. (1990). *Managing the Dynamics of New Technology*. New Jersey: Prentice Hall.

Noori, H., Munro, H., Deszca, G., and McWilliams, B. (1999). 'Developing the "Right" Breakthrough Product/Service: An Umbrella Methodology – Part A'. *International Journal Technology Management* 17(5): 544–62.

North, K., and Tucker, S. (1987). *Implementing Routine and Radical Innovations*. Lexington Books, Lexington.

O'Connor, G. C. (1998). 'Market Learning and Radical Innovation: A Cross Case Comparison of Eight Radical Innovation Projects'. *Journal of Product Innovation Management* 15: 151–66.

O'Connor, G. C., and Veryzer, R. W. (2001). 'The Nature of Market Visioning for Technology-based Radical Innovation'. *Journal of Product Innovation Management* 18: 231–46.

OECD. (1999). *Cellular Mobile Pricing Structures and Trends*. Paris: Directorate for Science, Technology and Industry.

OECD. (2003). *OECD Communications Outlook*. Paris: OECD Publications Service.

Orbell, J. (1993). 'Hamlet and the Psychology of Rational Choice Under Uncertainty'. *Rationality and Society*: January 1993, 127–40.

O'Reilly, C., and Tushman, M. L. (2004). 'The Ambidextrous Organization'. *Harvard Business Review* (April): 74–81.

Penrose, E. (1959). *The Theory of Growth of the Firm*. Oxford: Blackwell.

Perez, C. (1983). 'Structural Change and Assimilation of New Technologies in the Economic and Social Systems'. *Futures* (October): 357–75.

Petrick, I. J., and Echols, A. E. (2004). 'Technology Roadmapping in Review: A Tool for Making Sustainable New Product Development Decisions'. *Technological Forecasting & Social Change* 71: 81–100.

Pfeiffer, S. (1992). *Technologie Frühaufklärung: Identifikation und Bewertung zukünftiger Technologien in der strategischen Unternehmensplanung.* Hamburg: Steuer- und Wirtschaftsverlag.

Porter, M. E. (1980). *Competitive Strategy: Techniques for Analyzing Industries and Competitors.* New York: Free Press.

Porter, M. E. (1985). *Competitive Advantage – Creating and Sustaining Superior Performance.* New York: Free Press/Macmillan.

Porter, M. E. (1987). 'From Competitive Advantage to Corporate Strategy'. *Harvard Business Review* 3: 43–59.

Porter, M. E. (1989). *Wettbewerbsvorteile (Competitive Advantage).* Frankfurt: Campus.

Porter, M. E. (1996). 'What is Strategy?'. *Harvard Business Review* 74(6): 61–78.

Porter, M. E. (1998). 'Competitive Strategy in Emerging Industries'. *Readings in the Strategy Process.* Mintzberg: Henry & James Brian Quinn.

Prahalad, C. K., and Bettis, R. A. (1986). 'The Dominant Logic: a New Linkage Between Diversity and Performance'. *Strategic Management Journal* 7: 485–501.

Prahalad, C. K., and Hamel, G. (1990). 'The Core Competence of the Corporation'. *Harvard Business Review*: 79–91.

Quinn, J. B. (1980). *Strategies for Change: Logical Incrementalism.* Homewood, IL: Irwin.

Rafii, F., and Kampas, P. J. (2002). 'How to Identify Your Enemies Before They Destroy You'. *Harvard Business Review* (November): 115–23.

Ramsay, D. A., Boardman, J. T., and Cole, A. J. (1996). 'Reinforcing Learning, Using Soft Systemic Frameworks'. *International Journal of Project Management* 14(1): 31–6.

Reid, S. E., and Brentani, U. d. (2004). 'The Fuzzy Front End of New Product Development for Discontinuous Innovation: A Theoretical Model'. *Journal of Product Innovation Management* 21: 170–84.

Rice, M. P. (1996). 'Virtuality and Uncertainty in the Domain of Discontinuous Innovation'. IEMC: 528–32.

Rice, M. P., O'Connor, G. C., Peter, L., and Morone, J. G. (1998). 'Managing Discontinuous Innovation'. *Research Technology Management* (May–June): 52–8.

Roberts, E. B., and Berry, C. A. (1985). 'Entering New Businesses: Selecting Strategies for Success'. *Sloan Management Review* (Spring): 3–17.

Robinson, J. (1933). *The Economics of Imperfect Competition.* London: Macmillan.

Robinson, J. B. (1982). 'Energy Backcasting – A Proposed Method of Policy Analysis'. *Energy Policy*: December 1982, 337–44.

Rosenberg, N. (1995). 'Innovation's Uncertain Terrain'. *The McKinsey Quarterly* 3: 171–85.

Rothwell, R., and Wissema, H. (1991). 'Technology, Culture, and Public Policy'. In G. Rossegger (Ed.), *Management of Technological Change: Context and Case Studies.* Oxford: Elsevier Science: 3–23.

Ruggles, R. L. (1997). *Knowledge Management Tools.* Newton, MA: Butterworth-Heinemann.

Sanchez, R. (2001). 'Managing Knowledge into Competence: The Five Learning Cycles of the Competent Organization'. In R. Sanchez (Ed.), *Knowledge Management and Organizational Competence.* Oxford/New York: Oxford University Press: 3–37.

Sauber, T. (2004). 'Design and Implementation of a Concept of Structured Innovation Strategy Formulation'. Dissertation ETH, Zurich.

Savioz, P. (2002). *Technology Intelligence in Technology Based SMEs. Conceptual Design and Implementation.* Dissertation. Zurich: ETH Zurich.

Savioz, P. (2003). 'Competence Management with the Opportunity Landscape'. In H. Tschirky, H.-H. Jung and P. Savioz (Eds), *Technology and Innovation Management on the Move.* Zurich: Orell Füssli.

Savioz, P. (2004). *Technology Intelligence, Concept Design and Implementation in Technology-based SMEs*. Basingstoke: Palgrave Macmillan.

Savioz, P., Lichtenthaler, E., Birkenmeier, B., and Brodbeck, H. (2002). 'Organisation der frühen Phasen des radikalen Innovationsprozess'. *Die Unternehmung* (June): 393–408.

Schaad, D. (2001). *Modellierung unternehmensspezifischer Innovations-Prozessmodelle*. Zurich: ETH Zurich.

Schaible, J., and Hönig, A. (1991). *High-Tech-Marketing*. Munich: Frank Vahlen.

Schendel, D. E., and Cool, K. (1988). 'Development of the Strategic Management Field: Some Accomplishments and Challenges'. In J. H. Grant (Ed.), *Strategic Management Frontiers*. Greenwich: JAI Press: 17–33.

Schendel, D. E., and Hofer, C. W. (1979). *Strategic Management*. Boston: Little & Brown.

Schofield, B. A., and Feltmate, B. W. (2003). 'Sustainable Development Investing'. *Employee Benefits Journal* 28(1): 17–21.

Schumpeter, J. A. (1934). *The Theory of Economic Development*. Cambridge, MA: Harvard University Press.

Scigliano, D. (2003). *Das Management radikaler Innovationen*. Wiesbaden: Bayreuth.

Seibert, S. (1998). *Technisches Management – Innovationsmanagement, Projektmanagement und Qualitätsmanagement*. Leipzig: Teubner.

Shaklin, W. L., and Ryans Jr, J. K. (1984). *Marketing High Technology*. Lexington: Lexington Books.

Sharma, P., and Chrisman, J. J. (1999). 'Toward a Reconciliation of the Definition in the Field of Corporate Entrepreneurship'. *Entrepreneurship Theory and Practice* 23(3): 11–27.

Shenhar, A. J., Dvir, D., and Shulman, Y. (1995). 'A Two Dimensional Taxonomy of Products and Innovations'. *Journal of Engineering and Technology Management* 12: 175–200.

Sohn, S. Y., and Moon, T. H. (2004). 'Decision Tree Based on Data Envelopment Analysis for Effective Technology Commercialization'. *Expert Systems with Applications* 26: 279–84.

Song, X. M., and Montoya-Weiss, M. M. (1998). 'Critical Development Activities for Really New versus Incremental Products'. *Journal Product Innovation Management* 15: 124–35.

Stoelhorst, J. W. (2002). 'Transition Strategies for Managing Technological Discontinuities: Lessons from the History of the Semiconductor Industry'. *International Journal of Technology Management* 23(4): 261–86.

Strebel, P. (1992). *Breakpoints, How Managers Exploit Radical Business Change*. Boston: Harvard Business School Press.

Strebel, P. (1995). 'Creating Industry Breakpoints: Changing the Rules of the Game'. *Long Range Planning* 28(2): 11–20.

Suarez, F. F., and Utterback, J. M. (1995). 'Dominant Design and the Survival of Firms'. *Strategic Management Journal* 16: 415–30.

Teece, D. J. (1990). 'Contributions and Impediments of Economic Analysis to the Study of Strategic Management'. In J. W. Fredrickson (Ed.), *Perspectives on Strategic Management*. New York: Harper Business: 39–80.

Thierauf, R. J. (1999). *Management Systems for Business*. Westport: Greenwood.

Thomas, C. W. (1996). 'Strategic Technology Assessment, Future Products and Competitive Advantage'. *International Journal of Technology Management, Special Issue on Technology Assessment* 11(5/6): 651–66.

Tidd, J. (1995). 'Development of Novel Products through Intraorganizational and Interorganizational Networks'. *Journal of Product Innovation Management* 12: 307–22.

238   *Bibliography*

Trauffler, G., Tschirky, H., Csendes, M., and Biedermann, A. (2004). *An Uncertainty and Risk Reducing Process for the Strategic Management of Discontinuous and Disruptive Technology*. Seoul: PICMET.

Trommsdorff, V., and Schneider, P. (1990). 'Grundzüge des betriebswirtschaftlichen Innovationsmanagements'. In V. Trommsdorf (Ed.), *Innovationsmanagement in kleinen und mittleren Unternehmen*. Munich: Franz Vahlen: 1–25.

Tschirky, H. (2000). 'On the Path of Enterprise Science? An Approach to Establishing the Correspondence of Theory and Reality in Technology-intensive Companies'. *International Journal of Technology Management* 20(3/4): 459–74.

Tschirky, H. (2003a). 'The Concept of the Integrated Technology and Innovation Management'. In H. Tschirky, H.-H. Jung and P. Savioz (Eds), *Technology and Innovation Management of the Move*. Zurich: Industrielle Organisation: 43–105.

Tschirky, H. (2003b). 'The Technology Awareness Gap in General Management'. In H. Tschirky, H.-H Jung and P. Savioz (Eds), *Technology and Innovation Management on the move*: Zurich: Industrielle Organisation: 21–41.

Tschirky, H. (2005). 'From Managing Technologies to Managing Innovation driven Enterprises'. *Farewell Lecture at ETH*. Zurich: ETH Zurich.

Tschirky, H., and Bucher, P. (2003). 'Der Weg zum zukunftsfähigen Unternehmen'. *New Management* 6: 25–31.

Tschirky, H., Jung, H.-H, and Savioz, P. (2003). *Technology and Innovation Management of the Move*. Zurich: Industrielle Organization.

Tschirky, H., and Koruna, S. (1998). *Technologie-Management, Idee und Praxis*. Zurich: Orell Füssli.

Tushman, M. L., and Anderson, M. (1986). 'Technological Discontinuities and Organizational Environments'. *Administrative Science Quarterly* 31(3): 439–65.

Tushman, M. L., and Anderson, P. (1997). *Managing Strategic Innovation and Change*. New York: Oxford University Press.

Tushman, M. L., Anderson, P. C., and O'Reilly, C. (1997). 'Technology Cycles, Innovation Streams, and Ambidextrous Organizations: Organization Renewal through Innovation Streams and Strategic Change'. In Tushman and Anderson (1997) *Managing Strategic Innovation and Change*. New York: Oxford University Press: 3–23.

Tushman, M. L., and Nadler, D. (1986). 'Organizing for Innovation'. *California Management Review* 28: 74–92.

Tushman, M. L., and O'Reilly, C. A. (1996). 'Ambidextrous Organizations: Managing Evolutionary and Revolutionary Change'. In R. A. Burgelman, M. A. Maidique and S. C. Wheelwright (Eds), *Strategic Management of Technology and Innovation* (3rd edn). Boston: McGraw-Hill: 724–37.

Tushman, M. L., and O'Reilly, C. A. (1998). 'Unternehmen müssen auch den sprunghaften Wandel meistern'. *Harvard Business Manager* 1: 30–44.

Ulrich, H. (1984). *Management*. Bern: Haupt.

Ulrich, H., and Probst, G. J. B. (1988). *Anleitung zum ganzheitlichen Denken und Handeln – eine Brevier für Führungskräfte*. Bern: Haupt.

Utterback, J. M. (1994). *Mastering the Dynamics of Innovation, How Companies Can Seize Opportunities in the Face of Technological Change*. Boston, MA, Harvard Business School Press.

Veryzer, R. W. (1998a). 'Discontinuous Innovation and the New Product Development Process'. *Journal of Product Innovation Management* 15: 304–21.

Veryzer, R. W. (1998b). 'Key Factors Affecting Customer Evaluation of Discontinuous New Products'. *Journal of Product Innovation Management* 15: 136–50.

Vojak, B. A., and Chambers, F. A. (2004). 'Roadmapping Disruptive Technical Threats and Opportunities in Complex, Technology-based Subsystems: The SAILS Methodology'. *Technological Forecasting and Social Change* 71: 121–39.

Walsh, S. (1996). 'Commercializing of MicroSystems – Too Fast or Too Slow: SPIE'. *Int. Soc. Opt. Eng.*: 12–26, vol. 2881 (September 1996). Proceedings of SPIE, vol. 2881. Microelectronic Structures and MEMs for optical processing II ISBN: 0–8194–2279–7.

Walsh, S. T. (2004). 'Roadmapping a Disruptive Technology: A Case Study – the Emerging Microsystems and Top-Down Nanosystems Industry'. *Technological Forecasting and Social Change* 71: 161–85.

Ward, S., and Chapman, C. (2003). 'Transforming Project Risk Management into Project Uncertainty Management'. *International Journal of Project Management* 21: 97–105.

Welge, M. K., and Al-Laham, A. (1992). 'Strategisches Management, Organisation'. In E. Frese (Ed.), *Handwörterbuch der Organisation*, Vol. 3. Stuttgart: Poeschel: 2355–74.

Wenger, E. (1998). *Communities of Practice – Learning, Meaning, and Identity*. Cambridge: Cambridge University Press.

Wenger, E., McDermott, C. M., and William, S. (2000). *Cultivating Communities of Practice*. Boston: Harvard Business School Press.

Wieandt, A. (1995). 'Zur Entstehung von Märkten durch Innovationen'. *Betriebswirtschaftliche Forschung und Praxis* 47(4): 447–71.

Williams, R. L., and Chair, P. E. (1989). *Industrial Engineering Terminology* (rev. edn). Norcross, GA: Industrial Engineering and Management Press.

Wolfrum, B. (1991). *Strategisches Technologiemanagement* (2nd edn). Wiesbaden: Gabler.

Wright, R., Pringle, C., and Kroll, M. (1992). *Strategic Management: Text and Cases*. Needham Heights: Allyn and Bacon.

Wyk, R. J. v. (2002). 'Technology: A Fundamental Structure?'. *Knowledge, Technology and Policy* 15(3): 14–35.

Yates, J. F., and Stone, E. R. (1992). 'Risk Taking Behavior'. In J. F. Yates (Ed.), *The Risk Construct*. New York: Wiley: 1–25.

Yin, R. K. (1994). *Case Study Research – Design and Methods* (2nd edn): Sage.

Zahn, E., and Weidler, A. (1995). 'Verwertung technologischer Fähigkeiten'. In E. Zahn (Ed.), *Handbuch Technologiemanagement*. Stuttgart: Schäffer-Poeschel: 335–76.

Zehnder, T. (1997). *Kompetenzbasierte Technologieplanung: Analyse und Bewertung technologischer Fähigkeiten*. Wiesbaden: Deutscher Universitäts.

Index